PARENTS' GUIDE TO
SCHOOL SELECTION

in San Mateo/Santa Clara County

Third Edition

Nancy Ginsburg Gill

Haskala Press, Los Altos, California

PARENTS' GUIDE TO SCHOOL SELECTION

in San Mateo/Santa Clara County
Third Edition

Published by: Haskala Press
                       640 Orange Ave.
                       Los Altos, CA 94022
                       (415) 948-4648

Production and typesetting by: ASCI
                                  4600 El Camino Real, Ste 203
                                  Los Altos, CA 94022
                                  (415) 948-9477

ISBN: 0-9613846-2-X

TABLE OF CONTENTS

INTRODUCTION

When I was growing up in the old section of Los Altos in the 1950's, the neighborhood children went to either the local public school or a nearby Catholic school. When my husband and I moved back to the same neighborhood in the late 1970's with two children of our own, we discovered that the children living within a three block radius of our home attended twelve different elementary schools — five public and seven private[*].

In talking with friends and neighbors about schools, I saw how the great increase in school choices, both public and private, has created confusion and often panic among parents who want the best for their children. Fears of violence, teacher strikes, budget cuts, and declining academic standards have made parents leery of sending their children to the neighborhood public school. Highly publicized national studies lamenting the state of public education have intensified these concerns.

In the winter of 1980, after writing "Choosing a Private School" for *Parents* magazine, I decided to use my experience teaching in public and private schools, the research I had done as an education writer, and my interest in education issues to help parents through the baffling and often frightening process of finding a school for their child.

Since then, I have visited many of the schools described in the directory of this book. I have served on various public and private school committees, attended conferences and lectures, and talked with hundreds of parents and educators about the relative strengths and weaknesses of area schools.

This book is designed to clarify some of the confusing issues surrounding the public versus private school debate and give parents a better understanding of how to find the best school for their child.

After using the directory to identify the schools that will meet their needs financially, philosophically, and geographically, parents should evaluate schools for themselves, using the guidelines provided in the first part of the book.

No established elementary or secondary private school or public school district has been intentionally omitted from this book. Every reasonable effort has been made to see that the listings in the directory are accurate. The publisher and author assume no responsibility for any errors that may have been inadvertently made.

September 1984

1

---

[*] In this book, for the sake of simplicity, I use the term "private school" to refer to all non-public schools—parochial and private.

Introduction to the Second Edition of
Parents' Guide to School Selection

When the first edition of this book came out at the beginning of 1985, I was pleased to receive positive responses from many parents and educators. The fact that both private and public school educators liked what the book had to say made me feel that I had achieved my primary goal: to give parents an unbiased and balanced picture of their school options and offer guidelines that would help them make the best choice for their children.

However, it has been clear for several years that the book needed to be revised. Most obviously, the directory section of the book needed to be updated — private school tuitions have increased, some schools have closed while others have opened, and many public school districts have changed their grade configurations.

I also wanted to write a second edition so I could include some of the less obvious but more interesting and substantial changes that have occurred in the local education picture. In the early and mid-eighties, many public school districts were still struggling with shrinking enrollment. Now, many are bursting at the seams in the lower grades and instead of worrying about which schools to close, they are wondering how to get the funds for new school construction, struggling with the dilemma of needing classroom space that is currently rented by day care centers, and trying to cope with the challenge of educating a growing number of ESL — English as a second language — students.

Schools are doing a much better job meeting the needs of working parents. In 1984, working mothers often had great difficulty finding schools that provided on-site day care. That has changed dramatically. Now, it is the rare school — private or public — that doesn't have before and afterschool child care programs; those that don't usually have arrangements with day care centers which bus children to an afterschool day care facility. However, many working parents still find themselves in a quandary during school holidays as relatively few of these child care facilities stay open year-round.

With the growth of the elementary school population and the retirement of teachers who started teaching in the fifties and sixties, many schools are being infused with the energy of new and returning teachers. Some non-public schools have felt the negative side of the public school hiring spurt as they have

3

lost good teachers to the higher pay and better benefits offered by public schools, and when these schools seek new teachers entering the job market, they now have to compete with the public schools — something they rarely had to do during most of the seventies and the early eighties. Thus, private school tuition has increased substantially over the last decade since these schools can no longer attract and keep good teachers unless they attempt to keep up with the higher salaries paid by the public schools.

In the last few years, increased attention has been paid to middle school structure and curriculum and the needs of students in the eleven through fourteen year old age group. In the first edition of this book, I noted that most elementary schools spanned kindergarten through sixth grade, and most junior highs served seventh and eighth graders. In recent years, as financial and demographic pressures have meshed with pedagogical theory about the needs of the early adolescent, many elementary schools now end at fifth grade (or sometimes fourth grade) and many middle schools now include sixth graders. In fact, the traditional seventh and eighth grade junior high may be an endangered species.

Overall, I think parents are proceeding through the school selection process in a much more rational manner than they were in the early eighties. Families in general seem less negative about the public schools (rightfully so in most cases), and parents who are choosing non-public schools seem to be doing so less out of a misguided conviction that any school that charges tuition must be better than the public schools and more out of a careful examination of the benefits private schools can offer.

I hope that this book will continue to help all those parents who are struggling through the school selection process.

—November 1989

Introduction to the Third Edition of
Parents' Guide to School Selection

It is September of 1993, and although the second edition of the book has been sold out for many months, I was tempted to hold off the publication of the third edition for another few months. In November, California voters will be faced with a major initiative that if passed will dramatically affect the school choice process. Under the provisions of Proposition 174, parents will be allowed to use public school money, approximately $2600 a year, to pay tuition at any private school that serves at least 25 children and doesn't discriminate on the basis of race, ethnicity, color, or national origin. If the school voucher proposal wins public approval and survives the inevitable court battles over constitutionality, an increasing number of parents will agonize over school choice. Since many established private schools have no space for additional students, many new non-public schools will probably be established to serve parents wishing to use vouchers. If you are considering a new, unaccredited school, be sure that the people running the school are truly educators and are committed to offering quality education with competent teachers.

In the four years since I wrote the last edition of this book, California's recession has had ramifications for both public and private schools. The public schools have had to wait well into the summer to finalize their budgets, establish class sizes, cut or reinstate programs, and rehire (or not rehire) recently hired teachers. Many parents, alarmed by the increased class sizes and program cuts dictated by the state's ongoing budget crisis and fearful of violence and weapons on public school campuses, have sought a safer and more stable environment in private schools. On the other hand, the recession, rising private school tuition, and the prospect of spiraling college costs have sent some private school parents back to the public schools. Furthermore, many parents have discovered that while the big picture for public education in California is grim, local districts, through their use of parent involvement, business and community partnerships, and the creativity of teachers and administrators, still offer quality education to many of their students. Also encouraging is that most districts seem to be managing their internal relationships better so that the specter of teacher strikes is no longer a constant threat as it was a decade ago.

Once again, I am including CAP scores in the appendix, and this year am also including SAT scores. However, as in previous editions, I advise parents not to make too much of test scores. Sending your child to a school most people describe as "one of the best" simply because of its test scores and affluent student population does not guarantee that your child will have a wonderful experience and education. Furthermore, I have spoken with dozens of pleased parents whose children have attended schools that are considered "bad" because of a mixed student population and low test scores and yet have had wonderful experiences both socially and academically.

If you make an honest assessment of your child's needs and look for an environment full of enthusiastic, caring educators, chances are your search for the right school for your child will be a successful one.

HOW TO START
THE SCHOOL SEARCH

Make an honest assessment of your child's interests, strengths, and weaknesses.

Many children will do well wherever they go, and for their families, the school selection process is primarily a matter of finding the school that best meets parental expectations, practical needs, and education values. However, parents should first assess their child's personality, strengths and weaknesses. Some parents feed their own egos and need for status by pushing their children into prestigious schools that may not serve the child's needs at all. No one school is right for all children. A child who is easily distracted might need a structured learning environment, whereas a creative, self-motivated child would flourish in a more open, unstructured school. Children with low self-esteem often need a small school with a low student-to-teacher ratio, a place where they can feel important. More confident children often thrive on the variety and stimulation a large school can offer. Teachers who have worked with your child can be of great help in assessing the class size, amount of structure, and degree of academic pressure that will be best for him or her. If you have difficulty deciding what kind of school will be best for your child, you can also use the services of an education counselor.

Before you start visiting schools, decide what you want in a school.

You will have an easier time evaluating schools if you combine your assessments of your child's specific needs with your own practical requirements (e.g., on site day care, cost, distance from home) and your criteria of what qualities you think a good school should have. Some parents want structure, discipline, and lots of homework. Others want a more open learning environment, which allows children to learn at their own pace. The better sense you have of what you want in a school, the easier it will be to recognize the right school when you visit it.

You should also decide how involved you want to be in your child's school. Most public schools and some private schools welcome parental involvement in the classroom and on advisory committees. A few even require participation. Some private schools restrict parent participation to fund-raising efforts and write into their philosophies that volunteer aides are not used in the classroom. Thus, if you have the time and inclination to participate, look for a school that will welcome your involvement.

CONSIDER A PUBLIC SCHOOL

In spite of the many problems facing public education, the San Francisco Bay Area has many excellent public schools. Unless you want a school that offers religious instruction or a special program the public schools can't offer, you would be wise to start your school search by evaluating for yourself the education your child can receive free of charge. Talk to your public school administrators, teachers, and especially parents of current students. By following the "how to evaluate a school" guidelines, you should get a good feeling for the kind of education available in your assigned public school. You may find good teachers and exciting programs. Even if you are not satisfied with the public schools available to you, taking the time to evaluate them will give you a better idea of what you want in a private school.

FUNDING: Several decades ago financing of public education in California was a relatively simple but inequitable process, it was determined, for the most part, by the assessed value of local property and the extent to which communities were willing to pass local school bonds. However, in 1976, the State Supreme Court ruled in the Serrano v. Priest case that unequal funding among school districts was unconstitutional. In response to the court order, the Legislature passed a law to redistribute property taxes to reduce inequities. In 1984 the Superior Court declared that sufficient compliance with the Serrano decision had been achieved, and indeed, compared to most other states, there is relatively little disparity in how much each school district has to spend on each child.

The shift of school finances to state control became virtually complete in 1978 when Proposition 13 capped property taxes. It also limited the ability of local government to add to the state contribution by requiring two-thirds vote to pass local school bonds and parcel taxes. Most districts are "revenue limit" districts, i.e., they rely on the state for their funding. However, twelve districts in the area covered by this book are "basic aid" districts,[1] which means their property tax revenues exceed what the state would normally pay per student. These districts tend to have more money per pupil than other districts, and they are less vulnerable to the state's budget crises than are other districts. However, in recent years with property values declining and school enrollment increasing, many of these districts have also had to tighten their budgets and eliminate programs.

While Serrano mandated relative equity in what each district receives to educate each child, it did not cover all sources of funding. The resulting disparity is

9

---

[1] Belmont, Hillsborough, Las Lomitas, Portola Valley, San Mateo Union H.S., Sequoia, Fremont Union H.S., Los Gatos-Saratoga H.S., Mountain View-Los Altos H.S., Orchard, Palo Alto, Sunnyvale. Santa Clara Unified is projected to become a Basic Aid district in the 1993-94 school year.

illustrated in the appendix, which lists each district's revenue per student (average daily attendance). Many districts and some individual schools, primarily those serving wealthy communities, have established foundations, which in some cases raise hundreds of thousands of dollars annually to hire support specialists, buy new textbooks and equipment, and reduce class sizes. Furthermore, nine districts[2] in San Mateo and Santa Clara County, generally small districts serving affluent communities, have been able to win the required two-thirds vote to levy special parcel taxes to raise extra money for schools. When a district does succeed in passing such a measure, it demonstrates broad-based community support for the local public schools. A few very small districts get extra money because they qualify as necessary schools and require extra money per child to run a complete school program.

Many educators and legislators are hoping that the public will approve Proposition 170, an Assembly initiated amendment that will change the two-thirds requirement to a simple majority for local bonds for the construction and rehabilitation of school facilities. The state legislature is also considering a bill that will allow parcel taxes to pass with majority approval.

INTER AND INTRA DISTRICT TRANSFERS. In the summer of 1993, the state legislature passed AB 19 and AB 1114, which allow parents to send their children to any school within their district or in another district as long as space is available. However, if the transfer would have a negative impact on desegregation or if a school has already lost 1 to 3% of its students in a given year, the resident school district can prevent the transfer.

Even before AB 1114 was passed, many districts had an open enrollment policy, allowing parents to choose any school within the district as long as space was available. But by the early 1990's, districts were finding it increasingly difficult to honor these requests, since many schools, especially those deemed "the best," were packed with students from the school's attendance area.

In 1986, the state passed the Allen Bill allowing parents to place children in kindergarten through eighth grade in school districts in which their workplace is located. Districts are only required to grant such transfers as long as space is available and as long as such a transfer does not negatively impact a district's desegregation plan or cost the accepting district more money to educate the child than it would receive from the state in additional aid.

Although the Allen Bill, AB 1114 and AB 19 are well-intended efforts to give parents more choice in public schools, they are not expected to have a significant impact. Most school districts are experiencing a population spurt among their own residents and thus will probably grant few transfers under these bills. Moreover, Basic Aid districts (see explanation above) are unlikely to take large numbers of out-of-district students as their funding comes primarily from local taxes; these districts have a disincentive to take additional students because the state does not reimburse them for the extra cost of educating them. However, parents who feel their children can receive a better education in another district should inquire about an inter-district transfer under the provisions of these bills.

[2] Burlingame, Hillsborough, Los Altos Elem., Los Gatos Elem., Menlo Park, Oak Grove, Portola Valley, San Mateo-Foster City, Woodside.

Magnet Schools are used by some large school districts to help balance the student ethnic distribution of the district's schools. These schools emphasize one of a wide variety of areas such as performing arts, computer science and apprenticeship programs for training in specific job skills.

Alternative Schools. Many districts also operate alternative schools that have a different focus or philosophy than the neighborhood schools. If your district does offer such schools, start investigating them as soon as possible because these schools often have long waiting lists.

Back-to-Basics Schools generally have a teacher-directed, textbook approach to learning with a minimum amount of individualization. They often have a dress code and clearly defined homework and discipline policies. Grade levels are rarely combined, and parents are generally not used as classroom aides. Students and parents are often required to sign a written agreement to follow the rules and philosophy of the school. These schools appeal to parents who want a traditional, highly structured program for their children. They are especially effective for children who need firm guidelines and a quiet environment. Very bright or creative children sometimes find the structure and textbook orientation of these schools too confining.

Open Education Schools are characterized by student initiated activity, independent study, and freedom of movement in the classroom. Open schools are less textbook oriented than most schools and instead emphasize an inter-disciplinary and hands-on approach to learning. These schools often mix age groups and may require parent participation to achieve the low student-to-adult ratio necessary for individualized education. Open schools usually do not give graded report cards, but instead evaluate students through written comments and conferences. Open schools generally work best for creative, self-motivated children who thrive on freedom of choice, and they appeal to parents who want to be actively involved in their children's education. They are not appropriate for children who are easily distracted or who are overwhelmed by too many choices.

(Note: Most public schools belong in the middle of the educational spectrum between open schools and back-to-basics schools. In the 1970's many schools moved towards the open end of the spectrum; in the early 1980's, many public schools moved back towards a more structured model. In recent years, the emphasis on "school reform" has incorporated some of the ideas—e.g., integrated curriculum, collaborative learning, mixed age grouping— that typify "open" schools and were a part of the reform movements twenty-five years ago. All of this illustrates what is referred to as "the pendulum swing" in public education.)

Charter Schools. Under new legislation California allows school districts to abandon the 11-volume, 7,800 Education Code and create whatever kind of school the community wants, as long as its curriculum meets basic state education requirements. During the first application period to establish a charter school, San Carlos was the only school district in Northern California to apply for the program, but in future years other districts will probably take advantage of the opportunity to free themselves from the restrictions of the education code and establish new schools based on the shared vision of teachers and parents.

Continuation Schools. Almost every high school district offers a continuation program designed for students who have difficulty adjusting to regular school programs, who fail to attend classes according to district criteria, or who have already dropped out of the regular high school. These schools' academic programs are often individualized according to students' needs, and the student-to-teacher ratio is lower than that of the comprehensive high school. Some districts also offer Opportunity Programs directed at middle school students who have been evaluated as potential drop-outs. An increasing number of districts are implementing other programs to identify potential drop-outs and offer them specialized programs to motivate them to stay in school.

Education for the Handicapped. Every public school district provides special education programs for handicapped students. Resource specialist programs (RSPs) serve students who have identified learning handicaps but are able to spend most of the school day in regular classrooms. Specialists provide individual and small group instruction, conduct educational assessments, and coordinate the child's educational program with classroom teachers and parents. School districts also offer, either within the district or in cooperation with other districts, special day classes for students whose learning handicaps make it difficult for them to keep up with regular classroom work. School districts and the County Offices of Education also offer other programs for the more severely handicapped.

Under federal and state laws, public funding can be used to pay for sending handicapped children to specialized private schools. These laws state that if a resident school district does not provide an appropriate program for a handicapped child, that child may be funded at a non-public institution as long as that school has been certified by the California State Department of Education and can appropriately meet the needs of the student. Children evaluated as having specific learning disabilities are included in the laws' definition of handicapped. However, in recent years, as public schools have established more programs for the handicapped and as their own funds have dwindled, public school districts have understandably adopted much stricter qualification standards for public funding of private school placement. For more information on these laws, inquire at your public school district, the State Department of Education, or contact the **California Alliance for Special Education (CASE)** at (415) 928-2273. CASE offers free consultations about special education rights and services to parents and professionals and provides legal support, representation, and educational consulting to parents whose children need special education services.

The Parents' Educational Resource Center in San Mateo provides information for parents of students with learning differences. Resources include a special library, information/referral services, educational programs, guidance, and a parent newsletter. Phone: (415) 513-0920.

Gifted and Talented Education Program (GATE) is a state-funded program designed to offer special instruction to children identified as mentally gifted or talented. In the early 1980's, 50% or more of the students in some districts qualified for the program because they tested above a designated score — usually 131 — on intelligence tests. However, the funding is now based on a state-wide average which covers a lower percentage of the school population and may vary each year. Most districts, especially those with large numbers of high-testing children, have tightened the criteria for placement in GATE, and the method used to identify these students varies greatly from district to district. Most often districts use a combination of teacher or counselor recommendations, performance on intelligence tests, and demonstrated potential in leadership or performance art to identify children they think need more stimulation and challenge than they are receiving in the classroom. The expansion of the definition of giftedness has been applauded by those who recognize that giftedness can take many forms. On the other hand, increasing numbers of educators advocate integrating GATE programs into the regular classroom for they believe that all students deserve the kind of stimulating, enriching activities that typify instruction for the gifted.

The specific programs offered to GATE students vary from district to district. Most often, students are pulled out of their regular classrooms once or twice a week and given special instruction. Some districts use GATE funds to hire specialists to help the classroom teachers keep their exceptional students challenged. A few districts offer cluster programs, in which gifted students are placed together in self-contained classes designed to meet the needs of especially bright students. Once students reach junior high or middle school, clustering of gifted children occurs more naturally, as these children tend to be the ones taking foreign languages and advanced math and science classes. In high school, this natural clustering of the gifted increases as bright students — at least the academically motivated ones — group together in honors classes and the most challenging college preparatory classes.

Many advocates for gifted children are concerned that the current emphasis on heterogeneous grouping and collaborative learning, while perhaps beneficial to low achieving and average children, is detrimental to exceptionally bright, creative, and motivated students. If you have such a child and are considering a high school or middle school that has abolished ability grouping, you should investigate whether the curriculum adequately stimulates all students.

The California Association of the Gifted (C.A.G.) is an advocacy and information organization for teachers and parents of gifted children. To get information, write C.A.G., 426 Escuela, Suite 19, Mountain View, CA 94040 or phone (415) 965-0653.

Lyceum is a non-profit organization that offers afterschool, evening, and week-end enrichment seminars to Santa Clara County students in grades two through eight who score at or above the 98th percentile on an intelligence test. Parents can contact the GATE coordinator at their school or the County Office of Education for the phone number of this organization.

LOOK INTO THE HEALTH OF YOUR PUBLIC SCHOOL DISTRICT.
Learn how well the components of your public school district work by reading
local newspaper coverage of school board meetings and attending one or more
school board meetings. Try to answer the following questions: Do board members work well together for the good of the schools and the children, or are fac-
tions on the school board working against each other? Are teachers constantly
threatening to go on strike? Do they seem distrustful of the administration and
school board? Are teachers, administrators, parents, and the board working
together to solve problems and improve the schools? Are parents and teachers
given the opportunity to offer input when difficult decisions must be made
regarding the future of the schools? Do constant accusations and bickering char-
acterize the communication level within the school community, or is there a feeling of mutual respect? Find out if the administrators and teachers in your district
have improved the educational programs in their schools through implementing
joint ventures with local businesses and obtaining grants from private foundations.

WARNING TO NEWCOMERS: If you are buying or renting a home specif-
ically because you like a certain school in that neighborhood or like the idea of
living close to your child's school, don't assume that the Realtor is correct when
she or he tells you what school your child will attend. Be sure to check with the
school district to make sure that your child will be able to attend that school. In
recent years, some newcomers have been told that the only school with space for
their children is across town or have discovered that the house they have bought
is not in the school district they thought they were moving into. To save yourself this kind of disappointment and frustration, contact the school district before
you commit to a house or apartment.

CONDUCTING A PRIVATE SCHOOL SEARCH

One advantage private schools have over public institutions is that they don't have to be all things to all people. A private school can say, "These are our objectives, these are the methods we use to reach them, and these are the kinds of children we want to educate. If this is what you want and your child meets our qualifications, you are welcome to apply. Otherwise, go elsewhere." Therefore, parents searching for a private school should take special care in evaluating their child's needs and their own educational values.

As readers might notice when reading through the private school directory, school philosophies often sound very similar. "We offer a sound academic program while we develop in our students responsibility, self-confidence, and a concern for others." Visiting the school and talking with parents will help you determine whether you are comfortable with the environment and methods a school uses to achieve its goals. While some schools might work toward responsibility and academic excellence by offering a structured classroom environment and stressing homework, other schools seek to achieve the same goals by giving students the freedom to explore areas of study that interest them.

INQUIRE ABOUT THE CREDENTIALS AND BACKGROUNDS OF THE FACULTY. While many private schools hire only credentialed teachers, some do not. However, parents should not select a school purely on this basis. Many weak teachers have credentials; many excellent ones do not. Some private schools, especially secondary ones, look for staff with a variety of skills, advanced degrees, and practical experience in their subject matter, and consider the possession of a credential relatively unimportant. However, parents considering a school that does not require teaching credentials should carefully assess the caliber of teaching through parent and student evaluations and, if possible, class visitations.

CHECK THE FACULTY TURNOVER RATE. Although salaries at private schools are usually lower than those at public schools, private schools generally pride themselves on having dedicated, hard-working teachers. Up until the mid-1980's, young teachers in this area found that the only job opportunities were in private schools as shrinking enrollments and budget cuts brought public school hiring virtually to a halt. However, now that public schools are experiencing growing enrollment and many veteran teachers are retiring, capable young teachers and returning teachers have many more job choices. Although most private schools can't compete with public school salaries and benefits, many teachers who could get public school jobs stay on at good private schools for a number of reasons: small classes, close personal relationships with students, a minimum of disciplinary problems and bureaucratic red-tape, more control over curriculum, or in the case of religious schools, the opportunity to teach in a religious environment. A high teacher turn-over rate at a private school may indicate that a school does not offer enough of these advantages or that the salaries are dismally low.

CHECK ON THE SCHOOL'S FINANCIAL SOLVENCY. Few private schools can operate on tuition revenue alone. Most parochial schools are subsidized by their supporting church and therefore can offer private education at a relatively low cost to parents. Older schools often have substantial endowment funds and annual alumni fund-raising drives. Many schools rely on fund-raising efforts of parents to pay for special programs, scholarships and improvements. Almost all private schools publish some sort of annual financial report. If you are concerned about a school's financial solvency, do not be afraid to ask to read this report.

Proprietary schools operate under private ownership as profit-making ventures. Consequently, they cannot qualify for tax-exempt donations and must pay property taxes. Some educators are skeptical of any school run on such a basis. However, many proprietary schools are operated by dedicated educators and provide excellent programs. If you are interested in a proprietary school, check carefully to determine whether the school provides necessary services and materials to its students, sufficiently small classes, and adequate salaries to maintain a strong faculty while still making a profit for its owner.

UNDERSTAND THE DIFFERENCES IN PRIVATE SCHOOLS.

Carden Schools were started in the 1930's in New York City by Mae Carden and soon spread throughout the country. The curriculum is highly organized and stresses continuity from grade to grade. Reading, language and grammar instruction begin in kindergarten. The textbooks are privately printed and designed so that skills are taught in clear sequence. Emphasis on written and oral communication in a structured environment characterizes Carden schools. Carden teachers do not have to be credentialed by the state, but they must go through special Carden training and attend instructional seminars twice a year. Each Carden school runs independently — some as non-profit and some as proprietary institutions — but all must be accredited by the Carden Foundation. The degree of academic acceleration varies from school to school, depending on the abilities of the school's students.

Montessori Schools. In the early 1900's Maria Montessori, an Italian physician and educator, developed her ideas on education from observing slum children in Rome. Her belief that children have a great capacity for mental concentration, a desire to repeat activities, and a love of order led her to write influential books on education, which formed the basis for the Montessori method. Montessori schools stress the importance of a rich environment to provide children the opportunity to understand the world through sensory experiences. The Montessori teacher generally keeps a low profile, allowing children to move from one set of carefully designed materials to another as they wish. Montessori education stresses self-motivated learning and strives to develop self-discipline and self-confidence. San Mateo Elementary School District offers two very popular Montessori alternative schools to its families, but most Montessori schools in this area are proprietary. Because any school can use Montessori in its title, "Montessori" schools vary greatly in quality and approach.

Christian Schools. The label "Christian School" applies to schools that have an evangelical or fundamentalist approach to theology and integrate the Bible in almost all aspects of the school curriculum. Most are operated by churches which adhere to a literal interpretation of the Bible, but only a few require that students' families belong to a specific church. Christian schools usually use *A Beka* or other Christian texts; most use them along with secular textbooks, but some use these materials exclusively. Many of these schools offer specialized programs for students with learning disabilities. (Note: Some schools with Christian church affiliations are not considered "Christian Schools" in the above sense because they do not take an evangelical approach to religion, and they teach academic subjects in a secular manner.)

Roman Catholic Schools are committed to teaching the principles of the Roman Catholic Church while offering a strong academic program. However, Catholic schools can vary in their educational philosophy, structure, and overall flavor. Some are highly structured and traditional; others are more relaxed, open, and innovative. Catholic schools use state-adopted texts, often the same ones used in local public schools, and usually educate the same spectrum of children as are found in public schools. While most Catholic schools do not feel equipped to educate seriously handicapped children, some offer programs for those with mild learning disabilities.

Most Catholic elementary schools are parish (parochial) schools operated under the sponsorship of a specific church. Tuition at these schools is relatively low compared to the fees charged by other private schools, and the tuition discounts for siblings are substantial. A few Catholic elementary schools and most Catholic secondary schools are operated by religious orders. These nonparochial Catholic schools are usually more expensive than parish schools but tend to have smaller class sizes.

All Catholic schools give admissions priority to qualified Catholic applicants. They welcome non-Catholic students when space is available but expect all students to participate in the school's religious instruction.

Independent School is a term generally used for non-church affiliated, non-profit private schools, but some schools that belong to the National Association of Independent Schools (NAIS) and the California Association of Independent Schools (CAIS) do have religious affiliations. While independent schools may include the teaching of religious values and traditions in their philosophy, they teach academic subjects with a secular approach.

Independent schools tend to be more expensive than other private schools but usually have much smaller class sizes and are generally generous with financial aid. They are governed by boards of trustees and usually list preparation for high school or college as their primary goal. Because they are independent, these schools vary greatly in philosophy, structure, and academic programs.

Waldorf Schools, started in Germany in 1919 by Rudolf Steiner, stress the relationship between the physical, psychological, and the spiritual. Steiner believed that children pass through distinct stages of development and the Waldorf curriculum and teaching methods reflect these separate stages. In Waldorf schools, the class teachers continue from grade to grade with the same children and are responsible for their main subjects. Other teachers teach foreign languages, music, eurythmy (movement), crafts and games. Waldorf Schools do not use traditional textbooks in the early grades; instead the curriculum relies on oral presentations by the teachers and lesson books created by the children for each subject studied. Administrative decisions are made collectively by the faculty who work out of consensus.

Day-Care Originated Private Schools. In the last two decades, there has been a great increase in the number of schools that started out originally as preschool/day care centers and have responded to working parents' needs by expanding into elementary programs. These schools are generally owner-operated, stay open year-round, and include extended day care as part of the tuition. These schools vary greatly in quality and philosophy.

Other Schools. Some private schools listed in this book do not fall into any of the above categories. Most of these are either proprietary schools (see explanation on page 16) or are affiliated with a particular religion, e.g., Jewish, Episcopal, Seventh Day Adventist. Parents can learn about the philosophy and curriculum of these schools by reading the entries listed in the directory and contacting the schools.

HOW TO EVALUATE A SCHOOL

ASSESS THE LEADERSHIP QUALITIES OF THE PRINCIPAL (called the director, headmaster, or headmistress at many private schools). Your child's education will certainly be shaped largely by the quality of individual teachers; however, a strong principal can create an atmosphere that inspires staff members to put more energy into their jobs and fosters the high morale and family feeling that creates a sense of community among teachers, parents, and students. To assess the quality of leadership in a school, talk to parents, students, and teachers, and, if possible, arrange a meeting with the principal to help you answer some of the following questions:

- Do parents feel comfortable telephoning the principal when a problem arises that teachers cannot or will not handle? Are calls returned and, when necessary, conferences arranged?

- Does the principal support the staff, but still respond to legitimate complaints when parents feel teachers are not doing their jobs?

- Does the principal take the time to know the students? Does he or she make appearances on the playground, in the lunch area, and in classrooms, and participate in activities with students?

- Do students and teachers respect but not fear or hate the principal?

- Can the principal clearly describe the school's curriculum, and is he or she excited about the school's programs?

- When discipline problems arise in the classroom or on the playground, does the principal respond immediately and effectively?

If you get an affirmative answer to all or most of these questions, then you have found a place with one of the most important elements of a healthy school — strong leadership.

EVALUATE THE TEACHERS. In evaluating the quality of teaching at any school, parents should realize that no one teacher is perfect for all children and that no one school has only "star" teachers. Some children do best with hard-nosed disciplinarians who stretch students with demanding assignments and run a "tight ship" in the classroom. Others wilt under pressure and are happier and more productive with warmer, more nurturing teachers.

A lot of your information will come from talking with parents, but you should remember that tastes in teachers can be like tastes in movies — the reviews can be so different that you will wonder if people are talking about the same person. Unfortunately, many schools have at least one or two "lemons" — teachers who, according to almost everyone, are incompetent, burned-out, or just plain mean or indifferent. Schools usually also have at least as many "stars" — teachers whom parents and students praise for their extraordinary teaching abilities. Avoid schools that have a large number of "lemons" and look for one that has at least one or two "stars."

Class visits can help you judge the caliber of teaching at a school. Most public schools and some private schools welcome such visits as long as prior arrangements are made with the school office. Do not judge too harshly schools that do not allow such visits. Some schools, especially large private ones with many applicants, consider class visitations disruptive and logistically impossible. If a school does not allow classroom observation, ask to attend an open house or back-to-school night. Such a visit may give you an opportunity to talk to teachers or at least hear about and see the results of what goes on in the classroom.

Through classroom visits, attendance at open house, and discussions with parents and current students, try to answer the following questions:

- Do teachers explain material clearly and respond to questions without putting students down?

- Is the degree of discipline and control in the classroom what you want for your child? If you want a structured classroom, be sure that control is not achieved through fear or intimidation. If you want an open learning environment, be sure that freedom does not result in chaos.

- Do teachers discipline children without cruelty or sarcasm?

- Do teachers seem to enjoy their jobs and bring energy, enthusiasm, and empathy into the classroom?

- Are teachers willing to spend extra time — recess, lunch, or afterschool time if necessary — to explain material a child did not understand in class?

- Do teachers clarify class rules and the consequences of breaking the rules and follow through with consistency and fairness?

- Do teachers combine solid instruction in basic skills with projects and study units that generate excitement and intellectual curiosity? Even if you are primarily interested in a "basics" school, do not forget that stimulation of intellectual curiosity is probably the most important element of a good education. Ask parents if their children ever come home excited about what they are learning. When visiting classrooms, do you see only math dittoes and spelling tests covering the walls? Or is there evidence of more interesting assignments as well — creative writing samples, social studies projects, and science experiments?

You will probably never find a school where every teacher is wonderful, and it will be impossible to answer all of the above questions for every member of a school's faculty. But talking to members of the school community and spending time at the school should give you a good sense of how enthusiastic, caring, and competent a school's teachers are.

LOOK AT THE CURRICULUM. Asking questions and making observations about curriculum can also help determine whether a school will meet your expectations and be appropriate to your child's needs.

- Check to see that the textbooks are up-to-date.

- Try to determine whether the school achieves a healthy balance between development of basic skills and the exploration of ideas and thinking skills.

- Try to assess what ability level the school is geared toward, especially if the school stresses group instruction as part of its philosophy. If your child seems to fall above or below the ability norm of the general student body, ask how ability levels are handled. Are brighter children allowed to move ahead at a faster pace and given more challenging assignments? Or are they merely given 40 math problems instead of the normal 20 to keep them busy? Are slower students given extra help and more time to grasp concepts and complete work?

In specific areas, consider the following:

Reading: For decades, educators have debated the best approach to teaching reading. While the terminology has changed over the years, the issue is generally the same: proponents of phonics believe children should first learn the letters and the sounds the letters make so that they can decode words and learn to spell correctly. Advocates of what is now termed the "whole language approach" argue that the tedious drill and repetition of phonics instruction kills off enthusiasm for reading, and that children should be allowed to learn to read and write through the desire to express and understand what is important to them. Instead of beginning with the individual letters and sounds, the whole language approach de-emphasizes correct spelling and de-coding in the early years and instead concentrates on the "whole." Sounds are taught through rhythm, repetition and context. Critics of this approach argue that it doesn't give students the basic phonic skills needed to spell accurately and sound out unfamiliar words. This debate will probably continue indefinitely because children have different learning styles and no one theory fits all children. Most good teachers recognize the value of generating enthusiasm and interest in reading by exposing students to exciting literature at an early age, but at the same time know the importance of emphasizing, through multi-sensory techniques, the relationships of sounds and letters. Avoid primary grade teachers who are dogmatic about the best approach to teaching reading.

At the elementary level, look for schools that use a mixture of materials and techniques to stimulate interest in reading. Literature assignments, oral reading by the teacher and students, and regular outside reading assignments should be used instead of or in combination with traditional reading textbooks. Many schools — public and private — now set aside a specific time of day for school-wide silent, sustained reading to promote the concept that reading is a relaxing, enjoyable experience.

At the secondary level, an examination of required reading lists and syllabi will help you determine whether the school's curriculum is appropriate to your child's abilities and your values and expectations. While a few secondary schools still pride themselves on assigning only "classics" —e.g., Shakespeare, Dickens, Hawthorne—most are committed to a multicultural approach that reflects the rich diversity of our population and history. Whatever a school's philosophy about literature, the English classes should generate enthusiasm for reading and promote the ability to discuss and write about literature beyond the purely literal level of book reports.

Math: Math programs in the early primary grades should use manipulative materials to emphasize an understanding of concepts. Beware of schools that rely almost completely on rote learning of number facts without stressing mathematical concepts. Also look for programs that stress problem solving, logic, and real-life applicability.

Although many educators dislike ability tracking, it is difficult to avoid ability grouping in mathematics in secondary schools. Some students can breeze through Algebra I in the eighth or even seventh grade. Others have a great deal of difficulty grasping Algebra I in a year of ninth grade. Many middle schools now teach Algebra to large numbers of their eighth graders and a growing number of high schools offer Algebra I over two years to students who need a lot of practice and review to get through the course. Unfortunately, many schools assign their weakest math teachers to the weakest students and reward their "star" teachers with the accelerated classes. If you have a child who struggles with math, ask — not only administrators but also parents — about the school's policy regarding this issue. If you are considering a private high school, find out if the school offers options in its math program. If it doesn't, find out if the math program will fit your child's needs.

Composition: Look for a school that has defined expectations in the quantity and quality of writing it expects from students. A good writing program not only stresses the mechanics required for clear expression but also teaches the process of writing, exposes students to different kinds of writing, and inspires students to want to write. Beware of programs at either the elementary or secondary level that focus almost completely on grammar and sentence diagramming with little emphasis on actual composition. When evaluating secondary schools, ask parents and students how much writing is assigned, whether the assignments require higher level thinking skills than mere book reports, and if compositions are returned with meaningful teacher comments.

Science: Recognizing that most classroom elementary school teachers were not science majors, many private schools and some public school districts hire science specialists to enrich the science curriculum.

A good science program gives children the opportunity to observe, experiment, and use problem-solving techniques. A purely textbook approach to science, at either the elementary or secondary level, is one of the surest ways to stifle a child's natural curiosity about the world. Unfortunately, secondary school science teachers are under great pressure to prove the worth of their programs through student performance on Advanced Placement tests, and thus lab work often gets shunted aside for the easier and more testable textbook approach. The best science programs are those that prepare students to do well on the AP tests while maintaining the excitement and sense of discovery that comes from well-designed lab work.

Computer education: About a decade ago many schools enthusiastically invested in computers and then discovered that their staffs didn't really know what to do with them. Furthermore, much of the early educational software was disappointing as it was primarily limited to games and computerized workbooks and drills. In recent years, the quality of software has improved, and many more teachers have attended computer workshops and even developed their own programs. If a school appeals to you because it offers "computer education" and "computers in the classroom," you would be wise to investigate the degree of enthusiasm teachers express for using computers as an educational tool and the ability of the staff or district advisors to select high-quality software.

Social studies and history: By the time children complete the sixth grade, they should have a strong background in key events in American history, a respect for other cultures, and familiarity with world geography. Look for schools that teach these basic areas while generating interest in the subject matter through assigning historical fiction and using non-textbook activities like special projects, simulation games, field trips, movies (but beware of teachers who rely too much on movies to keep students entertained), guest speakers, and research papers.

At the secondary level, history classes should not be merely exercises in regurgitation. Look for programs that emphasize thinking, study, and research skills. A good history class should also include essay questions on the exams. Also look for schools that have realized the value of coordinating English and history instruction so that while students are studying American history, they are also reading American literature of the period.

The Arts: Some parents consider a strong arts program merely a frill; others consider the arts an essential part of a good education. If you are one of the latter, ask about a school's art, music, and drama programs. When public school districts were hit by the budget crunch of the 1970's, many of the first cutbacks came in the arts curriculum. Instrumental and chorus music teachers found their jobs cut or completely eliminated, and art specialists were relegated to volunteer status. In fact, many districts have come to rely on volunteer help using music and art volunteer docents to run programs formerly taught by paid specialists. These docent-run programs are often excellent, but many districts don't have a stable group of non-working parents to volunteer their time for the programs. Some elementary schools are blessed with classroom teachers who have a strong background in the arts, and thus, despite a shortage of parent art docents and the lack of funds to pay specialists, their students continue to get enriched exposure to the fine arts. Some innovative districts have won grants from the California Arts Commission to establish artists-in-residence programs which bring working artists to the schools to offer art education to both students and teachers.

Many private schools hire part or full time specialists to teach art, music, and drama. (In fact, having these specialists is often a draw that keeps teachers who aren't comfortable teaching this part of the curriculum in private schools. They are willing to work for lower pay, knowing they won't be responsible for teaching all aspects of their students' education.)

By the time children reach secondary school, parents usually have some indication of some special area of interest in the arts area. Often in high schools — both public and private — the success of a specific arts program is determined by a single individual. For example, on the San Francisco Peninsula, one public high school has an extraordinary chorus program, another a nationally known jazz band, and another an award winning marching band. One private school has an exceptionally strong drama program, another has an outstanding public speaking program, and another an excellent visual arts program. All of these programs are generated by the energy, enthusiasm, and expertise of one specific teacher. If your child has shown talent or interest in a specific area of the arts, you might want to look for a school that is known for its strength in that area.

EVALUATE THE SCHOOL ENVIRONMENT. Walking around a campus during school hours can be a helpful way of determining whether you will be happy with a school. Take note of the following:

Recess and lunch periods: Are recesses well supervised? Do children wander around aimlessly, or do most seem involved in games and playground activities? Are playground fights very common, and when they do occur, are they handled effectively? Do children toss litter around, or do they show a sense of pride in their school by using trash cans? Are the restrooms clean? Is there graffiti on the walls? Do children seem relaxed and happy?

The library: If a school has a library, is there a professional librarian, an aide, or a parent volunteer? Do students treat the library with respect? Is there evidence on the bulletin boards and walls of staff efforts to stimulate students' interest in reading? Are the books current, and is the collection appropriate to the size and age level of the student body? If a school cannot afford a librarian or a well-stocked library, and many good ones cannot, ask how the school stimulates interest in reading and teaches library skills.

The sounds of a school: When you walk by classrooms, is the dominant sound a teacher yelling at unruly students, or do you hear encouragement, lively class discussions, and occasional laughter. Do students speak to each other with kindness or with teasing and cruelty? Whether you want a highly structured school, an open one, or something in between, look for a school that makes learning a joyful experience in a calm atmosphere.

**SPECIAL THINGS TO CONSIDER WHEN LOOKING FOR AN ELE-
MENTARY SCHOOL.**

- If you need all day care for your child, closely examine what the before and after school activities involve.

  When I wrote the first edition of this book in 1984, the majority of elementary schools did not provide on site extended day care. Now, most do. However, parents should be certain that the school's child care program doesn't just mean sitting children down in front of a television set or turning them loose on a playground with minimal supervision. Look for a program that provides enriching activities provided by a trained, enthusiastic, and *stable* staff. Some child care operations pay employees so little that there is a constant turn-over of employees.

- If you are thinking of sending your child to a school some distance from your home, consider your child's social needs and your own sanity.

  In their zeal to give their children the best education, parents sometimes forget to include neighborhood friends as an important factor in the school selection process. If you do choose a school far from home and there aren't many other children in your area attending the school, sign your child up for neighborhood athletic teams or scout troops to give him or her the opportunity to make friends to play with during weekends and vacations. Furthermore, don't create an impossible situation for yourself by committing yourself to long drives unless you can do so without disrupting your home and work life, and you are confident that the stress of a long school commute won't adversely affect you or your child.

- Ask about a school's homework policy and consider whether it matches your needs and your child's abilities.

  If you want evening and weekend time to spend on family activities, a school that gives several hours of homework a night might be inappropriate. Inquire about the nature as well as the quantity of homework. Homework is useful if it broadens a child's interest in and understanding of classwork while developing good study habits. It is meaningless and potentially damaging if it is merely busy work or if the quantity is inappropriate to the age and ability of the child.

THINGS TO CONSIDER WHEN CHOOSING A MIDDLE SCHOOL

In recent years, educators have paid increasing attention to students in the preteen and early teenage years and the schools that serve these students. Formerly, these students were typically placed in junior high schools which treated the students as if they were just smaller versions of high school students. In 1986, a California study group issued a report that defined sixth, seventh and eighth grades as the "neglected grades." The concerns and recommendations of this group were echoed in the spring of 1989 in the Carnegie report on the Education of Young Adolescents. This report pointed out that "the guidance they [students] needed as children and need no less as adolescents is withdrawn" just as pressures to try drugs, alcohol, and early sex intensify. Parents evaluating schools for this age-group should look for schools which have in place pro-grams recommended by these study groups — programs which:

- de-emphasize rote skills and encourage critical and analytical thinking
- provide block scheduling or schools within schools to ensure that all students feel part of a community of teachers and students
- offer classes in health education
- minimize academic tracking.

Since private school programs for this age group are typically small, early adolescents at these schools usually do not experience the kind of anonymous, impersonal treatment typical of large public junior highs. However, some K-gr. 8 private schools in the area have difficulty keeping their students for the sixth, seventh, and eighth grade years. Many private school families, even some who plan to send their children to private high schools, switch to public middle schools — sometimes because the children themselves want the "rite of passage" experience of going to a new, bigger school that can offer more electives, social choices, and athletic opportunities.

In choosing a middle school, parents should consider their child's needs and personality. Confident children may love the novelty and stimulus of a large school that offers a full spectrum of electives, extensive athletic and extracurricular programs, and a broad range of social choices. Others may continue to need the security of knowing the principal and most of their classmates and teachers. However, parents should also note that a very small middle-school can be socially difficult for some children. This is often an age of intense cliquishness, and students who aren't part of the dominant social group can feel very socially isolated in a small school.

THINGS TO CONSIDER WHEN LOOKING AT SECONDARY SCHOOLS.

- Consider what size high school would be best for your child.

  Many students thrive in large high schools. They love the stimulation of broad course offerings, a diverse study body and a full menu of extra-curricular activities. Such students usually find their niche through special interests: sports, school government, music or drama. However, public school educators are beginning to realize what has long been clear to small independent school educators: many students get lost in large comprehen-sive high schools. They cut classes and fail to do assignments because they are convinced no one cares and they have no sense of connection to the teachers, administrators, or most of the students. To give students the opportunity to feel part of a community and to feel they are important, many school districts across the nation are establishing "schools within a school" and when possible small, self-contained public high schools. In this area, a few districts are following this trend; if such an option isn't available to you, and your child seems to be one who won't find a niche in a large high school, you might want to consider a small private school.

- Ask to see representative class syllabi, textbooks, and reading lists to determine whether the school's academic requirements are appropriate to your child's needs and abilities.

  If your eighth grader struggles through Jack London short stories, you probably should have second thoughts about sending him or her to a school that assigns Conrad and Hawthorne to all its ninth graders.

- Look for a school that offers extracurricular activities that will appeal to your child.

  Teenagers actively involved in extracurricular activities are more likely to be happy and stay out of trouble than those who merely go to classes and come home. Look not only for a school that offers programs in your child's special interest areas but also for one that encourages and allows broad participation in extracurricular activities so that he or she can develop new interests. (The segment on "Bruce Cohn" in *Four Families* at the end of the book illustrates why extracurricular involvement can be so important to a high school student's success and happiness.)

- Ask about the school's college counseling and career guidance program.

  Many public high schools have been forced to make drastic cutbacks in their counseling programs. If you choose a high school that offers little or no counseling, consider using a private counselor to help your child make college or vocational decisions. (Avoid those who make extravagant promises about their ability to get their clients into the *best colleges.*) Private high schools should provide thorough and personalized college counseling — check to see that they do.

- If you want your child to continue schooling after high school, ask to see the list of colleges and universities attended by recent graduates, and ask what percentage of students attend four year colleges after graduation.

  When students are surrounded by peers who are serious about preparing for college, they are more likely to take high school seriously. However, do not select a school because you think it is a feeder school to certain colleges (see page 36 for more on this topic.) Parents should also realize that many students attend two year colleges, not because they aren't qualified to go to a four year school but because family finances necessitate the bargain education community colleges provide. If a public high school serves a low socio-economic level and thus has a relatively small percentage of students going on to four year colleges, find out if it has a strong honors program for its motivated students.

  Two other indicators of the strength of a high school's academic program are its students' performance on Advanced Placement Tests and the pass rate of students enrolled at the University of California on the subject A Exam. Grades of 3, 4, or 5 on the exam qualify for credit at most of the nation's colleges. The California Department of Education releases statistics on the number of tests with a score of 3 or better measured as a percentage of the senior class of each public high school.

- If you have a child who doesn't seem interested in going to college and has lost interest in school, look for a high school that offers career apprenticeship programs.

Many students do poorly in high school because they feel that most of their classes are irrelevant. Consequently, many public high schools are working with the business community to establish programs that teach skills that students then use in afterschool apprenticeship programs. Such programs are designed to help students get good jobs immediately after high school or prepare them for further training. These programs motivate students to stay in school because they can see the practical application of what they are learning in the classroom.

- Ask about the school's policy towards ability grouping.

For years, educators have debated the pros and cons of ability grouping, sometimes referred to as tracking. Currently many influential educational researchers argue that all students should be exposed to the kind of challenging, stimulating curriculum typical of honors classes. Many school districts are moving in the direction of heterogeneous grouping in an attempt to give all students a rigorous, academic experience. However, some teachers and parents are concerned that the move away from ability grouping will result in a watering down of the curriculum and the loss of the stimulation normally associated with honors classes. Some schools have maintained their honors program but made them less exclusive by allowing any student willing to do the extra work to take the classes.

If you have a high achieving child and a school mandates heterogeneous grouping in most or all subjects, try to ascertain whether instructors successfully challenge all their students. If you have a student who doesn't shine academically and a school does track, find out if the school adequately stimulates its average and struggling students or whether these students get stuck with the least inspiring instructors and teachers who expect little of their students.

- Ask if a school has a community service program.

Educators have become increasingly aware that adolescents benefit when they help others. Meaningful community service increases students' sense of self-worth and promotes a sense of community responsibility. At the same time, it can help students overcome their own prejudices and misconceptions about those they are helping. Many secondary schools, public and private, have established programs that encourage and facilitate volunteer community service. Some private schools make such service a graduation requirement.

ASK WHETHER THE SCHOOL IS ACCREDITED. Accreditation certifies to other educational institutions and to the general public that a school meets established criteria and standards and has been evaluated by an official review board. Private schools that receive public funds to educate handicapped children must be certified as meeting certain standards by the California Department of Education, but California does not accredit private schools. If a school claims it is "accredited by the State" inquire further. Legally, private schools are merely required to register with their county office of education. This simple registration procedure is in no way a form of accreditation, but some schools try to make parents believe it is.

The Western Association of Schools and Colleges (WASC) is one of six regional agencies in this country authorized by the Department of Education to accredit public and private schools. Accreditation by this private agency is especially important for secondary schools because students from unaccredited schools may have difficulty getting into some colleges. To obtain WASC accreditation, a school must complete a thorough self-study, which is followed by a three-and-a-half day visit by a team of educators. The visitation committee evaluates the school on the basis of whether the school is accomplishing its stated objectives. Once full accreditation is granted, a review occurs at least every six years. If you are considering an accredited school, feel free to ask to read the accreditation report. A school is under no obligation to show it to you, but a refusal to do so should cause you some concern. WASC reports include a section commending the school for what the school does well and a section recommending what areas the school should work at improving. If the areas of recommendation are not merely trivial and address some concerns you have, ask the school what it is doing to implement the recommendations.

While virtually all public comprehensive high schools have WASC accreditation, public elementary and junior highs rarely apply as they are already subject to a high degree of accountability under state guidelines and controls. However, because there is virtually no state control over private schools, a growing number of private elementary and middle schools are applying for WASC accreditation. The accreditation process helps them evaluate and improve their programs while also assuring the public that the school meets established standards and provides a program that successfully implements its goals and philosophy.

Accreditation is not a guarantee of excellence, and a lack of accreditation does not imply an inferior program. Accreditation is a time-consuming and expensive process, and thus many good private elementary schools, especially new ones operating on a tight budget, do not choose to apply for it.

Other accreditation or certifying organizations mentioned in this book include:

The California Association of Independent Schools (CAIS) was established in 1939 to promote high academic and professional standards for its member schools. Secondary schools seeking CAIS membership must be accredited by WASC. All member schools are required to undergo a thorough self-evaluation every six years, followed by a visit from an evaluation committee. To be considered for membership in CAIS, a school must be in operation for at least six years; after two years of operation, a school may apply for provisional membership.

The Western Catholic Education Association (WCEA) has an evaluation procedure very similar to that used by WASC. The San Francisco Archdiocese, which oversees the operation of San Mateo County Catholic parish schools, and the Santa Clara County Archdiocese have chosen to certify their schools jointly with WASC.

The Association of Christian Schools International (ACSI) offers to its members an accreditation program similar to the WASC instrument. Many area ACSI schools are choosing to seek dual accreditation from both organizations.

Several other religious and education organizations accredit their member schools. In most cases, the accreditation process involves a self-study and a visit by outside educators.

ANSWERS TO FREQUENTLY ASKED QUESTIONS

Below are answers to some of the most frequently asked questions regarding school selection.

When should I start investigating schools?

Although you can't start talking to friends, neighbors, and pre-school teachers too soon about school choices, the fall term before your child enters school is usually the best time to start visiting schools and evaluating your public and private school choices. If you decide in October that you do not want what your public school district has to offer, you will have plenty of time to visit and apply to other districts or private schools. Few private schools, at least in this area, are interested in taking applications more than a year in advance. While an early start will maximize your options, don't despair if you start later. For every school with long waiting lists, many more have openings up until — and even after — the school year starts.

There are two important exceptions to this schedule. Private schools with preschool programs usually give priority to children coming from their pre-kindergarten program and therefore may not have many spaces left for children applying the winter or spring before kindergarten starts. Many parents have found that to ensure their children entry into these schools, they have to enroll them in the school's preschool program.

The hardest schools to get a child into can be public alternative schools; a few allow parents to sign up as soon as their child is born while others use a lottery system. If you live in a school district that offers alternative or magnet schools, phone the district office to find out when you should apply.

What should I do if a school recommends that my child wait a year before starting kindergarten?

A child must be five years old on or before December 2 to enter a California public school kindergarten. Many private schools use a similar cut-off date, but a few will allow younger children to enter their kindergartens if they feel the child is mature enough to handle the class work. A growing number of private schools require that entering kindergartners be five by September. Most schools give a kindergarten readiness test to determine a child's level of developmental maturity. On the basis of that test, the school may recommend that a child wait a year before entering kindergarten or that the child go into a transitional kindergarten, a pre-kindergarten program offered by many private schools and public school districts. These programs typically have a smaller student to teacher ratio than the regular kindergarten classes and take into account the shorter attention span and less developed motor skills of their students.

It has become very common, especially in affluent areas where parents can afford an extra year of preschool and where schools pride themselves on running "academic" kindergartens, to start children with fall birthdays a year later even if the child appears to be developmentally ready for kindergarten. This is especially common with boys because they tend to develop fine motor skills later than girls do and because parents often are apprehensive about their son being the smallest or youngest boy in the class.

Children who are developmentally, emotionally, or socially immature should be given an extra year to mature before starting school. If there is any doubt about your child's readiness, wait a year. Later, it will be far less painful to skip a child who is too advanced for his grade than it will be to have him repeat a grade.

Should I have my child tested before I start shopping for schools?

In most cases, testing is not necessary. However, if a child appears to have learning disabilities or seems *exceptionally* bright, testing might help you determine what kind of school will best serve your child's needs. You may be able to have your child tested without charge by your school district, or your pediatrician, the Family Service Association, or an educational counselor should be able to refer you to a reliable professional.

How important is it that reading be taught in kindergarten?

To a certain extent, this is one of those swing of the pendulum issues. Many educators in both public and private schools do not believe formal reading instruction should begin until first grade because they feel kindergarten should be a year for developing social skills, building self-confidence, and working on reading readiness. These educators point to studies that show a significant catch-up factor in reading ability — i.e., in studies of children with similar intelligence, those who aren't taught to read until first or second grade (or even later) catch up and often surpass in enthusiasm and ability those who were taught formal reading in kindergarten.

However, in the late 1970's and early 1980's, as the public reacted against the experimentalism of the previous decade, many parents demanded more structure and pressured the schools to include reading as part of the kindergarten curriculum. In response to that pressure, many public school districts and private schools set in place formal reading instruction in their kindergartens. Now, the pendulum seems to be swinging back as educators and parents are looking at these academic kindergartens and wondering if we're not pushing our children too hard.

Experienced kindergarten teachers realize that some of their students are ready to read and others aren't. A good program doesn't hold back those who are eager and ready to read, but doesn't pressure those who aren't ready. If you are considering a kindergarten that promises to teach all its students to read, be sure your child is developmentally ready for the tasks expected. Too much pressure on children early in their school careers can cause frustration and insecurity that might result in negativity toward school in general.

Can a child who starts out in public school change to a good private school later?

In most cases, yes. All private schools experience some natural attrition. Because of family moves, changes in family finances, or transfers to other schools, even the most competitive schools have occasional openings in the upper grades. And many private schools increase their class sizes in the upper grades, creating other openings. Therefore, a child who has done well in public school has an excellent chance of transferring to a private school.

Even parents with a child who has not done well in public school (a reason many parents consider making the switch) can find private schools willing to try to turn the child around. Some private schools are especially effective at taking under-achievers or "diamonds in the rough" and turning them into successes. However, some schools that take students with low test scores or grades make summer school attendance or the repetition of a grade a condition of acceptance.

Many parents are happy with public school for their children's elementary school education but wish to change them to private schools for their junior high and high school years. In most cases, secular private high schools accept students on the basis of test scores, grades, interviews, and recommendations. To most admissions people, a good student is welcome and past schooling is of relatively minor importance. The most competitive (i.e., most applicants for number of places) independent schools on the Peninsula all report that one half or more of their entering seventh graders each year come from public elementary schools.

Admittance to area Catholic high schools can be more difficult for the child who has attended a public elementary school since some Catholic high schools give priority to graduates of feeder parish schools. However, even these schools accept large numbers of public school products.

Should I forget about sending my child to a private school if the tuition is more than I can afford?

While some small private schools cannot afford to give scholarships, many of the large and well-established schools do. Parochial schools, where fees are relatively low anyway, usually give sibling discounts, and some try to set up a certain percentage of their budgets for scholarships for parishioners. Independent schools, which tend to charge the highest tuitions, are usually quite generous in granting financial aid. According to recent National Association of Independent Schools (NAIS) figures, 17% of the students at member schools receive some financial aid. Proprietary schools and new schools struggling to make ends meet tend to give few scholarships.

Are the best teachers in public or private schools?

Good teachers can be found in all kinds of schools — public and private, traditional and open. Public schools have more difficulty getting rid of weak teachers than do private schools, but private schools also have their share of "lemons." Because of public school pay increments for additional coursework and district in-service requirements, public school teachers are more likely to attend professional workshops than are their private school counterparts.

Ideally a school should balance the experience and wisdom of older teachers with the energy and enthusiasm of younger ones. When I wrote the first edition of this book, public school hiring of new teachers had been virtually non-existent for almost a decade, so few had that healthy balance. At the time I predicted that would soon change. It has. Now that public schools are experiencing a growth in enrollment at the same time veteran teachers are retiring, they are hiring many new teachers. Some of those are former private school teachers attracted by the more attractive pay and benefits that public schools can offer.

Often, especially at the secondary level, it is easier to be a good teacher at a private school than a public one. Because class sizes are usually smaller, teachers can assign more written work and respond more thoroughly. Private school teachers don't have to put up with as many discipline problems or as much red-tape as do their public school counterparts. And private school teachers can expect more support from parents; when parents are paying a hefty sum for tuition, they're more likely to make sure their children complete their assignments and attend classes. Because of these advantages, many excellent teachers remain at private schools despite the lower pay.

Why are the "best" public schools — the ones that score the highest on the statewide tests — always in the most expensive communities?

High-priced neighborhoods have a concentration of well-educated professionals, and there's an obvious correlation between the academic achievement of the parents and their children's ability to do well on standardized tests. Furthermore, these areas have few rental units, and therefore teachers don't have significant student turnover during the school year. Another explanation for the expensive housing/high test score correlation is that when children of affluent parents do struggle academically, their parents have the financial resources to send them to specialized private schools or pay for extensive tutoring.

Another aspect of the high-priced neighborhood that helps improve the schools is the availability of energetic, capable volunteers (many of whom were once themselves teachers) — parents who have the luxury of not working full-time and can serve as classroom, music, art, and library aides. These parents also have the time to be active members of their P.T.A.s. Furthermore, many affluent districts have set up foundations to raise extra money for the local schools and used the donated funds for such "extras" as library books, computers, and science aides and equipment.

Should I believe people when they tell me that a certain school or district is good or bad?

Unfortunately when people talk about "good" and "bad" schools, they usually are referring to the population a school serves and not the quality of the teachers, principals, and programs. Certainly, the "good" schools described above offer many advantages because they are working with children who may be easier to teach and are blessed with parents who support the schools in countless ways. However, many schools that look bad when judged by standardized test scores are excellent if they are judged by the caliber of their programs and staff. An administrator in one local district described in glowing terms the best school in his district: a school full of committed, dynamic teachers led by a wonderful principal; however, he admitted that few people would describe this school as the best or choose to send their children there because it serves the poorest, most transient segment of the district. On the other hand, he told me that the school that is considered the district's best, i.e, has the highest test scores, is actually one of the worst—has the most burned out teachers and uninspired leadership. Before ruling out what everyone says is a bad school or district, you would be wise to investigate for yourself in what way a specific school is good or bad.

What kind of school will be best for my very bright child?

Many area public and private schools have excellent programs for bright students. If you have a child who is extraordinarily bright, look for either a specialized school for the gifted or one that has flexible and imaginative teachers who can keep your child intellectually stimulated while encouraging social interaction with peers. Avoid placing an exceptionally bright child in a highly structured school which emphasizes group instruction and focuses primarily on basic skills.

Who should consider a boarding school?

Sending children to boarding school for their high school education is less common in California than it is on the East Coast. However, parents might consider boarding school if:

- family problems interfere with a child's academic and emotional well-being;
- a child needs a change of environment to get a second chance academically;
- they cannot find an acceptable school in their own community;
- a child seems to need the close interpersonal relationships and total school environment offered by good boarding schools.

If you are considering a boarding school, you can save yourself time, money, and disappointment by using the services of an educational counselor — an expert who specializes in matching students with appropriate schools. Avoid counselors who charge schools a commission for each student they place. Write the Independent Educational Counselors Association, 38 Cove Rd., P.O. Box 125, Forestdale, MA 02644 for names of reputable counselors in this area.

What school will give my child the best chance of getting into a prestigious college like Stanford or Harvard?

Admissions people from the most competitive private colleges assert that students with good grades, high test scores, and impressive talents and extracurricular activities will have a good chance of acceptance no matter what high school the student attends. Some area high schools, public and private, consistently have a high percentage of students accepted at prestigious colleges. However, these students are generally accepted because of their abilities and achievements and not because of any special influence their schools have.

Parents should select high schools on the basis of philosophy, course offerings, quality of teaching, and the ability of the school to meet the student's needs. Parents who place their child in an academically competitive high school may find that because the competition is stiffer and the courses are more demanding, the child's grades are lower than they would be in a school with a more average spectrum of students. Consequently, selecting a high school with a good track record in college admissions can backfire if the school is chosen primarily because parents think it will be a stepping stone to a prestigious college.

DIRECTORY OF PUBLIC SCHOOL DISTRICTS

Hester School, San Jose, 1891.

EXPLANATORY NOTES FOR PUBLIC SCHOOL LISTINGS

If you do not know what school district you reside in, telephone your County Office of Education listed at the beginning of each county's district listings. School districts are listed alphabetically by county and your district of residence can tell you your child's assigned school.

In the spring of 1993, every school district in San Mateo and Santa Clara counties was asked to complete a questionnaire for the third edition of this book. Some districts filled out these questionnaires completely and took advantage of the opportunity to share with the public a description of the programs offered in their schools. Others provided only basic information.

Class and school size: Because of enrollment changes and contract agreements with teacher unions, average and maximum class sizes may vary from year to year. Many public schools use paid and volunteer instructional aides, thus making the adult-to-student ratio lower than the stated class size indicates. The average class size in junior and senior high schools varies greatly from course to course; academic classes usually have fewer students than do physical education and typing. In many districts, a maximum class size is set as part of the contract agreement with teachers. In instances where a class exceeds the stated maximum, the district must get approval from the teacher or hire an extra classroom aide. Districts were also asked to state the average enrollment of their schools.

On site day care is noted as **EDC**. Districts were asked to indicate which of their schools have on-site day care and whether these programs are available to parents during school holidays. On site day care is offered by a variety of providers: non-profit agencies such as the YMCA and city recreation departments, and proprietary day care centers. Some districts indicated which providers serve their schools, but most did not. Principals often have a list of licensed day care homes and local day care centers that serve children attending their schools.

Transportation: During the years of budget cuts, bus service was one of the first items slashed in most districts. A few districts, especially those in which students live great distances from school campuses or in which children must take dangerous routes to school, have retained transportation services. All districts must by law provide transportation for handicapped students.

Alternative programs: Districts were asked to explain alternative programs (see page 11) in some detail. Some high school districts did not describe programs such as independent study or work study because they do not operate as alternative schools. All unified and high school districts have continuation schools (see page 12).

Transitional Kindergartens (Trans Kdg.): Districts were asked to indicate if they offer a program for children who are legally old enough to attend kindergarten but who are not developmentally ready.

GATE: As is explained on page 13, programs for students designated as gifted or talented vary greatly from district to district. School districts were asked to indicate how their schools serve their GATE students.

Open/Closed Campuses: Many of today's high school campuses are open — i.e., students are free to come and go during lunch and their free periods. Other districts, in response to parental and community concern, have maintained or reinstated closed campuses and thus forbid students to leave campus during the school day without permission. Some districts have a modified form of the open campus — e.g., students may leave campus only during lunch or only if they are seniors.

Couns:student ratio: High schools were asked if they have a counseling staff serving their student body and to indicate the ratio of counselors to students.

High School districts were also asked the percentage of graduates attending four year and two year colleges, and the percentage of students participating in extracurricular activities. Some districts did not have this information available.

DISTRICT BOUNDARIES
SANTA CLARA COUNTY

ELEMENTARY, HIGH SCHOOL & UNIFIED SCHOOL DISTRICTS

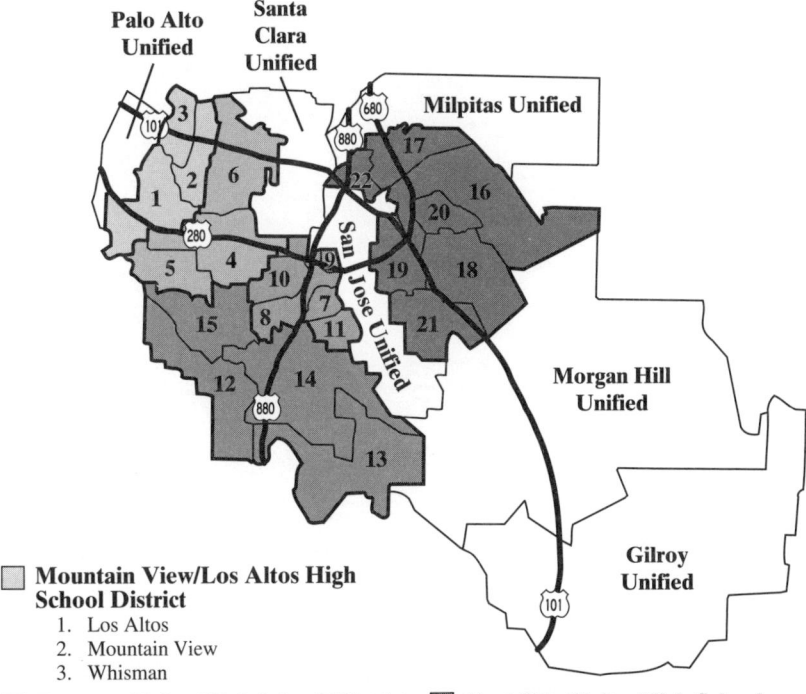

Mountain View/Los Altos High School District
1. Los Altos
2. Mountain View
3. Whisman

Fremont Union High School District
4. Cupertino
5. Montebello
6. Sunnyvale

Campbell Union High School District
7. Cambrian
8. Campbell
9. Luther Burbank
10. Moreland
11. Union

Los Gatos/Saratoga Joint Union High School District
12. Lakeside
13. Loma Prieta
14. Los Gatos
15. Saratoga

East Side Union High School District
16. Alum Rock
17. Berryessa
18. Evergreen
19. Franklin McKinley
20. Mount Pleasant
21. Oak Grove
22. Orchard

Palo Alto Unified School District

San Jose Unified School District

Santa Clara Unified School District

SANTA CLARA COUNTY PUBLIC SCHOOL DISTRICTS

Santa Clara County Office of Education
(408) 453-6500

ALUM ROCK. 2930 Gay Ave., San Jose 95127. (408) 258-4923. Larry Aceves, Superintendent. Eighteen K-gr. 5 elem. schools, six gr. 6-8 middle schools. EDC at some schools. Avg. class size 30, max. 34. Transportation for K-gr. 5 students who live more than 1.5 miles from school; for gr. 6-8, more than 2 mi. away. All sites have programs for gifted students. Most schools offer bilingual education. Sheppard Mid. School has school-age mothers' program.

BERRYESSA UNION. 1376 Piedmont Rd., San Jose 95132-249. (408) 923-1800. G. Herbert Wadley, Ed. D., Superintendent. Ten K-gr. 5 elem. schools (one elem. school houses a 6th-7th grade classroom), avg. school size 550; three gr. 6-8 middle schools, avg. class size 32, max. 34. Some transportation. EDC at all elem. schools except Cherrywood. Music programs in gr. 4-8. Summer programs. GATE: resource teacher assists classroom teacher in providing higher levels of instruction, afterschool programs offered in all schools. Instrumental music in elem. schools; band & orchestra in mid. schools. Parent participation alternative programs for 10 elem. classrooms located at 3 sites. Home School study offered as an alternative education program. District is developing outcomes for measuring student progress; alternative assessment models being used in 2 schools. English Language Development (ELD) at all schools. Migrant program. School site councils develop educational plans for their schools. District foundation.

CAMBRIAN. 4115 Jacksol Dr., San Jose (408) 377-2103. B.R. Groves, Superintendent. Four K-gr. 5 elem. schools, avg. school size 475, aides in K-gr. 5; one gr. 6-8 mid. school, 700 students. Avg. class size 28, max. 31. Transportation avail. to some elem. students for fee. Bagby, Farnham, Fammatre have EDC. Summer academic programs for gr.1-8. Instrumental music. Computer labs at each school. Programs for GATE students planned at school site to meet students' needs. Clubs and after-school programs at mid.

school. Decision-making and drug awareness curriculum in all schools. Reading intervention for 1st graders. Write to Write computer program at Bagby. The district "has a strong academic focus" and it strives to "build strong self-esteem in its children."

CAMPBELL UNION. 155 No. 3rd St., Campbell 95008. (408) 364-4200. Marcia Plumleigh, Superintendent. Eight K-gr. 4 elem. schools, avg. school size 530; three gr. 5-8 middle schools, avg. school size 925. Avg. class size 29, max. 33; aides used in some K-gr. 4 classes. Transportation. EDC at all elem. schools. Elem. schools have computers in classrooms and/or in labs. Computer labs and instrumental music at all mid. schools. All schools have business partnerships. GATE: clustering as well as special course offerings at mid. schools. After school programs: Odyssey of the Mind; performing arts. Summer programs: special ed., ESL, core academics, music, gr.4-8 proficiency.

CAMPBELL UNION HIGH SCHOOL DISTRICT. 3235 Union Ave., San Jose 95124. (408) 371-0960. Bruce Hauger, Ed D., Superintendent. Four high schools; three have closed campuses. 2-3 counselors at each school. 70% of grads. go to college. Avg. class size in most departments, 28. 9th grade English classes, 20.

Blackford Alternative High School offers special programs and independent study.

CUPERTINO UNION. 10301 Vista Dr., Cupertino 95014. (408) 252-3000. Patricia Lamson, Superintendent. Eighteen K-gr. 6 schools, avg. class size 30, avg. school size 500-600; four gr. 7-8 jr. highs, avg. class size 31, avg. school size 700. Limited transportation. EDC at all elem. sites, open school holidays, hours vary by site. Extended day instrumental music, jr. high chorus & band, elementary chorus. Variety of summer programs include core and enrichment, special education, jr. high proficiency. All schools have GATE programs. District provides comprehensive array of integrated, school -based services designed to meet the needs of all students including extended learning, special education and English as a second language. Extensive community partnerships. Nationally recognized as a leader in technology, the district has adopted as a major goal the development of a comprehensive technology plan that embraces instructional and administrative technology as an effective tool for students and teachers. District foundation raises approximately $300,000/yr.

"The mission of the Cupertino Union School District is to provide its students with a classical education from which they gain the knowledge, skills, and attitudes that foster an enjoyment of learning, a respect for themselves and others, and the ability as responsible citizens to fulfill their right to self-determination."

Faria Academics Plus Program: 10155 Barbara Lane, Cupertino 252-0706. K-gr. 6. Whole group instruction by teacher in a structured class environment; required homework four nights a week.

McAuliffe Alternative Elementary Program: 12211 Titus Ave., Saratoga 253-4596. K-gr.6, individualized curriculum, integrated learning, family participation required, low adult-to-child ratio allows a great deal of individual attention.

EAST SIDE UNION HIGH SCHOOL SCHOOL DISTRICT. 830 N. Capitol Ave., San Jose 95133. (408) 272-6400. Joe Coto, Superintendent. Eleven high schools, avg. enrollment 2200. Avg. class size 30, max. 35. 6 periods/day. Closed campuses. 30 AP courses offered, 6 languages. Tutorial assistants. 1 couns: 800 students. 80% of students participate in extracurricular activities. 35% attend 4 yr. colleges; 30% attend 2 yr. colleges. Academy program for at risk students. No ability grouping.

East Side Magnets: Police Academy, Business Occupations, Leadership and Communications, Aerospace Science, Pre-Engineering, Mega Tech, Teaching Academy, Medical/Health Services, and Manufacturing Industrial Technology. Priority given to students who sign up for magnet programs in April of 8th grade year. Placement depends upon available space and ethnic and racial balance.

EVERGREEN SCHOOL DISTRICT. 3188 Quimby Rd., San Jose 95148. (408) 270-6800. James Smith, Superintendent. Four K-5 elem. schools, seven K-6 elem. schools, three gr. 6-8 mid. schools. Avg. class size 30. Transportation. Summer programs for gr. 4-8, Chapter 1, migrant and special education students. GATE students receive 200 minutes of qualitatively different education; honors program in mid. schools. Music programs in middle schools. The district's philosophy is "sharing a commitment to excellence."

FRANKLIN-McKINLEY. 645 Wool Creek Dr., San Jose 95112. (408) 283-6000. 13 elem. schools (grade configurations vary), avg. school size 650, avg. & max. class size 30; two gr. 6-8 mid. schools, avg. school size 1000. 8 elem. & 1 mid. school operate year-round. Most elem. sites have EDC, avail. during school holidays. Avg. & max. class size 30. Transportation for K-6 students who live 1 1/4 miles or more from school; for gr. 7-8 students who live more than 1 1/2 miles away. GATE: resource teachers at elem. schools. Slingerland program avail. at Franklin & Stonegate. Cooperative program with homeschooling families. Independent study avail. for middle school students. Si Se Pueda ("Yes I Can) Counseling Program for at-risk students. Quest (skills for adolescents), Cooperative Learning Program. Summer programs for migrant students and for students needing remediation; Valdez Math program. Services available through district office include health care, probation officer, Project Crackdown, family counseling, and child care.

FREMONT UNION HIGH SCHOOL DISTRICT. 589 W. Fremont Ave., P.O. Box F, Sunnyvale 94087. (408) 735-6060. Betty A. Pacheco, Superintendent. Five comprehensive high schools, enrollments range from 1099-1757. Avg. class size 32.5. Max. class size in 9th grade English is 21. 7

per./day. Spanish, French, & German taught at all campuses. Mandarin Chinese at some. Open campus policy. Numerous business and community partnerships. Tutorial centers. 40% attend 4 yr. colleges; 45% attend 2 yr. colleges. Basic Aid District.

The Institute of Computer Technology (ICT) is a computer educational institution dedicated to providing students, teachers and community members opportunities for career development in an increasingly technological society. It is operated as a joint powers venture by Fremont Union, Sunnyvale Elementary and Los Gatos-Saratoga High School Districts. This joint venture of education and industry is designed to provide basic computer literacy for the community, train students for entry level jobs after high school, and offer sophisticated technical education for the college-bound student. For more information phone 736-4291.

Middle College, an alternative program located on the campus of De Anza Community College, is designed for juniors and seniors who are academically very capable but for a variety of reasons are not performing up to their potential. By interacting with a more mature role group and taking advantage of advanced course work, students develop responsibility and a sense of self-direction.

Phoenix High School, the district's continuation school, operates on the philosophy that at risk students can succeed by giving them a sense of power and involvement with their own educational program.

District's Vision Statement: "Our youth become lifelong learners; informed and active citizens of the world; knowledgeable and self-directed members of the workplace; and discerning participants in the arts."

GILROY UNIFIED. 7810 Arroyo Circle, Gilroy 95020. (408) 847-2700. Kenneth A. Noonan, Superintendent. Nine K-gr. 6 elem. schools, range from 250-800 students, aides used according to programs; two gr. 7-8 jr. highs, avg, school size 900. Avg. class size 30, max. 32. Transportation. Music specialists for gr. 1-6; instrumental music gr. 5-12. Computer labs in all schools. Business partnerships in most schools. GATE: pull-out programs, cluster program at Rucker. Summer school programs. Spring sign-ups for open enrollment and alternative programs.

Brownell Fundamental School is the district's magnet fundamental school for K-gr. 6 The school has a structured and highly disciplined learning environment and emphasizes oral reading, reading comprehension, composition, spelling, mathematics, handwriting, patriotism, morals, social skills, and responsibility. Educational technology is incorporated throughout the curriculum. Homework is a primary focus, and there is a dress code. Parents & students required to sign a contract to uphold the school's guidelines. 842-3135.

Eliot School serves students whose performance on the Slingerland Pre-reading Inventory demonstrates that they need information delivered through a multisensory approach. Specially trained teachers use the Slingerland Program, a multisensory method of language instruction. Classes are grouped by grade level and held to a maximum of 25 students. 842-5618.

El Roble Bilingual Magnet is a K-gr.6 bilingual program that offers a transition program for Spanish-speaking students and an enrichment program for English-speaking students. Students learn to communicate naturally in two languages. Through the use of computers, science materials, math manipulatives, laser disc programs video and other multi-media technology and cooperative learning strategies, comprehension is enhanced and academic achievement assured. Bilingual resource teacher and paraprofessionals support the program.

Gate Cluster Program at Rucker School serves children in gr. 3-6 who have been identified as gifted and exhibit identified strength in language arts. Students use computers & video equipment on regular basis; extended day program offered in Theater Arts program.

Las Animas Science/Math Magnet. K-gr. 6 provides a heterogeneous student population with educational experiences that promote higher order thinking skills, utilizing math & science as a focus of instruction. Two science labs, full-time science specialist & instructional assistant, technology in all classrooms, outdoor life lab, field trips & assemblies related to science, math and technology.

Gilroy High School, 2000 students. Avg. class size 32, max. 35. 30% attend 4 yr. colleges, 30% attend 2 yr. colleges. Closed Campus. 1 couns: 500 students. 60% of students participate in extra curricular activities. School-wide tutorial program, GATE, 10 AP classes, bilingual ed., French, Spanish. Business partnership w/ IBM. Oasis (drop-out recovery program), pregnant minors/child care program, student assistance program, Drug Abuse Prevention Council. Heterogeneous grouping.

LAKESIDE JOINT UNION. 19621 Black Rd., Los Gatos 95030. (408) 354-2372. Martin St. John, Superintendent. One K-gr. 6 school, 146 students; jr. high students go to Fisher Jr. High in Los Gatos S.D. Avg. class size 22.6, max. 30. Transportation. EDC: 12-6, open during school holidays. Computer lab, Art Scope, life science gardening program in school garden. Pull-out GATE program. Summer programs, EDC in afternoons. District foundation raises about $13,500/yr. "We are a one school district with active supportive staff and parents."

LOMA PRIETA UNION. 23800 Summit Rd., Los Gatos 95030. (408) 353-1101. Lee Tinder, Superintendent. One K-gr. 5 elem. school, 350 students; one gr. 6-8 middle school, 170 students. District also offers program for 100

47

homeschooled students. Avg. class size 25. EDC at K-gr. 5 school (may be expanded to middle school), open all weekdays during the year. New technology program at both schools. New building will be completed in 1994. 4 wk. summer school. GATE: in class individualization. The district prides itself on California and National Recognition Awards for middle school, high academic expectations, teacher leadership in curriculum and staff development, and 80% parent involvement.

LOS ALTOS. 201 Covington Los Altos 94022. (415) 941-4010. Dr. Marge Gratiot, Superintendent. Six K-6 elem. schools, avg. class size 28, max. class size 31, aides used in all classes, avg. school size 400. Two gr. 7-8 jr. highs, avg. class size 26, max. class size 32, approx. 400 students per jr. high. Trans. Kdg. Computer writing labs at every school. All campuses have EDC. Bullis, Springer & Loyola have day care during school holidays. Summer school, technology lab. GATE: accelerated math, some pullout. District offers music, PE specialists, art classes at schools, elementary science labs, computer programs. District Foundation raises approx. $350,000/yr. Parcel tax of $168/yr. passed by 81.3%. All schools are Calif. Distinguished Schools, 2 are National Blue Ribbon Schools.

"Our goal is to foster higher level thinking and problem solving skills in students through a strong, content-based, rigorous curriculum and a nurturing cooperative environment."

LOS GATOS-SARATOGA HIGH SCHOOL DISTRICT. 17421 Farley Rd. West, Los Gatos 95030. (408) 354-2520. Dr. Tod R. Likins, Superintendent. Two high schools; 1450 students at Los Gatos H.S., 900 at Saratoga H.S. Avg. class size 28, max. 34. 7 per./day. Daily & weekly tutorial periods. Open campus. 1 couns.: 400 students. 60% of grads attend 4 yr. colleges; 32% 2 yr. colleges. 75% of students participate in extra-curricular activities. French, Spanish, Italian, German, Japanese; 8 AP courses including computer science. Combined mean score on SAT over 1100; 80% who take AP exams score 3 or higher; in top 1% of Calif. high schools. Basic Aid District.

The Institute of ComputerTechnology: See listing under Fremont Union High School District.

Mark Twain Alternative High School: offers programs for students needing or desiring closer attention and individualized instruction.

LOS GATOS UNION. 15766 Poppy Lane, Los Gatos 95030. (408) 395-5570. Stephen D. Benbow, Superintendent. Four K-gr. 5 elem. schools, one gr. 6-8 middle school. Aides in K-gr. 5. Avg. class size 26, max. 30. EDC at all elem. campuses, operated by Rec. Dept. Day care at one campus during spring & winter breaks. Summer programs in special ed., competency, Rec. dept. GATE: gr. 3-5, pullout for enrichment and special studies. District offers instrumental music, computers, art docent program, substance abuse education. District foundation raises about $75,000/yr.

LUTHER BURBANK. 4 Wabash Ave., San Jose 95128. (408) 295-1813. Donna Elder, Superintendent. One K-gr. 8 school. Avg. class size 30, max. 32. Aides in gr. K-8. Trans. kdg. EDC: 2:30-6; available during school holidays. Summer school. Child Development Center offers child care for 3 yr. olds-3rd grade. On-site medical clinic. Counseling program for families & children. Computer lab. Bilingual kindergarten program. District works closely with the Sheriff's Dept. & participates in the DARE program.

MILPITAS UNIFIED. 1331 E. Calaveras Blvd., Milpitas 95035. (408) 945-2300. John K. H. Mackay, Superintendent. Nine K-gr. 6 elem. schools, avg. school size 550; two gr. 7-8 mid. schools, avg. school size 600 students; one high school, 2300 students. Avg. & max. class size 32. Trans. Kdg. Alternative high school for at-risk students. EDC at some elem. campuses. Summer school programs at all levels. GATE classes for gr. 4-8. Counselors at high school. Special programs: bilingual, E.S.L., limited English proficient, Indian Education, vocational ed., migrant education.

Milpitas Unified School District's mission is "to equip each student with the most challenging and comprehensive education the student's abilities and motivation allow."

MONTEBELLO. 15101 Montebello Rd., Cupertino 95014. (408) 867-3618. Janet H. Schwind, Superintendent; Jean Chandler, Principal. One K-gr. 6 elem. school, about 35 students; gr. 7 & 8 students go to jr. high in Cupertino S.D. Avg. class size 12, max. 18. Aides used in kdg. Transportation (contribution solicited). GATE: individualized placement program within regular setting. LD: pullout help; those who need more help granted interdistrict transfers. Music, school play, field trips. Students are given individual attention within small group setting.

MORELAND. 4710 Campbell Ave., San Jose 95130. (415) 379-1370. Jim Ritchie, Ed.D., Superintendent. Eight, K-gr.5 elem. schools, avg. school size 450; two gr. 6-8 mid. schools, avg. school size 600. Avg. class size 30, max. 32. Some aides in K-gr. 5. Transportation. Trans. Kdg. EDC at all elem. sites, closed on school holidays. Summer school for K-gr. 7 and special ed. Choral music for gr. 4-5; instrumental music gr. 4-8. Computer labs; classroom computers in 2 schools; all schools have writing Technology Plans. GATE: program varies in elem. schools, afterschool GATE program for gr. 6-8. ESL centers, ESL aides and tutors; pre-school special ed; on site counseling. District education foundation.

MORGAN HILL UNIFIED. 15600 Concord Circle, Morgan Hill 95037. (408) 779-5272. Eleven elem. schools, two mid. schools, one high school.

MOUNT PLEASANT 14265 Story Rd., San Jose 95127. (408) 928-1200. Ida Jew, Superintendent. Three K-gr. 4 schools, one gr. 5-6 school, one gr. 7-8 mid. school. Avg. class size 31, max. 33. Avg. school size 510. Some transportation. EDC at Valle Vista from 6:30 a.m.-6:30 p.m., open during school holidays. Computer labs at each school. GATE: pull-out and interest groups.

MOUNTAIN VIEW. 220 View St., Mountain View 94041. (415) 968-6565. Patricia Bubenik, Superintendent.

Four K-gr. 5 elem. schools, one gr. 6-8 middle school. Avg. class size 25. Max. class size: K-gr. 3, 27; gr. 4-8, 30. EDC avail. at all schools, all open during school holidays. Variety of summer school programs. Parents are encouraged to visit and volunteer in classrooms. GATE: pull-out in gr. 3-5. Programs for learning disabled students include 7 special day classes, CHAC counselors. Special programs: young astronauts, shadowing (students spend day at work sites), peer counseling & tutoring, in-school scouting, migrant education programs, ESL. Project Cause, a partnership between the district and the community, implements programs to motivate students to stay in school. Mtn. View Schools Fund has provided over $25,000 for art & music enrichment and library resources.

MOUNTAIN VIEW-LOS ALTOS UNION HIGH SCHOOL DISTRICT. 1299 Bryant Ave., Mtn. View 94040. (415) 940-4650. Dr. Donald Phillips, Superintendent. Two high schools, avg. enrollment 1350. Both high schools selected as California Distinguished Schools. Avg. class size 27, max. 36. 7 periods/day. Tutorial & career centers staffed with paid paraprofessionals, job shadowing. Open campus. 1 couns:375 students; freshmen guidance monitoring program. 45% of grads. attend 4 yr. colleges; 43% attend 2 yr. colleges. 35-50% of students participate in extra-curricular activities. 9 AP courses; Spanish, German, French, Latin. Basic Aid District.

The Learning Community, c/o Los Altos High School, 948-6571, X69. The Learning Community is a supportive environment in which students join to seek personal meaning in the pursuit of learning. Students earn 25 credits per semester toward graduation requirements while participating in minicourses, lectures, discussions, field experiences, student-initiated studies, interpersonal communication seminars, and service projects. Preference is given to applicants who possess a commitment to self-improvement and a willingness to cooperate with others in building a learning community and in creating a better world.

OAK GROVE. 6578 Santa Teresa Blvd., San Jose 95119. (408) 227-8300. Tim Cuneo, Superintendent. Seventeen K-gr. 6 elem. schools, avg. enrollment 400-500 students; three gr. 7-8 junior highs, avg. enrollment 800-900. EDC at some sites. District-wide business partnerships at individual schools. Variety of summer school programs.

ORCHARD. 711 Gish Rd., San Jose 95112. (408) 998-2830. Dr. Donna Elder, Superintendent; Helen Lund, Principal. One K-gr. 8 school, 360 students; on site EDC, open during school holidays. Avg. class size 28, max. 32. Transportation. Afterschool recreation and enrichment programs include computers, art, drama. Interdistrict transfers granted for day care needs. Basic Aid District.

PALO ALTO UNIFIED. 25 Churchill Ave., Palo Alto 94306. (415) 329-3700. James Brown, Superintendent. Eleven K-gr. 5 elem. schools, two gr. 6-8 mid. school, two gr. 9-12 high schools. Trans. Kdg. Avg. class size in K-gr. 8, 27.5 Some transportation. EDC at all elem. sites; open during school holidays. Classroom visits encouraged at all schools except Hoover. Register for schools under open enrollment in Feb-March. Alternative school students accepted by lottery. Needs of gifted students met through classroom enrichment. Complete scope of special education programs. Spectra Art (identified by Carnegie Foundation as one of seven quality art programs in the nation), traveling music, and PE teams. Basic Aid District. District Foundation.

Ohlone Alternative School, 950 Amarillo Ave., 855-8408, is an "open education" K-gr. 5 program with classrooms characterized by pupil-initiated activity, independent study, and a relaxed, informal atmosphere. Classes, except kindergarten, are organized into two year, cross-age groupings and students progress at their own rate. The school emphasizes human relations and a problem solving approach to arguments. Competition is de-emphasized. Grades are not given.

Hoover School, 800 Barron Ave., 856-1377, offers a structured K-gr. 5 alternative with primary emphasis on the basic academic skills, subject matter, and the establishment of good study habits. The school is characterized by a quiet, orderly environment; self-contained single-grade classrooms; teacher-initiated and directed activities; regular measurement of student progress through testing and grades.

Palo Alto and Gunn High Schools: Avg. class size 28.5, avg. enrollment 1,150 students. 7 periods/day. Gunn has one counselor: 300 students. Paly has 18 teacher-advisors with a ratio of about 1:80 and 1 couns.:567 students. Tutorial centers. 78% of grads. attend 4 yr. colleges; 18% attend 2 yr. colleges. District offers 14 AP classes; Spanish, French, German, Latin, German, & Japanese; honors classes; ROP classes; music, drama, myriad of electives and a variety of options for completing high school.

SAN JOSE UNIFIED. 1605 Park Ave., San Jose 95128. (408) 998-6000. Dr. Linda Murray, Superintendent. Twenty-eight K-gr. 5 elem. schools; seven gr. 6-8 mid. schools; seven high schools. Trans. Kdg. Avg. & max. class size 30.5. Transportation provided for K-gr.5 students who live 1.5 miles or more from their school, gr. 6-12 students who live 2.5 or more from their school, or students for whom walking would be hazardous. Extensive Bilingual Programs offered throughout district for Limited English Proficiency students and for

English speaking students wishing to become proficient in a second language. GATE: programs offered at each elem. site according to each school's resources and environment; many programs incorporate technology, the sciences, fine arts and the development of leadership skills. EDC avail. at 14 elem. sites. Extensive business partnerships through the Adopt-a-School program. High schools have closed campuses and provide tutorial centers. Honors & advanced placement classes at all high schools. Guidance deans at high schools, counselors at mid. schools. Summer school at all levels.

In 1985 the Federal Court ordered SJUSD to desegregate its schools. As a result, the district offers parents and students a wide variety of program and school choices. Areas of emphasis include science, writing, foreign languages, foreign language immersion, language arts, mathematics, intensive academic studies, visual and performing arts, communications, and aviation/aerospace. Secondary school options also include Center for College, Career, and Lifetime Learning Experiences; Agri-Science/Business and Environmental Science; International Baccalaureate/Aviation/Aerospace; and Professional Studies. The Career-Occupational Preparation program prepares students for work or advanced career training.

To obtain the district's <u>Choices Catalog</u>, parents should contact the district office. Each year parents of prospective kindergartners, sixth and ninth graders are asked to visit schools that interest them, and then at one of two enrollment centers fill out forms listing their choices. The district gives as many families as possible their first choice within mandated ethnic ratios and space availability.

SANTA CLARA UNIFIED. 1889 Lawrence Rd., P.O. Box 397, Santa Clara 95052. (408) 983-2000. Dr. Bob Carter, Superintendent. Fifteen K-gr. 5 elem. schools, avg. class size 30; three gr. 6-8 mid. schools, avg. class size 29, max. 33, avg. school size 943. EDC at all elem. sites. GATE: pull out for gr. 4-5. One elem. & one mid. school have "state of the art" technology in every classroom. Two high schools, avg. class size 29.6, max. 33, avg. school size 1540. High schools have tutorial centers, 1 couns: 350 students. 6 periods/day. 15-20% of grads. go to 4 yr. colleges, 50%+ to 2 yr. The district has a very active partnership program with over 30 private sector partners. "The priority of the district is to provide a quality education for all students." Parents should sign up for alternative programs in April. The district is projected to become a Basic Aid district during the 1993-94 school year.

Basics + Formal Education Program. Millikin School, 2720 Sonoma Place. 985-6310. This alternative school is open to any youngster in the Santa Clara Unified School District whose parents desire a more structured method of teaching. The program places high value on teaching academic skills in a self-contained setting. Emphasis is placed on a phonetic approach to reading and all subjects are taught in a traditional manner.

Open Classroom Alternative, Westwood School, 435 Saratoga Ave, 985-6355. The Open Classroom school provides a loving and enriching environment where children can learn in their own way, at their own pace. The program emphasizes the involvement of parents in the classroom so that learning can be an on-going process at home and school. Parent participation is required, or parents can pay for a substitute. Children receive individualized instruction and many choices of learning experiences. The primary objectives of this program are to develop in students a positive self-image, social responsibility, competence in the basic skills, aesthetic judgment, and creativity.

Wilson High School offers an independent study program.

SARATOGA. 20460 Forest Hills, Saratoga 95070. (408) 867-3424. Mary Gardner, Superintendent. Three K-gr. 5 elem. schools, avg. class size 28, max. 30, aides in all grades, 300-450 students per school; one gr. 6-8 mid. school, 700 students, avg. class size 31, max. 32. EDC at all elem. sites, open on school holidays. Vocal music for K-gr. 5; instrumental gr. 5-8. Business partnerships, computer labs, mentorships for highly gifted (e.g., NASA mentorship in science), accelerated math & science programs, French Connection (5th grade exchange program). GATE coordinator and classroom teachers present GATE programs to all students. Vertical acceleration for students who master subject material. Students generally achieving at two yrs. above grade level, test scores in 99 percentile. District foundation raises about $200,000/yr.

SUNNYVALE ELEMENTARY. 830 W. McKinley Ave., Sunnyvale 94086. (408) 522-8200. Seven K-gr. 6 elem. schools, avg. school size 600, aides in all classes; one gr. 7-8 jr. high, 1200 students. (In 1994 a second middle school will open and 6th grades will be part of mid. schools.) Avg. class size 29, max. 32. All elem. sites have EDC. All schools have at least one business partner, some have several. All schools have computer labs. GATE integrated into regular curriculum, some extra afterschool activities. Register in May for open enrollment or Basics program. Summer programs in basics and core gr. 7-8 program. District Foundation raises about $40,000 to support growth of technology in district. Basic Aid District.

Columbia School Basics Program. K-gr. 8. 739 Morse Ave., Sunnyvale 94086. 522-8247. Focuses on basic skills, parent cooperation and discipline.

Vargas Elem. School, rebuilt and modernized for re-opening in '93, emphasizes technology and has a television/video studio, location of SV public access TV station. The station is available to all Sunnyvale students.

The Institute of Computer Technology. See listing under Fremont Union High School District.

UNION. 5175 Union Ave., San Jose 95124. (408) 377-8010. Dr. Janice Smith, Superintendent. Eight K-5 elem. schools, avg. school size 396; two gr.6-8 mid. schools, avg. school size 700. EDC at 6 elem. sites.. GATE: pull-out for gr. 3-5 students one morning/wk. Computer lab at each school. Strong staff development program. Summer school programs for spec. ed. students and those lacking in proficiency in subject areas.

WHISMAN. 750-A San Pierre Way, Mtn. View 94043. (415) 903-6900. Eve T. Bressler, Ed. D., Superintendent. Three K-4 elem. schools, avg. school size 350, avg. & max. class size 27, aides used in K-gr. 4; one gr. 5-8 mid. school, 650 students, avg. & max. class size 30. Trans. Kdg. EDC offered by YMCA at Monte Loma & Theuerkauf School from 7 a.m.-6 p.m. Transportation. Computer labs at Crittenden & Whisman, interactive multi-media at all schools, classroom computers, business partnerships, Community School of Music & Art, hands-on science. GATE program offered after school through Hewlett Packard and Structure of Intellect Evening. Afterschool sports at Crittenden Mid. School. All schools use a variety of instructional strategies so that each child can achieve "personal best." Active parent groups, fall walk-jog and other community events. Evening parenting classes held in both English and Spanish. Variety of summer school programs.

DISTRICT BOUNDARIES
SAN MATEO COUNTY

ELEMENTARY, HIGH SCHOOL &
UNIFIED SCHOOL DISTRICTS

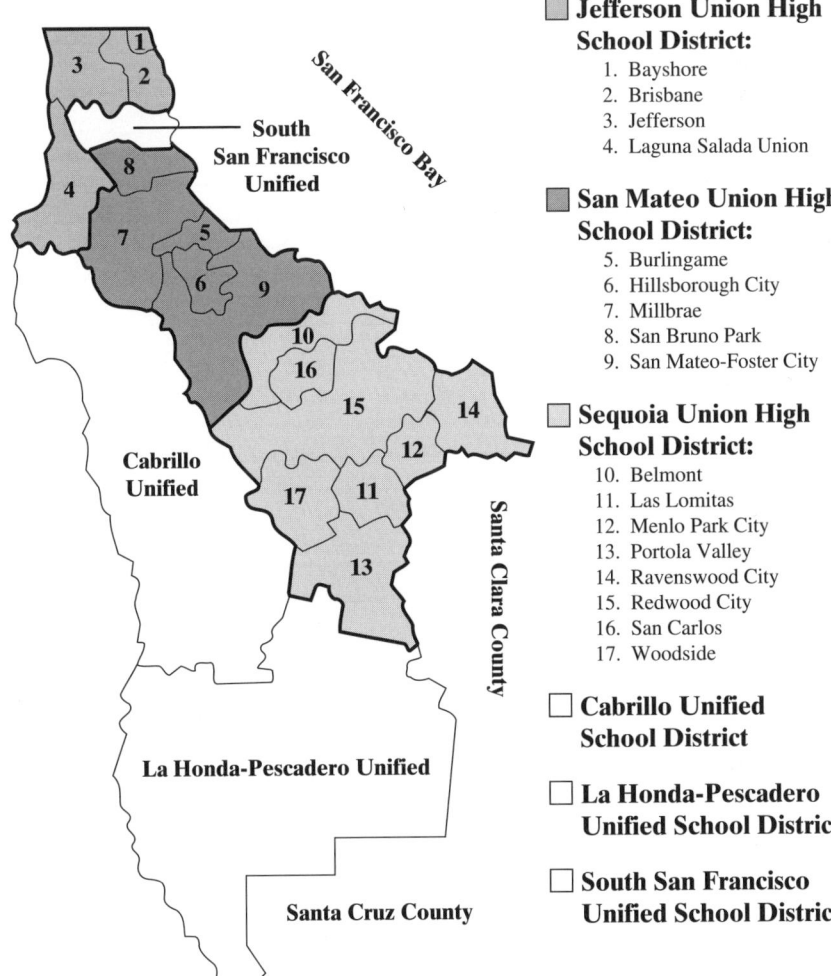

Jefferson Union High School District:
1. Bayshore
2. Brisbane
3. Jefferson
4. Laguna Salada Union

San Mateo Union High School District:
5. Burlingame
6. Hillsborough City
7. Millbrae
8. San Bruno Park
9. San Mateo-Foster City

Sequoia Union High School District:
10. Belmont
11. Las Lomitas
12. Menlo Park City
13. Portola Valley
14. Ravenswood City
15. Redwood City
16. San Carlos
17. Woodside

Cabrillo Unified School District

La Honda-Pescadero Unified School District

South San Francisco Unified School District

SAN MATEO COUNTY PUBLIC SCHOOL DISTRICTS

San Mateo County Office of Education
(415) 802-5300

BAYSHORE. 1 Martin St., Daly City 94014. (415) 467-5443. Winifred Kum, Superintendent. One K-gr. 4 elem. school, avg. class size 28, max. 30, aides in all grades; one gr. 4-8 mid. school, avg. class size 28, max. 31. One two-year kdg. class. EDC avail. through Bayshore Child Care within a block of both schools, 7 a.m.-6 p.m., open during school holidays. Beginning & intermediate band, beginning & advanced choir. Computer lab at mid. school. Radio station operated by mid. school students. Several business partnerships. Summer programs: proficiency, Kids at Risk Services, Futures.

BELMONT. 2960 Hallmark Dr., Belmont 94002. (415) 593-8203. Carol Worthington, Superintendent. Three K-gr. 5 elem. schools, avg. enrollment 450 students; one gr. 6-8 mid. school, 650 students. Avg. class size 25.5, aides used in primary grades. EDC at elem. sites, open during school holidays. Partnership with City of Belmont for afterschool sports programs & summer recreation programs. Adopt-a-school programs at all schools. Summer school programs for gr. 1-7. Classroom music for K-gr. 5 integrated into curriculum. GATE: afterschool program at elem., clusters & advanced placement for gr. 6-8. PTA raises approx. $100,000/yr. Basic Aid District.

BRISBANE. 1 Solano St., Brisbane 94005. (415) 467-0550. Anne Ladd, Superintendent. One K-gr. 5 elem. school, one K-gr. 6, avg. school size 168, avg. class size 25, max. class size 31; one gr. 6-8 middle school, 180 students, avg. class size 25, max. class size 30. Some transportation. One elem. school has day care. Band & choral group. Drama, computer lab, Adopt-a-School, Quest, journalism, humanities, art. GATE: pull-out for gr. 3-8. Chapter 1 & ESL programs. Summer school programs. District foundation raises about $20,000/yr.

BURLINGAME. 2303 Trousdale Dr., Burlingame 94010. (415) 692-5097. Robert E. Beuthel, Superintendent. Four K-5 elem. schools, avg. school size

320, avg. class size 30, max. class size 32; one gr. 6-8 mid. school, 650 students, avg. class size 28. EDC at all elem. schools. Chorus & band from gr. 3-8. Computer labs at all schools. District Foundation raises about $30,000/yr. Summer school for K-gr. 3; fee-based summer academy for gr. 4-8.

"Burlingame School District offers a strong instructional program with active staff and community participation and district-level support. The creativity, energy, and intelligence of school and district staff allow students to thrive and share the joy of learning in a stimulating environment."

CABRILLO UNIFIED. 498 Kelly Ave., Half Moon Bay 94019. (415) 712-7100. Jane Martin, Superintendent. Four K-gr. 5 elem. schools, enrollment varies from 70 to 622 students; one gr. 6-8 mid. school, 718 students; one high school, 834 students. Avg. class size: elem. 30, h.s. 28; max. 33-34. Transportation. Trans. Kdg. EDC at all elem. sites, open during school holidays at Farallone, El Granada, & Hatch. Summer programs at all levels. GATE: pullout enrichment for gr. 3-5; accelerated classes gr. 6-12. District also has migrant education and bilingual programs. **King's Mountain Alternative School** offers smaller classes and individualized instruction in a unique rural setting.

Half Moon Bay H.S.: Bilingual tutorial center, bilingual program, advanced placement program, GATE, vocational ed. One couns: 175 students. 70% of students participate in extracurricular activities. 30% of grads. attend 4 yr. colleges; 50% attend 2 yr. colleges. "All students will be provided a comprehensive program that meets individual needs and strengths. District emphasizes support in both academic and interpersonal growth."

HILLSBOROUGH. 300 El Cerrito Ave., Hillsborough 94010. (415) 342-5193. Marilyn Loushin-Miller , Superintendent. Three K-5 elem. schools, avg. school size 250; one gr. 6-8 mid. school, 400 students. Avg. class size 25, max. 29. Aides in K-gr. 5. Trans. Kdg. Vocal music in K-gr. 8; instrumental music gr. 3-8. All schools have extensive multi-media programs, computer labs and computers in classrooms, TV studio at Crocker Mid. School, extensive electives, 2 for. languages, 1 required in gr. 6-8. Summer school programs. GATE programs integrated into total program. Crocker Mid. School cited by Royal Academy of Sciences in Sweden as one of the best schools in the world. Basic Aid District.

JEFFERSON ELEMENTARY. 101 Lincoln Ave., Daly City 94015. (415) 991-1000. Joseph M. DiGeronimo, Superintendent. Nine K-gr. 6 elem. schools, three K-gr. 5 schools, avg. school size 474; two gr. 7-8 mid. schools, avg. school size 645. Avg. class size 28, max. 33. Aides in gr. K-6. EDC 7 a.m.-6 p.m. at Edison, Columbus, Kennedy, Wilson, Roosevelt, Webster; program at Edison open during school holidays. Chorus & instrumental music programs. Summer school programs in core/proficiency, special ed. & Chapter 1. GATE: one day a week pull-out for elem.; advanced courses for mid. school. Reading specialist at each school.

JEFFERSON UNION HIGH SCHOOL DISTRICT. 699 Serramonte Blvd., Suite 100, Daly City 94015. (415) 756-0300. Robert Gross, Ed.D. Superintendent. Five high schools. Enrollment varies from 400-1600. Some campuses open, some closed. Oceana H. S. offers Humanities core, open to any student in the district. Health careers core at Serramonte. Avg. class size 28, max. 34. 6 per./day. Tutorial centers. 1 Couns: 450 students & special counselors. Special program for low-achieving 9th graders. Bi-lingual programs. A.P. classes at all levels. Spanish, French, German.

LA HONDA-PESCADERO UNIFIED. 620 North St., Pescadero 94060. (415) 879-0286. Roger Yohe & Judith Frost co-superintendents/principals. One K-gr. 6 elem. school, one pre K-gr. 5, avg. # of students 160, avg. class size 25, max. class size 31, aides used in special ed. & primary grades. One gr. 6-8 mid school (located on elem. site), 60 students, avg. class size 28, max. class size 30; one gr. 9-12 h.s. Trans. Kdg. EDC at elem. schools from 3-6 pm. Transportation. Enrichment & instrumental music. Computer labs at elem. sites. Partnerships with P.G. & E. Intensive language, migrant, bilingual classes, state pre-school program at Pescadero Elem. Summer programs. Challenger program for GATE students.

Pescadero High School: 86 students, avg. class size 14, max. class size 26. 70% of students involved in extra-curricular activities. 35% of grads. go to 4 yr. colleges, 20% to 2 yr. college. Open campus. 1 couns: 90 students. Environmental studies, honors world literature, computer hypercard, Spanish.

LAGUNA SALADA. 375 Reina del Mar, Pacifica 94044. (415) 359-1641. Dr. Marc Liebman, Superintendent. Seven K-gr. 5 schools, two K-gr. 8 schools, avg. class size 28-30, max. 32, avg. enrollment 350; two gr. 6-8 mid. schools, avg. class size 30, max. 32, avg. enrollment 500. Mid-year kdg. for students who turn five between Dec. and 2nd semester. EDC at or near all school sites, open 6 am-6 pm. GATE: integrated for gr. 3-5, special periods for gr. 6-8. Enrichment, academic, & proficiency summer programs. Spring enrollment for Kdg. & alternative programs. District Foundation.

Vallemar Structured School's general purpose is "to provide for a strong academic program...All classroom activities will be teacher-initiated, directed and supervised...Discipline will be firm, fair, and consistent...Homework is assigned a minimum of three nights a week." Parents are expected to support the concepts of the Structured School and students must adhere to a behavior and dress code. Current students and children with siblings in the school are given priority. Parents should contact school to be placed on waiting list. 359-2444.

The Alternative Class is an ungraded K-gr.8 program designed to "equip all students with the ability to make intelligent choices and the desire to contribute to their community." The program provides individualized instruction; reinforcement of positive academic, social, and emotional growth; opportunities for students to make academic choices; cross grade instruction. Parent participation is required and parent-teacher conferences take the place of grades. 355-0413.

LAS LOMITAS. K-gr.8. 1011 Altschul Ave., Menlo Park 94025. (415) 854-2880. Dr. Charla Rolland, Superintendent. One K-gr.3 school; one gr.4-8. EDC open during school holidays. Avg. class size 24, max. 30. Transportation. Extensive programs in music, art, computers & PE. Trans. Kdg. District Foundation raises about $100,000/yr. Basic Aid District.

MENLO PARK. 181 Encinal Ave., Atherton 94027. (415) 321-7140. Dr. Judy Rogers-Bianchi, Superintendent. One K-gr. 5, one K-gr. 2, one gr. 3-5; enrollment at elem. schools 300-500. One gr. 6-8 mid. school, enrollment 440. Avg. class size: K, 23.7; gr. 1-2, 24.6; gr. 3-8, 28.5. Aides in K-gr. 2, some in upper grades. EDC at Encinal 7:30 am-6 pm, open school holidays. Art & music specialists; science specialist for gr. 4-8, P.E. specialist for gr. 6-8. Computers, woodshop (gr. 6-8), music, band. Several summer school programs. GATE programs designed & implemented by classroom teachers & GATE coordinator. District foundation raises about $260,000/yr.

MILLBRAE. 555 Richmond Dr., Millbrae 94030. (415) 697-5693. Karen K. Philip, Superintendent. Four, K-gr. 5 elem. schools, avg. # of students 400, avg. class size 27; one gr. 6-8 middle school, 700 students, avg. class size 27. Max. class size 32. Tutorial learning center. EDC at all elem. sites, avail from 7 a.m.-6 p.m., open during school holidays. GATE pullout in gr. 4-5; summer program for gr. 3-4 Instrumental music in gr. 4-8. Summer school programs: GATE for gr. 3 & 4; core program; proficiency; enrichment.

PORTOLA VALLEY. 4575 Alpine Rd., Portola Valley 94028. (415) 851-1777. James Shroyer, Superintendent. One K-gr. 5 elem. school, 435 students, avg. class size 23, aides in all grades; one gr. 6-8 middle school, 165 students, avg. class size 23. Private day care housed on Corte Madera campus, avail. from 12-6, open on school holidays. Vocal music & band. Business partnership with Hewlett Packard; computer labs at both schools. Classroom visits during several days in the spring. Interdistrict transfers encouraged. Art, science, & music specialists in K-gr. 5.

RAVENSWOOD. 2160 Euclid Ave., East Palo Alto 94303. (415) 329-2800. Dr. Charlie M. Knight, Superintendent. Four K-gr. 8 schools, two K-gr. 4 schools, two gr. 5-8 schools. EDC avail. at all sites. Early entrance program for 4 yr. olds. Transportation. Avg. class size 28, max. 29. Summer programs. Every school adopted by a business. Extensive co-operation with community agencies, corporations, foundations, Stanford University. District-wide curriculum integrates math and science into the the district's thematic instructional approach to learning. District philosophy: "All children will succeed when they are presented an enriched curriculum in a caring, nurturing environment."

Flood School Math/Science Technology School thematically integrates the curriculum with science at its core. Instruction is hands-on; computer and science lab instruction is coordinated with the classroom to extend and support learning. Students must meet a variety of criteria for acceptance and parents are expected to take an active role in their children's success by monitoring homework, attending school meetings and functions, and providing volunteer assistance.

Parent Child Intervention Program is designed to serve at risk and developmentally delayed infants and toddlers exposed to drugs

REDWOOD CITY. 815 Allerton St., Redwood City 94063. (415) 365-1550. Dr. Ronald F. Crates, Superintendent. Twelve elem. schools, grade configurations vary, enrollment ranges from 175 to 740, avg. class size 28, max. 30; two gr. 6-8 mid. schools, avg. school size 975, avg. class size 29, max. 30. EDC at all elem. schools, 6:30 a.m.-6:30 p.m., avail. during school holidays. Summer school programs include programs for pre K-gr. 8, Stanford Math Institute for gr. 6-7, Woodside Priory math program for gr. 8. GATE: Cluster for K-gr. 6, honors program for gr. 7-8. Peer counseling, "Quality Education Program," Bilingual Newcomer Center.

Orion School is an alternative school with a flexible, non-competitive classroom structure that encourages self-motivation, self-discipline and self-evaluation. Students use a "hands-on" approach to learning and learn problem solving, decision making, and communication techniques. Parent participation is strongly encouraged. Beginning in 1994-95, the school will also have a Spanish Immersion Strand. 3150 Granger Way. 363-0611.

In 1994-95, the district will have five magnet school programs, which will all have a technology component: Hoover, K-gr. 5, math; Garfield, K-gr. 5, communication arts & performing arts; Cloud, K-gr. 8, communication arts; Clifford & Selby, K-gr. 8, science.

SAN BRUNO PARK. 500 Acacia Ave., San Bruno 94066. (415) 244-0133. Dr. Theresa Daem, Superintendent. Six K-gr. 6 elem. schools, enrollment ranges from 206 to 498 students; one gr. 7-8 int. school, 565 students. EDC at some sites Summer school programs. Strong afterschool sports program.

SAN CARLOS. 826 Chestnut St., San Carlos 94070. (415) 593-7626. Don Shalvey, Superintendent. Five K-gr. 5 elem. schools, avg. enrollment 350 students; one gr. 6-8 mid. school, 700 students. Avg. class size 28, max. 32. Four elem. schools have day care from 2:30-6 p.m., open during school holidays. Summer school: academic and spec. ed. for gr. 4-8. GATE: integrated in regular classroom and pull-out in gr. 3-5. Instrumental music in gr. 4-8., vocal music specialist. All schools have business partnerships, community-based performance assessment, "Harvest of the Mind" creativity festival, technology labs. Afterschool enrichment programs in technology, arts & foreign languages. The district has been chosen to operate one of California's first charter schools to open in Sept. '94. Specific information will be available in Nov. '93.

SAN MATEO-FOSTER CITY. 300 28th Ave., San Mateo 94403. (415) 312-7700. Dr. Richard J. Damelio, Superintendent. Fourteen K-gr. 5 elem. schools, avg. class size 25-27, if classes go over 32 extra assistance given, avg. school size 500; four gr. 6-8 mid. schools, avg. class size 27, avg. school size 750. District operated EDC (The Children's Annex) offered at 11 sites from 7 a.m.-6 p.m., open during school holidays. Choral music for K-gr. 5; instrumental music for gr. 4-5; band & orchestra for gr. 6-8. 13 schools involved in adopt-a-school program. School-based re-structuring underway at each school. All middle schools have networked computer labs. Summer school programs: enrichment, proficiency, ESL, spec. ed., Children's Annex. GATE students transported once a week to I.D.E.A. Center, an enrichment oriented learning lab. All middle schools and two elem. schools have site-based GATE programs. A self-contained class for highly gifted fourth and fifth grade students housed at Laurel School. Pull out programs and special day classes available for RSP (learning handicapped students). Several district schools are piloting other organizational structures (reduced class size & team-teaching) to better meet the needs of RSP students. Three of the last four S.M. County Teachers of the Year from the district. In 1991 the community passed by over 71% a parcel tax to reduce class size and a $33 million bond measure for facilities. District foundation raises about $175,000/yr. For more information about the following alternative schools phone 312-7720.

Montessori Programs for K-gr.5 at Horrall and Parkside Schools. The Montessori philosophy (see pg. 16) is "implemented through the use of specially designed sequential materials and a prepared environment. The program attempts to develop a child who is interested in the process of learning rather than just the end product. The child chooses his/her own work, and, in this way, builds autonomy and independence...the Montessori classes also incorporate all the district's goals as an integral part of their program."

Turnball Learning Academy is an innovative community center for lifelong learning for children & adults. The academy requires family members to participate actively in the education of their children either at the school site, at home or in the community. The Academy will be multi-ethnic and some classes will be bilingual, taught in both Spanish & English.

Fiesta Gardens International School offers an immersion program that leads to full literacy in Spanish & English. The school offers a challenging curriculum through a global perspective. Native English and Spanish speaking students study together in the same classroom. The immersion program will be offered in kindergarten and 1st grade in the '93-94 school year and a grade will be added each year until the program includes the fifth grade.

SAN MATEO UNION HIGH SCHOOL DISTRICT. 650 N. Delaware St., San Mateo 94401. (415) 348-8834. Dr. Nicholas Gennaro, Superintendent. Six high schools, avg. school size 1200, avg. class size 33. 20 students in 9th gr. Eng. classes. 6 periods/day. Transportation for students living more than 3.5 miles from campus. Closed campus at two sites. One couns: 500 students.

17 AP courses offered. French, Spanish, Italian, Japanese, Latin. Performing Arts programs at each site. 42% of grads. attend 4 yr. colleges; 33% attend 2 yr. colleges. 30% of student body participates in extra curricular activities. District offers program in Principles in Technology at 5 campuses. Drug & Alcohol Abatement Program, Elizabethan Arts Festival. Burlingame and Hillsdale High Schools operate a "traditional school" program for students from any attendance area in the district. Basic Aid District.

SEQUOIA UNION HIGH SCHOOL DISTRICT. 480 James Ave., Redwood City, 94062. (415) 369-1411. Merle Fruehling, Superintendent. Four high schools. Avg. enrollment 1500. Avg. class size 28, max. varies in subject area. 7 per./day. One couns.: 275 students. 45% of students participate in extracurricular activities. Business partnership with each school. Literacy Center. District is moving towards heterogeneous grouping but will continue to offer AP courses, honors & advanced standing classes. 10 AP classes offered. German, Japanese, Spanish, French & Latin. Academies Programs, Alternative Study Center, School-Age Mothers Program. 48% of grads. attend 4 yr. colleges; 38% attend 2 yr. colleges.

SOUTH SAN FRANCISCO UNIFIED. 398 B St., South San Francisco 94080. (415) 877-8700. Dr. Richard Rigg, Superintendent. Ten K-gr. 5 elem. schools, avg. class size 29. Three gr. 6-8 middle schools, avg. class size 28, avg. school size 756. Two gr. 9-12 high schools, one continuation school. EDC at 8 elem. sites from 7 am-6 pm. Summer programs for K-gr. 4 & gr. 9-12. Tutorial Centers at elem. sites. ESL classes. Model technology school at Skyline.

District High Schools: avg. school size 1400, avg. class size 28, 6 periods/day. Students tracked in English classes. 1 AP class. Spanish, French, Italian. One couns.: 550 students. 70% participate in extra-curricular activities. Special programs include Capitol Focus, Project Close-Up, History Day, Mock Trial, large well-equipped Business Department, ESL program. 10% of grads. attend 4 yr. colleges; 45% attend 2 yr. colleges. Scholarships available for good athletes with good grades who will attend college.

WOODSIDE. One K-gr. 8 school, 430 students. 3195 Woodside Rd., Woodside 94062. (415) 851-1571. Avg. class size 25; max. class size 28; aides in K-gr. 5. Full day kdg., 8:30-2:30. EDC: 7:30-6, open during school holidays. Full music program includes chorus, band, strings. Extensive art program. Computers in all classrooms. Spanish instruction in gr. 1-8. Full time P.E. specialist. Math & art specialists. Technology program. Summer programs: enrichment & privately run sports camp. District foundation raises approx. $100,000/yr.

DIRECTORY OF PRIVATE SCHOOLS

Convent of the Sacred Heart (now called
Sacred Heart Schools), Menlo Park, 1915.

EXPLANATORY NOTES FOR
PRIVATE SCHOOL LISTINGS

In the spring of 1993, every private school registered with the offices of education in Santa Clara and San Mateo Counties and listed as having at least 12 students was sent a questionnaire. A few schools wished only to be listed in the directory and stated that parents should telephone the school office for further information. Others chose not to respond to all of the questions. No private school was deliberately excluded from the survey or omitted from this directory.

Schools are divided by county into three sections–— elementary, secondary, and special education. If a school fits into more than one category, it may be cross-referenced. The elementary schools are listed by geographical groupings from south to north, and then divided into three categories: Roman Catholic, other religious affiliations, and secular. Those listed in the last category include independent, proprietary, Montessori, and Carden schools.

Note: All information in the directory portion of this book was provided by the schools themselves. The author can not guarantee that the information provided is accurate. Parents should use the directory merely as a tool to ascertain what schools might meet their needs, and then evaluate the schools for themselves, using the guidelines provided in the first section of this book and their own parental instincts.

School day hours are noted as **SDH.** Some schools indicated kindergarten hours, but many did not.

Extended day care is noted as **EDC.** Most, but not all, private schools that have extended day care charge extra for this service. If you need extended day care but are interested in a school that doesn't offer it, ask whether local day care centers or licensed homes serve children from the school.

Class size: Average and maximum class size can vary from year to year and by grade and course offering. Many schools use aides and/or specialists in areas like physical education and music so that the student/staff ratio is smaller than the average class size, but only a few schools indicated that ratio on the questionnaire.

Tuition: Schools were asked to list their tuition and incidental fees for the 1993-94 school year. Preschool fees are not listed. Most schools raise tuition at least every two or three years; many raise it annually. Unless otherwise noted, the tuition listed is per year.

Scholarships: Schools were asked to indicate whether they grant scholarships and then asked to approximate the percentage of students receiving financial aid. Because the amount of financial aid available often varies year-to-year, many schools just indicated **fin. aid avail.** to show that tuition reductions are granted to needy students when possible. Some schools reserve scholarship money for students who are already in the school but whose families can no longer afford tuition.

Transportation: Many private schools can be reached by public transportation, and most schools help parents arrange car pools. When schools offer transportation for an extra charge, this service will be indicated in the listing.

Special programs: Schools were asked to list any special facilities and programs beyond basic academic instruction. Some did this in great detail; others did not. Therefore, some schools may have extras like computer labs and afterschool sports even though they did not list them.

Application procedures: Many schools have application deadlines, but most schools continue taking students as long as space is available. Almost all schools give priority to siblings of students currently enrolled in the school as long as the sibling is academically qualified. Schools with religious affiliations also give priority to members of the sponsoring church. To the best of the author's knowledge, no school listed in this directory discriminates on the basis of race, color, or national origin.

Accreditation: See explanation on page 28.

Secondary Schools were asked to indicate whether they have a closed or open campus (see explanation on page 40) and what percentage of their graduates attend four and two year colleges. They were also asked for their average SAT scores (see explanation in appendix) for the years between 1991 and 1993 and the percentage of students who usually take the test; some schools provided this information but many did not.

Philosophy: The third paragraph of each listing includes the school's stated philosophy but does not convey the author's own evaluation of the extent to which that philosophy is carried out.

Special Education: Schools that specialize in serving students with special needs are listed in the Special Education section for each county. Many private schools will take students with learning differences if they feel the student can benefit from their program; schools were asked to indicate whether they have on-site learning disability (**LD**) specialists to help those students.

SANTA CLARA COUNTY PRIVATE ELEMENTARY SCHOOLS

Gilroy ◆ Morgan Hill
CATHOLIC SCHOOLS

ST. CATHERINE SCHOOL. 17500 So. Peak Ave., Morgan Hill 95037. (408) 779-9950. Jeff Smoker, Principal. Est. 1963. Non-profit.

K-gr. 7; 251 students. $1980. Incidentals $240. Fin. aid avail. SDH: 8:40-2:50. EDC: 7a.m.-6 p.m. Avg. & max. class size 35. Uniforms. Classroom art, vocal music program, computer lab, afterschool sports. Feb. registration but late registration taken through June. Acceptance based upon interview, test results, report card and school recommendation. Waiting list. Accredited by WCEA and WASC.

"St. Catherine operates upon Catholic Christian principles. The school provides quality education in academic areas, daily religious instruction and an environment that nurtures and enables growth in Christian values."

ST. MARY SCHOOL. 7900 Church St., Gilroy 95020. (408) 842-2827. Christa Hanson, Principal. Est. 1871. Non-profit.

K-gr. 8; 190 students. $1840-$2420 Reg. fee $155; materials $75. Fin. aid avail. SDH: 8:30-3. EDC: 7 a.m.-6 p.m.; $2-$3/hr. Avg. & max. class size 35. Uniforms. Departmentalized junior high; enrichment programs in math and science, literature and art; computer education in modern facility featuring 18 Mac. computers; sports program. Waiting list. Accredited by WASC & WCEA.

"The mission of St. Mary School, in partnership with parents, is to provide a program of academic excellence in a Christian environment based on Catholic beliefs."

NON-CATHOLIC RELIGIOUS SCHOOLS

ADVENTIST CHRISTIAN SCHOOL. 1575 Mantelli Dr., Gilroy 95020. (408) 842-8504. Connie Jespersen, Principal. Est. 1980. Non-profit.

K-gr. 9; 30 students. $250/mo. Inc. fees $250. 10-20% receive fin. aid. SDH: 8:15-3; option of half or full day kindergarten. EDC can be arranged. Avg. class size 15-20. Uniforms. Music & computer programs. New facilities with four new classrooms, large playground on five acres. Admissions subject to board approval. Accredited by Pacific Union Conference of Seventh Day Adventists.

The school's "main purpose is to provide a Christian education for children with teachers who not only provide students with academic direction but also help them become acquainted with Jesus Christ and become well-rounded, responsible citizens."

SOUTH VALLEY CHRISTIAN. 145 Wright Ave., Morgan Hill 95037. (408) 779-8850. Dr. Earl Nordby, Director. Est. 1976. Non-profit.

PreK-gr. 8; 175 students. Young K (4 yr. olds, half day), $2000; K-gr. 8, $2200. Reg. fee $100. SDH: 8:30-3. EDC: 6:30 a.m.-6:30 p.m. Avg. class size 20, max. 24. Dress code. Tutoring to help students catch up. Students score above norm on Stanford Achievement Tests. Interview & testing required of new students. Applications taken as long as space available. Member of ACSI.

"Education is complete when knowing Christ is the ultimate goal of that process. The Creator and His creation are inseparable subjects at our school, and together provide a foundation for successful living as they are understood by our students."

SECULAR SCHOOLS

GAVILAN HILLS ACADEMY. 6901 Monterey St., Gilroy 95020. (408) 842-7455. Marguerite L. Kennedy, Administrator. Est. 1970. Proprietary.

K-gr. 12; 52 students. Gifted and accelerated programs. Special needs students accepted. All students are accepted and placed according to ability and not age. Summer school. Students accepted any time space available. No waiting list.

"We specialize in classes for gifted and accelerated students. Each student works at his or her own level in every subject. Homework is strictly enforced."

San Jose

CATHOLIC SCHOOLS

FIVE WOUNDS. 1390 Five Wounds Lane, San Jose 95116. (408) 293-0425. Mrs. Barbara McCallion, Principal. Est. 1960. Non-profit.

K-gr. 8, 239 students. $1280-$4030. Sibling discounts. Inc. fees $250-$350. Fin. aid avail. SDH: 8:10-2:55. EDC: 6:30 a.m.-5 p.m. Avg. class size 27, max. 35. Uniforms. Entrance test. Computer classes. Accredited by WCEA & WASC.

"Five Wounds School is a distinctive place of faith formation, continually striving to proclaim the message of Jesus, to enhance academic excellence, to promote the ministry of service, and to create a Christ-centered atmosphere where Gospel values are fostered and lived."

HOLY FAMILY EDUCATIONAL CENTER. 4848 Pearl Ave., San Jose 95136. (408) 978-1355. Kenneth Boegel, Director. Est. 1986. Non-profit.

PreK-gr. 8. K, $1200; gr. 1-8, $2000 (additional children $1450.) Reg fee $125. Fin. aid avail. SDH: 8:15-2:45. EDC: 7 a.m.-6 p.m.; $2.40/hr. Avg. class size 33, max. 35. Uniforms. 6th grade science camp, parent enrichment seminars, student prayer services, computers in all classes, student service projects. Kindergartners must be 5 by Sept. 1. Priority to siblings. Applications available at end of Jan. Waiting list. Accredited by WASC & WCEA.

"The mission of Holy Family is to build a Catholic Christian community through study, prayer, service & community. Our goals are to integrate the 'total child,' and support parents as primary educators. We use volunteers from parish and parent community to foster a climate of community involvement."

MOST HOLY TRINITY. 1940 Cunningham Ave., San Jose 95122. (408) 729-3431. Sister Susan Barry, Principal. Est. 1965. Non-profit.

K-gr. 8; 290 students. $2295. Inc. fees $180. Fin. aid. avail. SDH: K, 8:15-11:30; gr. 1-8, 8:15-2:50. EDC: 7 a.m.-6 p.m.; $2.25/hr. Avg. & max. class size 35. Uniforms. Computer education offered at all grades; P.E. regular part of the curriculum; fine arts programs by professional artists offered to all students. Application deadline June 1. Waiting list for some grades. Accredited by WASC & WCEA.

"Most Holy Trinity is one of the pastoral elements of Most Holy Trinity parish. Together we express our fidelity to the Word of God through Witness, Service, and Sacraments. Our community reflects the multi-cultural and multi-economic richness of the city where a safe, nurturing environment provides students with the opportunity to reach their full potential."

QUEEN OF APOSTLES. 4950 Mitty Way, San Jose 95129. (408) 252-3659. Marianna Willis, Principal. Est. 1964. Non-profit.

K-gr. 8; 281 students. In parish $2115; out-of-parish $2385. Materials fee $230. SDH: 8:00-2:40. AM & PM kdg. EDC: 6:30 a.m.-6 p.m. $135/mo., 20hrs./$60, $4.75/hr. Avg. class size 31, max. class size 35. Specialized reading gr. 1-3, computer lab. Afterschool sports for gr. 5-8, Spanish gr. 7-8. Accelerated 8th gr. math at Mitty. Summer extended day care for K-gr. 5 for enrolled students. Accredited by WASC & WCEA.

"We emphasize basic skills in a warm, friendly atmosphere and seek to nurture Christian values by developing self-esteem, respect for others, and responsibility. Parents are encouraged to participate in school activities and help in fund-raising."

ST. CHRISTOPHER. 2278 Booksin Ave., San Jose 95125. (408) 723-7223. Arlene Ernst, Principal. Est. 1955. Non-profit.

K-gr. 8; 620 students. $2150. Sibling discounts. Fin. aid avail. SDH: 8:25-2:50. EDC: 7 a.m.-6 p.m. Avg. class size K, 30; gr. 1-8, 35. Max. class size 35. Uniforms. Extensive computer program, science teachers, LD teacher. After school sports program. Reg. period Feb. 1-Feb. 28. Accredited by WCEA & WASC.

"We attempt to develop the potential of each student and strive to teach students to lead a full Christian life making God, Christ, the Church and others the focus in their lives."

ST. FRANCIS CABRINI. 15325 Woodard Rd., San Jose 95124. (408) 377-6545. Sister Patricia Layman, Principal. Est. 1963. Non-profit.

K-gr. 8, 583 students. $2400. Inc. fees $180. No scholarships. Avg. class size 33, max. 35. SDH: 8:15-2:45. EDC: 6:30 a.m.-6 p.m. Afterschool sports for gr. 5-8. Apply anytime. 4 wk. summer program in July with day care, academics, play. Accredited by WCEA & WASC.

"St. Francis Cabrini is a Catholic school committed to educating the whole child in cooperation with the parents."

ST. JOHN VIANNEY. 4601 Hyland Ave., San Jose 95127. (408) 258-7677. Sr. Michele A. Murphy, Principal. K-gr. 8; 620 students. EDC: 7-6. Non-profit. Accredited by WCEA & WASC.

ST. LEO THE GREAT. 1051 W. San Fernando St., San Jose 95126. (408) 293-4846. Gloria Pearce, Principal. Est. 1916. Non-profit.

K-gr. 8; 280 students. SDH: K, 8:15-12:30; gr. 1-8, 8:15-2:45. EDC: 12:30-6, closed on school holidays. Avg. class size 30, max. 35. P.E., school counselor, computers, enrichment program, afterschool sports for gr. 5-8. No specific application deadline. Accredited by WCEA & WASC.

"The mission of St. Leo the Great School is to create a Christian environment in which students of diverse social and cultural backgrounds are able to develop the self-confidence, love of learning, and sense of responsibility needed to help them discover and use their God-given potential."

ST. MARTIN OF TOURS. 300 O'Connor Dr., San Jose 95128. (408) 287-3630. Kevin Eagleson, Principal. Est. 1955. Non-profit.

K-gr. 8; 350 students. $2670. Inc. fees $200. 10% receive fin. aid. SDH: 8:15-2:45. EDC: 7 a.m.-6 p.m. $3/hr+ $40 reg. fee. Avg. & max. class size 35. Uniforms. Accredited by WASC & WCEA.

"St. Martin of Tours is a parish school rich in the tradition of Catholic education."

ST. PATRICK CATHEDRAL. 51 North Ninth St., San Jose 95112. (408) 283-5858. Ms. Yvonne Gomez, Principal. Accredited by WCEA & WASC. Non-profit.

Preschool-gr. 8; 320 students. $2000, sibling discounts. $25 reg. fee, books $225. Sibling discounts. Fin. aid. avail. SDH: 8:15-2:45. EDC: 7 a.m.-6 p.m., $2.25-$2.50/hr., drop-in $3/hr. Avg. & max. class size 36. Uniforms. L.D. teachers on campus 2 days/wk. On staff counselor, classroom music, P.E., computers, science specialist, drama, afterschool dance program. Begin taking applications in Jan. Waiting list. 4 wk. academic & enrichment summer school. Accredited by WCEA & WASC.

"Saint Patrick School is a faith community where teachers and students pray together and are supported and united by their bond in Christ...We recognize our obligation to provide quality education, which will maximize the realization of each child's potential: spiritual, physical, intellectual, cultural, social."

ST. VICTOR. 3150 Sierra Rd., San Jose 95132. (408) 251-1740. Sister Sharon Ann Breden, CSJ, Principal. Est. 1964. Non-profit.

K-gr. 8. In parish, $1750; out-of-parish, $2000. Fin. aid avail. Inc. fees $100. SDH: 8:00-2:30. EDC: 7 am-6 pm., $35-$70. Avg. class size 37, max. 40. Uniforms. Computer lab, library, student government, school choir, after school sports. Admissions based on entrance test, teacher-student & principal-parent interview. Reg. in Feb., entrance test in March. Waiting list. Accredited by WCEA.

"St. Victor's provides an environment for the development of Gospel values and the living out of Christian community. We the faculty believe strongly in the Christian message, a faith community, and the service of others. We accept the responsibility to challenge our students to make those Christian goals a part of their immediate lives."

NON-CATHOLIC RELIGIOUS SCHOOLS

ACHIEVER CHRISTIAN. 800 Ironwood Dr. San Jose 95125. (408) 264-6789. Eugene Birdsall, Superintendent. Est. 1971. Non-profit.

Preschool-gr. 6. $200-258/mo. $250 reg. fee. No scholarships. SDH: 8:30-3. EDC: 7 a.m.-6 p.m. Avg. class size 20, max. 25. Dress code. Swimming, computer classes, music, science labs, Spanish. Testing and therapy for L.D. students. Apply for fall by March 1. Waiting list. Summer camp sponsored by First Baptist Church.

"The school provides a strong academic program with a Biblical world view. A loving, disciplined environment."

APOSTLES LUTHERAN. 5828 Santa Teresa Blvd., San Jose 95123. (408) 578-5012. Paul Bauer, Principal. Est. 1970. Non-profit.

K-gr. 8; 191 students. Church members $1900; non-members $2800. Scholarships for church members only. SDH: K, 8:30-11:45; gr. 1-8, 8:30-3:05. EDC: 6:30 a.m.-6 p.m., $1.75/hr. Avg. class size 21, max. 29. Dress code. Instrumental music lessons, choir, drama, remedial reading, full girls' and boys' athletics. Apply by July 15 for reduced rate. Summer programs in reading, computer, art, basketball camp.

"We strive for excellence in Christian education."

CAVALRY CATHEDRAL ACADEMY. 2165 Lucretia Ave., San Jose 95122. (408) 298-7622. Doris Upshur, Administrator. Est. 1980. Non-profit.

K-gr. 8; 100 students. Church members K, $213/mo., gr. 1-8 $250/mo.; non-members K, $237/mo., gr. 1-8, $282/mo. Sibling discounts. Application fee $50; reg. & books $150. Fin. aid avail. SDH: K, 8:10-11:30; gr. 1-8, 8:10-2:45. EDC: 7 a.m.-6 p.m.; $2.25/hr. Avg. class size 15, max. 25. Computers. Uniforms. Accredited by ACSI.

The school's goal is to "equip tomorrow's leaders today."

CHRISTIAN COMMUNITY ACADEMY. 1523 McLaughlin Ave., San Jose 95122. (408) 279-0846. Kenneth Van Meter, Director. Est. 1978. Non-profit.

K-gr. 12, 250 students. $2400-$3200. Inc. fees $290. No scholarships. SDH: K, 8:30-12; gr. 1-12, 8:30-3:15. EDC 7 a.m.-6 p.m. $2/hr. Avg. class size 23, max. 29. Uniforms. PE, Spanish, music for all K-6 students. Families must attend Bible-believing church. Priority given to siblings and on basis of application date. Apply by July 30th. Open-door policy, parents invited to visit anytime. Waiting list for some grades. 6 wk. summer program. Candidate for WASC & ACSI accreditation.

"The school is an extension of home and church. Enrollment is a partnership to assist parents to fulfill their responsibility to educate their children. Traditional academic program. Biblically integrated."

EAST VALLEY CHRISTIAN. 2715 South White. Rd., San Jose 95148. (408) 274-6644. Pastor Nelson, Director; Cheri Ortiz, Admissions. Est. 1988. Non-profit.

K-gr. 12; 107 students. $250/mo. Reg. fee $100. No scholarships. SDH: (all grades) 8:30-3. EDC: 6:30 a.m.-6 p.m. $86/mo. or $2/hr. Uniforms. Accredited by A.C.E.

"Accelerated Christian Education is an individualized curriculum that allows students to work at own level of performance."

EITZ CHAIM ACADEMY. 3001 Ross Ave., San Jose 95148. (408) 978-5822. Rabbi Lapin, Director. Est. 1988. Non-profit.

Preschool-gr. 8; 47 students. $500/mo. + book & reg. fees. Avg. class size 10, max. 15. SDH: K, 8:30-2; upper grades, 8:30-3:30. Uniforms. ESL program.

The school provides "a Torah education for all children."

LIBERTY BAPTIST. 2790 S. King Rd., San Jose 95122. (408) 274-5613. Tom Chaffin, Elem. Principal; David Kiser, High School Principal. Est. 1969. Non-profit.

Jr. K (for 4 yr. olds)-gr. 12; 500 students. Jr. K, $1955; K, (all day) $2395; gr. 1-5 $2385; gr. 6, $2495; gr. 7-11, $2795; gr. 12, $2839. Books $95, enrollment fee $45. No scholarships. SDH: 8:30-3:25. EDC: 7 a.m.-6 p.m. Avg. class size 25, max. 27. Dress code. Band & drama for gr. 4-12. Well developed athletic program in jr. and sr. high. Apply anytime. Waiting list in some grades.

MILPITAS CHRISTIAN SCHOOL, INC. 3435 Birchwood Lane, San Jose 95132. (415) 945-6530. Judy Morasci, Principal. Est. 1973. Non-profit.

Transitional K-gr. 8. 520 students. K, $215/mo., gr. 1-5, $264/mo., gr. 6-8, $288/mo. SDH: 8:30-2:30 or 3. EDC: 6:30 a.m.-6:30 p.m. Closed only on legal holidays. Avg. & max. class size 25 with teacher and aide. Computer, music, P.E. classes. Afterschool keyboard, Spanish & French classes . We provide tutoring for L.D. students and also refer those with special needs to other agencies. Daycare summer camp. Candidate for ACSI & WASC accreditation.

"MCS provides quality education in a supportive Christ-centered environment. Christian values from a biblical perspective are taught along with a sound academic program."

ST. STEPHEN'S. 500 Shawnee Ln., San Jose 95123. (408) 365-2927. Sharyl Leggate, Head of School. Est. 1978. Non-profit.

Episcopal, preschool-gr. 6; 300 students. $1000-$2800. Additional enrollment and testing fees. No scholarships. SDH: 8:30-3. EDC: 7:15-5:45; $2.25-$2.50/hr. Avg. class size 18- 20, max. 22-24. Uniforms. Chorus, P.E., part-time resource specialist for LD students. Apply in March. Placement test required. Waiting list in most classes. Summer day care. Accredited by National Association of Episcopal Schools.

"We strive to develop each student's spiritual, intellectual, physical, social and cultural capacities by involving them in the Circle of Education with God, Parent, School and Community. Within this creative, loving Christian environment, each child will develop his or her own unique character."

ST. TIMOTHY'S LUTHERAN. 5100 Camden Ave., San Jose 95124. (408) 265-0244. B. Torgerson, Principal. Est. 1979. Non-profit.

Preschool-gr. 5 Jr. Kdg. & K, $1820; gr. 1-6, $2440. Inc. fees $200. SDH: 9-3. EDC: 7-9 a.m., $60/mo.; 3-6 p.m., $85/mo. Avg. class size 18, max. 22. Music, art. Registration & screening for fall in Feb. Waiting list. Accredited by Evangelical Lutheran Education Association.
"We provide a Christ-centered environment where children can develop to their fullest potential."

SAN JOSE COMMUNITY CHRISTIAN SCHOOL. 480 S. McCreery Ave., San Jose 95116. (408) 729-9300.

SECULAR SCHOOLS

CHALLENGER. 1325 Bouret Dr., San Jose 95118. (408) 723-0111. Mrs.Darlene Wilson, Director; Lois Huang, Admissions. Est. 1963. Proprietary.

K-gr. 8. 367 students. K, $3951; gr. 1-5, $4176: gr. 6-8, $4473. Books $100. Fin. aid avail. SDH: K-gr. 8, 9-3:30. EDC: 7 a.m.-6 p.m., $927/yr., not available during school holidays. Avg. class size 20, max. 25. Uniforms. After school dance, foreign language, karate, music & art lessons. Admissions test. Waiting list. Summer program. Accredited by National Independent Private Schools Association.

"Challenger has high academic and comportment standards."

2nd San Jose campus is at 880 Wren Dr. Nancy Cyester, Principal. (408) 448-3010. Preschool-gr. 5; 193 students. All other information is the same.

ALMADEN COUNTRY SCHOOL. 6835 Trinidad Dr., San Jose 95120. (408) 997-0424. Kathleen Peterson, Director. Est. 1982. Proprietary.

Preschool-gr. 8. $1750-$4100. Inc. fees $350. Fin. aid avail. SDH: 8-3:05. EDC: 8 a.m.-6 p.m, $1900-$2900.   Avg. & max. class size 20. Uniforms. Computer science, music, art, drama, science, P.E., French, field trips. Admissions procedure includes two day evaluation. 6 wk. academic and creative arts summer camp.

"Our focus is on rigorous academics balanced with broad enrichment programs in fine arts and sciences. The atmosphere is wholesome, and discipline is administered with kindness."

CASA DI MIR MONTESSORI. P.O. Box 4804, San Jose 95150-4804. (408) 866-7758. Sheila Dubin, Board President. Est. 1991. Non-profit.

Gr. 1-6; 37 students. $400/mo. $250 one-time capital development fee; $100 materials fee; $50 field trips. Fin. aid avail. Teacher, student ratio: lower grades 1: 13; upper grades 1:16. SDH: 8:30-3. EDC available from separate program next door. Spanish Program. Field trips a regular part of the studies. Accredited by American Montessori Society.

"The aim of Cas di Mir Montessori is to encourage and nurture the creative, spiritual and developmental growth of children as well as their cognitive growth by means of active, self-directed learning and harmonizing individual mastery with group collaboration."

DE YOUNG. 730 Camina Esquela, San Jose 95129. (408) 725-1555. Lorin De Young, Director. Est. 1975. Proprietary.

Young Kdg. (4 yrs.)-gr. 12; 52 students. Tuition varies according to program child enrolled in. No scholarships. Books $120. SDH: 9-2:30. Avg. class size in YK-gr. 6, 8; max. 12. Avg. class size for gr. 7-12, 12; max. 24. Structured classes, individualized instruction as needed. Family-like atmosphere. For admission, child visits school, then parents, teacher & child confer. School accepts children who respect others.

"...Our parents want us to discipline their children, as we develop in them self-discipline; to respect their children, as we inculcate in them a respect for others;...In other words, they want an alternative to what is being passed off today as education. They want to be partners with us in a return to educational excellence — where high standards prevail."

EAST HILLS. 30 Kirk Ave., San Jose 95127. (408) 258-6595. Jane Lockrem, Director. Est. 1981. Non-profit.

K-gr. 3; 35 students.. K, $2000; gr. 1-3, $2900. Inc. fees: K, $425; gr. 1-3, $515. No scholarships. SDH: K, 8:30-12; gr. 1-3, 8:30-3. EDC planned for the future. Max. class size 16. Applications accepted until classes are filled. Classroom visits welcome. Parent owned and operated school. Summer programs from June 14-Aug. 20.

"East Hills Elementary offers a stimulating learning environment for kindergarten through fourth grade students. One of the most important components of the East Hills' approach is that our credentialed staff teach the total child. We consider academic, social, and physical development in order to bring children to their full potential. The program features individualized attention through small classes, active learning experiences, and a positive approach to developing self-discipline and social skills."

HARKER SCHOOL. 500 Saratoga Ave., San Jose 95129. (408) 249-2510. Howard E. Nichols, Headmaster. Est. 1893. Non-profit.

Jr. K-gr. 8; 697 students. Day students, $8840; 5 day boarding, $15,530; 7 day boarding, $17,970. Inc. fees $200-$600. 10% receive fin. aid. SDH: 8:15-3:15. EDC: 7 a.m.-5:30 p.m., no additional charge. Avg. class size 17, max. 23. Transportation. Uniforms. 15 acre campus includes new kdg. facility, computer and science labs, jr. Olympic swimming pool, tennis courts, library, gymnasium/auditorium, large playgrounds and athletic fields. New jr. high complex will be complete in 9/94. Drama, dance, music, art, afterschool sports program, regularly scheduled extra-help classes. Admissions criteria: entrance exams, school records, character evaluations. Brochures, videos available. Students performing average to above-average academically considered for admissions. 6 wk. summer programs include academics, enrichment, sports, recreation, computer camp, summer caravans. Accredited by WASC, CAIS, ACA & WAIC.

"The Harker School endeavors to develop well rounded young citizens. Through comprehensive programs of sound academics and character development, the school provides an alternative for parents who are seeking a rigorous and balanced education for their children."

MULBERRY. 1980 Hamilton Ave., San Jose 95125. (408) 377-1595. Ruth Kaplan, Director. Est. 1963. Non-profit.
Preschool-gr. 4 (will add gr. 5 in '94). K, $250/mo.; gr. 1-4, $335/mo. Reg. fee $25-$60. No scholarships. SDH: K, 9-12; gr. 1-4, 9-3. EDC: 7:30-6 p.m., $3/hr. Avg. & max. class size 16. Motor program with motor specialist, educational specialist, music teacher. Open enrollment begins March 1 and continues until classes are full. Waiting list. 6 wk. summer program with single week sessions.

"Mulberry provides a multi-sensory, manipulative enrichment program which challenges children's thinking and encourages children to learn and grow at their own pace. Mulberry's small classes allow children to have individualized programs."

PRIMARY PLUS. 3500 Amber Dr., San Jose 95117. (408) 248-2464. Vaughn Beckman, Principal. Est. 1969.

Preschool-gr. 6. $280-$440/mo.; $440/mo. with full day care. Books and materials, $100; reg. fee, $50. No scholarships. SDH: 8:30-3. EDC: 6:30 a.m.-6 p.m. Avg. class size 18, max. 22. Individualized instruction. Science, art, music, computer, science along with academic basics. After school dance, drama, crafts, clubs, cooking, computer science. School operates year round. Waiting list for some grades. Summer program includes swimming, tennis, karate, dance.

The school seeks "to provide an educational setting that will be staffed with warm, personally interested adults who will give the students the message that learning is exciting and establish a learning environment that will allow the children to experience the maximum amount of success possible."

SMALL WORLD. 730 Camino Escuela, San Jose 95129. (408) 257-7320. Gloria Lewis, Director. Est. 1973. Non-profit.

Preschool-gr. 5. $97/wk. Reg. fee $30, supplies $50. Fin. aid avail. SDH: 8:30-3:30. EDC: 6 a.m.-6 p.m., included in tuition. Avg. & max. class size 24. Gymnastics, dance program, field trips, computer classes for all ages. On site sibling care for preschoolers & infants. May register up until the first day of school. Summer camp includes thematic curriculum, field trips, swimming lessons. School closed only for the 7 legal holidays.

"All children learn at different rates and in different ways. Small World School offers a variety of activities and techniques to meet all children's needs."

TOWER ACADEMY. 2887 McLaughlin Ave., San Jose 95121. (408) 578-2830. Joyce Nelson, Director. Est. 1983. Proprietary.

Preschool-gr. 3. $89/wk. Reg. fee $45, books $55. No scholarships. 6:30 a.m.-6:30 p.m. EDC included in tuition. Avg. elem. class size 15, max. 20. School closed only 8 days/yr. Summer program includes swimming, tennis, dance, computer program, field trips, and sleep-overs.
Tower Academy "provides a warm, comfortable environment for children to grow, learn and explore the world, to begin new friendships, to express themselves, and to develop a sense of independence through thinking and reasoning skills."

Campbell ◆ Los Gatos ◆ Saratoga
CATHOLIC SCHOOLS

SACRED HEART. 13718 Saratoga Ave., Saratoga 95070. (408) 867-9241. Sister Aileen Donahue, Principal. Est. 1957. Non-profit. K-gr. 8. $2900. Sibling discounts. Inc. fees $180. Fin. aid avail. SDH: K, 8:30-11:30, 12-3; gr. 1-8, 8:30-3. EDC: 7:15-6; $2.50/hr. Avg. class size 33, max. 35. Uniforms. Extensive computer program, music, art, science, afterschool sports. On site reading specialist. Apply in Jan. Accredited by WASC & WCEA.

"The mission of Sacred Heart School is to offer students a Christian education from which they can draw the inspiration to live as Jesus did; to respect themselves and one another as well as to become citizens of the Church and the world community. Sacred Heart School accepts the responsibility to lead students to the skills, knowledge and behaviors which will equip them to meet life's challenge with faith and courage."

ST. LUCY'S. 76 East Kennedy Ave., Campbell 95008. (408) 378-7454. Sr. Jolene Schmitz, Principal. Est. 1953. Non-profit.

K-gr. 8; 300 students. In parish, $2100; out of parish $2415; non-participating $2550; reg. fee $160. Sibling discounts. Fin. aid avail. Avg. class size 30, max. 35. SDH: 8:30-3. EDC: 6:45 a.m.-6 p.m. $2/hr. Uniforms. Instructional aides. Specialists for LD reading, computer science, music & physical education. Upgraded computer lab used by all students regularly. Waiting list. Accredited by WCEA & WASC. Non-profit.

"The school believes that each child is a unique human being with the right to an education, and each student needs to develop spiritually, emotionally, and intellectually; this is made possible through the development of a strong sense of self-esteem."

ST. MARY. 30 Lyndon Ave., Los Gatos 95030. (408) 354-3944. Sister Nicki Thomas, Principal. Est. 1954. Non-profit.

Gr. 1-8; 245 students. In parish, $2020; out-of-parish, $2550; non-Catholics, $3050. Reg. fee $150. 5% receive fin. aid. SDH: 8:15-3 p.m. EDC: 3 p.m.-6 p.m., $2-$2.50/hr. Avg. class size 30. Max. class size, gr. 1-3, 30; gr. 4-8, 35. Uniforms. Computers, Spanish, music, art. Motor perception for gr. 1 & 2. Afterschool sports gr. 5-8. Entrance tests in April. Waiting list. Accredited by WASC & WCEA.

"St. Mary's Catholic School is a Christian Community which teaches Catholicism as a way of life, provides an education consistent with the highest standards, instills in its students an appreciation for learning as well as a sense of personal responsibility to themselves, their families and community."

NON-CATHOLIC RELIGIOUS SCHOOLS

CAMPBELL CHRISTIAN. 1075 W.Campbell Ave., Campbell 95008. (408) 370-4900. Carter Lambert, Principal. Est. 1979. Non-profit.

K-gr. 6; 160 students. Half day K, $2205; full day K, $2810; gr. 1-6, $2915. Reg. & testing fee $150. Fin. aid avail. for returning students. SDH: K (half day) 8-12; other grades 8-3:00. Avg. class size 20-25, max. 25. Uniforms. All academics approached from Christian point of view. Computers in elem. grades. Assertive discipline. Students accepted on basis of entrance tests and recommendations from previous schools. Accredited by ACSI.

"With Christ and the Bible as the basis of the school philosophy, children are educated to do their best academically, to treat others with respect, and to develop self-confidence. A Bible-based curriculum combined with a dedicated teaching staff that truly enjoys teaching increases the likelihood that both spiritual and academic goals can be met."

COVENANT LIFE ACADEMY. 1300 Sheffield Ave., #14, Campbell 95008. (408) 371-5141. Doyle De Graw, Principal. Est. 1981. Non-profit.

K-gr. 8; 60 students. $24000. Books $100. No scholarships. SDH: K, 8:15-12; gr. 1-8, 8:15-2:50. Avg. class size 15, max. 20. Uniforms. Art, Spanish, music. Ongoing admissions.

"We are a Christian school that operates with the purpose of assisting Fathers in their responsibility of educating their children."

LOS GATOS CHRISTIAN. 16845 Hicks Rd., Los Gatos 95032. (408) 268-1502 (elem.); 268-5252 (jr. high). Linda Smedley, Director. Est. 1977. Non-profit.

Jr. Kdg.-gr. 8; 426 students. K-gr. 6, $2680; gr. 7-8, $3040. Inc. fees: $290-$310. SDH: 8:30-3. EDC: 7 a.m.-6 p.m., $2.00/hr. Avg. class size 23; max. class size varies by grade. Dress code. Uniforms optional. P.E. & music programs, afterschool sports, computers. Small group tutorial programs in language & math to help L.D. students succeed at grade level. Admission by application and interview. No deadline. Kdg. evaluation in April for following year. Waiting list in some grades.

"Los Gatos Christian School seeks to offer a Christ-centered traditional education as a ministry of Los Gatos Christian Church."

MOUNTAIN BIBLE CHRISTIAN SCHOOL. 23946 Summit Rd., Los Gatos, 95030. (408) 353-2302. John Haak, Director. Est. 1982. Non-profit.

K-gr. 5; 19 students. $1800. 10% sibling discounts. SDH: 8:45-1:15. Avg. class size 9, max. class size 12. Rural setting in Santa Cruz Mts. Apply by May 15.

"Each child is precious to God and we seek His guidance in training each one to know and serve Him according to their abilities."

SAINT ANDREW'S. 13601 Saratoga Ave., Saratoga 95070. (408) 867-3785. Rev. Julian Lentz, Headmaster. Est. 1961. Non-profit.

Preschool-gr. 8; 400 students. $5000. Inc. fees vary. Fin. aid. avail. SDH: 8:30-3; EDC: 7:30-5:30, $2/hr. Avg. & max. class size 22. Uniforms. Daily chapel and religious instruction geared to students of many religious backgrounds. Afterschool sports for gr. 6-8. French or Spanish required of all students. Summer programs for preschool and K; sports camp. First inquiry best in Jan. or Feb. Preference given to siblings and parish members; otherwise, first come, first served. Waiting list for all grades. Accredited by National Association of Episcopal Schools.

"The goal of Saint Andrew's School is to develop as fully as possible the intellectual, spiritual, physical and social capabilities of each student. We are a structured school with high academic standards in an atmosphere of religious concern and community, catering to students of many diverse traditions."

SAN JOSE CHRISTIAN. 1300 Sheffield Ave., Campbell 95008. (408) 371-7741. Al Kosters, Principal. Est. 1959. Non-profit.

Preschool-gr. 8. K-gr. 4, $3091; gr. 5-8, $3234. Reg. fee $115. SDH: K, 8:30-11:45; gr. 1-8, 8:30-3. EDC: 7 a.m.-6 p.m.; $2.10/hr.; closed only on major holidays. Avg. class size 16, max. 28. Dress code. Computers, field trips, band, music, choir, art, 6th grade outdoor ed. Parents expected to actively participate in worship and activities of a Bible-believing church, and/or sincerely desire to have their child receive a Christ-centered education. Waiting list for kdg. Accredited by C.S.I.

"We believe the Bible to be true, infallible, the ultimate source of truth about God and all of creation. San Jose Christian School exists to train young people for Christian life and service. We offer a balanced program emphasizing spiritual, academic, physical, and social growth and a curriculum that recognizes that Christ is Lord of all creation."

VALLEY CHRISTIAN. 220 Kensington Way, Los Gatos 95032. (408) 559-4400. Claudia Lee, Principal; Dr. Clifford Daugherty, Superintendent. Est. 1969. Non-profit.

K-gr. 5, 277 students. $3333; Fin. aid avail. SDH: K, 8:30-11:50; gr. 1-gr. 5, 8:30-2:45. EDC: 7 a.m.-6 p.m.; $2.50/hr. Avg. class size 24. Max. class size: K-2, 25; gr. 3-5, 28. Dress code. Learning disabilities program, math lab. The Discovery Center provides educational assistance for students experiencing learning difficulties. Music theory, band, orchestra, graded choirs, vocal ensembles, physical ed. & art specialists, computer lab, Bible classes, weekly chapel, noon sports. For admission, recommendation by educator & pastor of

Evangelical, Bible-believing church required. Summer programs for school-age children Jun. 1-Aug. 20; $85/wk or $20/day. Accredited by ACSI and WASC.

"Valley Christian Elementary School seeks to provide students of Christian families an excellent academic education, founded upon and integrated with God's word."

WEST HEIGHTS CHRISTIAN. 19380 Bear Creek Rd., Los Gatos 95030. (408) 395-2273. Pastor Gary Alexander, Principal. Est. 1980. Non-profit.

K-gr. 12; 33 students. $1200-$1800. Reg. fee $35. Sibling discounts. SDH: K, 9-1; gr. 1-12, 9-3:30. Kindercare 1-3:30. Avg. class size 12, max. 15. Uniforms. Redwood trails & pond, rustic beauty. Enrichment in arts, hiking, nature, musicals, field trips. Abeka & B. Jones curricula, creation science. Daily Bible classes. Gr. 7-12 use self-paced Accelerated Christian Education curriculum. Applicants must regulary attend a Christian church where the Bible is believed to be the only infallible Word of God. Parent participation required. Applicants interview with pastor/principal to adapt program. Accredited by A.C.S.I.

"West Heights is dedicated to training Christians to love, serve and depend entirely upon Jesus Christ."

WEST VALLEY SEVENTH-DAY ADVENTIST SCHOOL. 95 Dot Ave., Campbell 95008. (408) 378-4327. Perry Rogers, Principal. Est. 1948. Non-profit.

K-gr. 8; 120 students. $185-$200/mo. Inc. fees $200. No scholarships. Avg. class size 18, max. 25. SDH: K, 8:25-2:45; gr. 1-8, 8:25-3:15. EDC: 6:30-6 p.m., $1.50/hr. Dress code. Band, choir, private lessons available. Application deadline Aug. 20 but can apply later. Students admitted on basis of order of application and test scores. Accredited by Central California Conference of Seventh-Day Adventists.
"We stress academic excellence and character-building."

YAVNEH DAY SCHOOL. 14855 Oka Rd., Los Gatos 95030. (408) 358-3413. Est. 1981. Non-profit.

PreK-gr. 5; 115 students. $5300. Books & supplies $250. Fin. aid avail. SDH: 8:30-3:30. EDC available through Jewish Community Center. Avg. class size 15, max. 19. Teacher/student ratio 1:8. Dual language program, ESL, special program for children with no Hebrew background. Apply anytime. Waiting list. Accredited by Solomon Scheter Association and CAIS.

"Yavneh offers a comprehensive general studies and Judaica studies education in a nurturing environment which fosters creative and critical thinking. Our students are prepared to be good citizens and knowledgeable Jews."

SECULAR SCHOOLS

DENMAN. 5051 Lone Hill Rd., Los Gatos 95032. (408) 448-5345. Anne P. Denman, Owner/Director. Est. 1983. Proprietary.

K-gr. 6; 28 students. K, $235/mo; gr. 1-6, $265/mo. Supply fee, $150; testing fee $25. No scholarships. SDH: 9-3. EDC: 7 a.m.-6 p.m. (for gr. 1-6), $3/hr. Avg. class size 12, max. 16. Uniforms. Music, Christmas program, poetry in all grades. Because of small classes can work with students with learning disabilities. Summer activity program: learning workshops, field trips.

"We are an academic institution. The school day is devoted primarily to academic pursuits. We offer thorough and effective instruction in basic skill areas. Our objective is to make each grade level a successful academic experience for each child. We use small classes, individual attention, encouragement, praise and discipline to achieve our goals."

HILLBROOK. End of Marchmont Drive, Los Gatos 95030. (408) 356-6116. Robert M. Clements, Headmaster; Diana Clayton, Admissions Director. Est. 1936. Non-profit.

Preschool-gr. 8; 290 students. Jr. K & K, (8:45-1:30) $3750: full day K & gr. 1-8, $6,750 Inc. fees, $175. 11% receive fin. aid. SDH: 8:45-3:15. EDC: 7:30 a.m.-5:30 p.m., $2.30/hr. Transportation avail. for $1400/yr. Avg. class size 18, max. 24. Dress code. Specialists teach P.E., art, music, Spanish, woodshop, science, typing, math, library. Outdoor education trip for gr. 6-8. Typing in gr. 5 & 6; computer skills in gr. 7 & 8. Six wk. summer school and camp. Apply by January. Admission based on test scores in upper grades, readiness in lower grades and suitability to school program in all grades. Preference given to siblings. Waiting list. Accredited by WASC & CAIS.

"The school seeks to balance a family atmosphere with high academic standards and to graduate students who are confident about their abilities. We encourage students to do their best. We actively seek minority students."

LOS GATOS ACADEMY. 220 Bel Gatos Rd., Los Gatos, 95032. (408)358-1046. Jean Spinner, Director. Est. 1988. Non-profit.

Preschool-gr. 8; 101 students. $525/mo. Ski trip, $215. No scholarships. SDH: 9-4; EDC: 4-5:30, $50/mo. Van Service avail. Extensive art and dance program. Campus on 9 beautiful acres. Year round enrollment. School runs through summer with same hours and cost.

"We use the study methods of L. Ron Hubbard. Students move at their own pace and learn for application and use in life."

OLD ORCHARD SCHOOL. 400 W. Campbell Ave., Campbell 95008. Gr. 6-8 at 250 Virginia Ave., Campbell. (408) 378-5935. Idanthea B. Weston, Director. Est. 1971. Proprietary.

PreK-gr. 8. Full day K, $4890; gr. 1-5, $5210; gr. 6-8, $5250. Supplies, $100. No scholarships. SDH: 8:30-3. EDC: 7 a.m.-6 p.m., $2.75/hr. (Not open during summers or holidays.) Avg. class size 20, max. 22. Uniforms. French taught in K-gr. 5, Latin in gr. 6-8. Music, drama, art. Monthly field trips. For admissions students come for 3 day audit. Siblings given priority, then according to date of application. Waiting list in lower grades. Summer programs in creative writing.

"Students are taught to read with insight, write with clarity, speak effectively, and listen with curiosity and concern. Because education includes the development of character, creativity and confidence, Old Orchard School supplements the academics with a program of fine arts to help shape well-rounded individuals."

PRIMARY PLUS. 1870 Bucknall Rd., Saratoga 95070. (408) 370-0357. Infant care-gr. 2. See listing for San Jose secular schools.

SOUTH VALLEY CARDEN SCHOOL OF ALMADEN. 220 Belgatos Rd., Los Gatos 95032. (408) 356-9126. Mrs. Evelyn K. Musavi, Director. Est. 1977. Proprietary.

Jr. K-gr. 8. $5100; inc. fees $50. No scholarships. SDH: 8:30-3:15. EDC: 6:30 a.m.-6 p.m. Avg. class size 15, max. 22. Dress code. Music, French, Latin, daily PE, computers taught by special subject teachers. Art, drama, 7000 volume library. All students who can benefit from program accepted on a first come-first serve basis. LD specialist avail. for students who need extra support. Waiting list in some grades. Classroom visits permitted. Summer sport & survival camp, all summer. Accredited by Carden Educational Foundation.

"We believe that all students can and will learn when the teacher teaches. The Carden method is a sound, non-theoretical integrated, sequential method that emphasizes the basic skills of reading, writing, and math. Classical literature is read, homework and study habits emphasized. Personal responsibility, reliance on self, and sound character development are nurtured and guided which in turn promote a healthy self-esteem."

Milpitas
CATHOLIC SCHOOLS

ST. JOHN THE BAPTIST. 360 South Abel St., Milpitas 94035. (408) 262-8110. Judith A. Perkowski, Principal. Est. 1987. Non-profit.

PreK-gr. 8; 278 students. $2000. Reg. fee $210. Fin. aid avail. SDH: K, 8:20-11:30, 10:00-1; gr. 1-8, 8:20-3:00. EDC: 6:30 a.m.-6 p.m., $10/day. Avg. class size 35, max. 40. Uniforms. Computer lab, music program, P.E., afterschool sports and jr. high program. On site LD specialist. Priority given to families of St. John's & St. Elizabeth's parishes. Application process should begin in Jan.; deadline March 1. Waiting list. Accredited by WASC & WCEA.

"This school, the Catholic Church, and our families have joined together in partnership. Together, we are dedicated to providing a caring, Catholic environment in which our students can achieve their full potential as productive, responsible members & leaders of tomorrow's world."

NON-CATHOLIC RELIGIOUS SCHOOLS

FOOTHILL SEVENTH-DAY ADVENTIST SCHOOL. 1991 Landess Ave., Milpitas 95035. (408) 263-2568. Robert Hicks, Principal. Est. 1979. Non-profit.

K-gr. 8; 120 students. $250/mo. Reg. fee $100. Church members can apply for worthy student fund. SDH: gr. K-gr.8 8-3:15. EDC: 6:30 a.m.-6 p.m. also avail. during Xmas & spring vacations. Avg. class size 15. Computer instruction, music, gymnastics. Private music lessons available. Summer school. Accredited by Central California Conference of Seventh-Day Adventists.

"Our intention is that each child will come to know God as a personal being who really cares...develop thinking skills that will serve as a basis for comprehension and understanding,....respect others, regardless of their abilities, appearance, or heritage, and experience success."

SECULAR SCHOOLS

RAINBOW BRIDGE CENTER. 1500 Yosemite Dr., Milpitas 95035. (408) 945-9090. Jeff Mair, Administrator. Karen Hill, Principal. Est. 1983. Proprietary.

Preschool-gr. 6; 280 students. $112/wk. No scholarships. SDH: 8:30-2:30. EDC: 6:30 a.m.-6 p.m.; cost included in tuition. School closed only on major holidays. Avg. class size 26, max. 29. Gymsters, swim lessons, many outings to nearby park, music lessons, karate, computers, foreign languages, drama. Summer program includes swim lessons and curriculum review. Entrance test. Enrollment for new students begins in March and continues until classes fill. Waiting list.

"We expect children in every grade and in every subject area to learn to the limits of their ability, master basic skills, and overcome specific difficulties as they occur."

Cupertino ◆ Santa Clara ◆ Sunnyvale
CATHOLIC SCHOOLS

RESURRECTION. 1395 Hollenbeck, Sunnyvale 94087. (408) 245-4571. Toni Amodio, Principal. Est. 1965. Non-profit.

Jr. K-gr. 8; 350 students. K & Jr. K, $1875-$2375; $2000 parishioners, $2000; non-parishioners, $2800. Sibling discounts. $80 reg. fee. Fin. aid avail. to parishioners after 1 year in school. SDH: K, 8:30-12 or 12-3; gr. 1-8, 8:30-3. EDC: 6:30-6. Avg. class size 35, max. 37. Uniforms. Computers, art, music, P.E. in all grades. Educational TV, science camp for 6th graders, field trips, professional counseling, 8th grade retreat, Christmas production with all students. Enrollment begins in late Jan. Afterschool sports program. Summer camp. Accredited by WCEA & WASC.

"Resurrection School seeks to develop the individual student's full potential mentally, morally and physically by providing a Catholic education emphasizing academics, critical thinking, love of learning, self-esteem, and care and concern for others, with full support from parents and parish in a Christian-centered, caring environment."

ST. CLARE. 725 Washington St., Santa Clara 95050. (408) 246-6797. Sister Virginia Crilly, Principal. Est. 1856. Non-profit.

K-gr. 8; 300 students. In parish, $2400; out of parish $2758; non-Catholic $2676. Inc. fees $220. Sibling discounts. Fin. aid avail. after one year in school. SDH: 8:15-3. EDC: 6:30 a.m.-6 p.m. Uniforms. Avg. & max. class size 35. Computers, art, P.E. Waiting list in some grades. Accredited by WASC & WCEA.

"St. Clare's is a Catholic school with Christian values and priorities. Our school is a Christian community which respects the dignity and worth of all people."

ST. CYPRIAN. 195 Leota Ave., Sunnyvale 94086. (408) 738-3444. Sister Mary Leonard, Principal. Est. 1968. Non-profit.

K-gr. 8. 228 students. $1805/yr. Reg. fee $125. Fin. aid avail. SDH: 8:30-2:45. EDC: 7 a.m.-6 p.m., $2.50/hr. Uniforms. Computer lab, band, art class, P.E. gym, playground. Waiting list in some grades. Accredited by WASC & WCEA.

"We are a multi-cultural Catholic community with sequentially developed curriculum and extensive parental involvement...We assist students to address with Christian insight the multiple challenges which face individuals and society."

ST. JOSEPH OF CUPERTINO. 10120 N. De Anza Blvd., Cupertino 95014. (408) 252-6441. Mary Lyons, Principal. Est. 1956. Non-profit.

K-gr. 8; 250 students. $2100-$4525. Inc. fees, $200. Fin. aid avail. SDH: 8:25-3. EDC: 7 a.m.-6 p.m., $2.25/hr. Avg. class size 29, max. 35. Special program for learning disabled students. Art, music, computer & science labs, library, afterschool sports and drama. Applications open in Jan., testing in March. Waiting list for some grades. Summer day care program. Accredited by WCEA & WASC.

"St. Joseph of Cupertino is a Catholic parish school which fosters a sense of spirituality and a feeling of community. We have a strong academic program which challenges students to do their best. Family involvement is an important aspect of our parish and school."

ST. JUSTIN. 2655 Homestead Rd., Santa Clara 95051. (408) 248-1094. Kathy Almazol, Principal. Non-profit.

K-gr. 8. $2100. Reg. fee $160. Fin. aid avail. SDH: K, 8:15-11:50; gr. 1-8, 8:15-3:00. EDC: 7 a.m.-5:45, not avail. on school holidays. Avg. & max. class size 35. Science and computer labs. Instrumental music, art teacher, science consultant for K-gr. 5, P.E., departmentalized jr. high. Apply Jan. 30-March 31. Accredited by WASC & WCEA.

The school is "committed to spreading the Gospel message of peace and justice. Students are asked to participate in parish & school programs benefitting those in need. St Justin provides a warm nurturing environment and an excellent academic foundation with gifted teachers and staff."

ST. LAWRENCE. 1971 St. Lawrence Dr., Santa Clara 95051. (408) 296-2260. Priscilla Murphy, Principal. Est. 1961. Non-profit.

K-gr. 6; 263 students. $2680. Inc. fees, $200. 5% receive fin. aid. SDH: 8-3:00. EDC: 7 a.m.-6 p.m., $2.80/hr. Avg. class size 36, max. 40. Uniforms. Music, library, computers, PE, gymnasium, pool. Afterschool sports for gr. 5 & 6. Applications available in Jan., testing in March. Summer camp open to all students. Accredited by WCEA & WASC.

St. Lawrence Elementary School strives "to maximize each child's potential in a Christ-centered community of learners."

ST. MARTIN. 597 Central Ave., Sunnyvale 94086. (408) 736-5534. Rosemary Griggs, Principal. Est. 1953. Non-profit.

K-gr. 8. 240 students. $1600-$2000. Sibling discounts. Inc. fees $200 . Fin. aid avail. SDH: 8:30-3. EDC: 6:30 a.m.-6:00, $3/hr., sibling discounts. Avg. class size 30, max. 35. Uniforms. Instrumental band for gr. 4-8, computers, choir, afterschool sports. On site L.D. specialist. Waiting list in some grades. Accredited by WCEA & WASC.

"We strive to provide an environment in which the teaching of Jesus Christ can be learned and lived. Secondly, we seek to create an atmosphere of learning that will produce knowledgeable and creative individuals with high self-esteem and a desire for continuous learning."

NON-CATHOLIC RELIGIOUS SCHOOLS

BETHEL LUTHERAN. 10181 Finch Ave., Cupertino 95014. (408) 252-8512. Est. 1978. Non-profit.

Preschool-gr. 3. Jr. K, $195/mo; K, $205/mo.; gr. 1-3, $280/mo. $100 reg. fee. No scholarships. SDH: 9-3. EDC: 7 a.m.-9 a.m., $4; 3-6 p.m., $6. Avg. class size 18-20, max. 20. Music director & Spanish teacher. Enrollment begins in March for following year. 10 wk. summer program for preschool-gr. 6 beginning in June. Accredited by American Lutheran Education Association.

"Our role is to provide children with the tools they need to access their own possibilities, to guide the natural curiosity and joy of learning, and to help them become lifelong learners, problem solvers and thinkers in a loving Christian environment."

THE LUTHERAN SCHOOL OF OUR SAVIOR. 5825 Bollinger Rd., Cupertino 95014. (408) 252-0250. Carl Moody, Principal. Est. 1958. Non-profit.

Jr. K-gr. 8; $235/mo., sibling discounts. Reg. fee $175. SDH: 8:30-3. EDC: 7 a.m.-6 p.m; $450/yr. for a.m., $900/yr. for p.m. Avg. class size 25, max. 27. Dress code. Inter-school sports include volleyball, basketball, and track. Children & parents must agree to school's philosophy and regulations. Waiting list in some grades.

"The school is owned and operated by The Lutheran Church of Our Savior and has as its primary purpose the obligation of developing in its students such attitudes, habits, and skills as are necessary to the building of a life dedicated to the services of God and man."

NEIGHBORHOOD CHRISTIAN. 1290 Pomeroy Ave., Santa Clara 95051. (408) 241-8837. Est. 1981. Non-profit.

K-gr. 6; 85 students. $2350. Testing fee $35; Inc. fees $120. 10-15% discount for church members. SDH: 9-3. EDC: 6:30 a.m.-6 p.m.; under separate management (408-984-3418.) Avg. class size 15, max. 18. Dress code. Full day academic kdg. featuring Slingerland program. Music, physical education, art, non-denominational Bible-study, computer. Students accepted on first come-first served basis. Waiting list for some grades. Summer enrichment through day care. Accredited by ACSI.

"With its small teacher-pupil ration and warm, disciplined atmosphere, the school emphasizes academic excellence, high moral standards, and respect for each other."

NEW COVENANT SCHOOL. 220-A Blake Ave., Santa Clara 95051. (408)249-3993. Pastor Kim C. Gossett, Director. Est. 1987. Non-profit.

K-gr. 7; 53 students. $176-$193/mo. $100 books & reg. fee. No Scholarships. Avg. & max. class size 13. Dress code. SDH: K, 8:30-12; gr. 1-7, 8:30-3:30. EDC: until 6 p.m.; $2.25/hr. Bible-based, Abeka curriculum. Enroll anytime through Sept. Summer Bible Day Camp.

"We prepare, equip and train our children according to the principles of the kingdom of God that they come to understand their relationship to God and the world they live in. Ours is a spirit filled, non-denominational, loving Christian atmosphere."

SOUTH PENINSULA HEBREW DAY SCHOOL. 1030 Astoria Dr., Sunnyvale 94087. (408) 738-3060 or (415) 965-8390. Bonnie Thompson, Principal. Est. 1972. Non-profit.

Preschool-gr. 8. K, $4308; gr. 1-8, $5150. Fin. aid avail. SDH: K, (Sept.-Dec) 8:30-12, (Jan.-June) 8:30-1:30; gr. 1-8, 8:30-3:30. EDC: 7:30 a.m.-6 p.m. Yearly fees or drop-in @ $5.50/hr. Computer classes, science lab, library, ESL for students from other countries. Should apply by May. School visit and interview required. The school is designed for Jewish children who can handle the curriculum.

"The Hebrew Day School provides both general and Jewish education under one roof…it offers a chance for a more integrated educational experience…and spending the full day at the Day School with its warm and reinforcing Jewish environment leads the child to a more lasting identification with his or her people and heritage."

SUNSHINE CHRISTIAN. 445 S. Mary Ave., Sunnyvale 95050. (408) 736-3286. Yvonne Waters, Director. Est. 1979. Non-profit.

Preschool-gr. 4. 10 month plan: $379/mon. for school and day care, $279/mon. for school only; 9 month plan: $421/mon. full time, $309 for school only. No scholarships. SDH: 8:30-2:30. EDC: 6:30 a.m.-6 p.m., closed on school holidays. Avg. class size 18, max. 25. Ballet, gymnastics, drama. Summer program includes swimming & bowling lessons and field trips. Accredited by ACSI.

The school strives to "initiate and nurture our relationship with Jesus Christ in ourselves, our community, our church, our family, and wherever our influence extends."

SECULAR SCHOOLS

ADVENTURES IN LEARNING. 980 Pomeroy Ave., Santa Clara 95051. (408) 247-4769. Annegret Albrecht, Principal. Est. in 1982. Proprietary.

K-gr. 6; 50 students. $235-$295/mo. Materials fee $190. No scholarships. SDH: K, 8:30-2; gr. 1-6, 8:30-3. EDC: 7 a.m.-6 p.m.; $1.25/hr. Avg. class size 15, max. 20. Uniforms. French, music, drama, yoga, karate. Applications accepted throughout the year. Classroom visits permitted 9 a.m.-12. Six wk. summer school, child care all summer. Swimming & karate available at extra cost.

"We provide a superior learning environment to encourage the development of academic excellence and personal growth. These goals are achieved through a strong academic program and small classes."

CARDEN EL CANTO. 615 Hobart Terrace, Santa Clara 95051. (408) 244-5041. Mr. William A. Ries, Director. Est. 1973. Proprietary.

Jr. K-gr. 8, 364 students. $4500; testing fee, $100; reg. fee, $200. Some fin. aid avail. SDH: 8:30-3. EDC: 7 a.m.-5:45; $1.25-$2.00/hr. Avg. class size 22, max. 24. Dress code. Music, art, French, daily PE, library studies, afterschool sports. Admissions based on in-house test. Waiting list in some grades. Accredited by Carden Foundation.

"We give academic tools and strive for academic excellence in a pleasant setting. The Carden method strives to preserve the dignity of the student and to meet his individual needs."

CHALLENGER SCHOOL. 1185 Hollenbeck Ave., Sunnyvale. (408) 245-7901. Josie Calicdan, Director. Preschool-gr. 8. See listing for Challenger School under San Jose Secular Private Schools.

ONE WORLD MONTESSORI. 20220 Suisun Dr., Cupertino 95014. (408) 255-3770. Rebecca Keith, Administrator. Est. 1979. Non-profit.

Infant-gr. 6. $4700 full day. Reg. fee $30; insurance $120. No scholarships. SDH: 9-3. EDC: 7:30 a.m.-6:30 p.m. Avg. class size 33, max. class size 44. Music, gymnastics, drama, art, & foreign language offered after school. Summer school for children enrolled includes swimming, field trips, arts & crafts, sports, and gymnastics. For admission parents must observe classes then children are interviewed. Waiting list. Siblings & children with previous Montessori training given admissions priority. Accredited by AMS.

"Utilizing a system of manipulative materials, we have created an environment in which the child can be challenged to develop independently at his or her own pace...The Montessori method of education strives to equip the child not only with academic skills but also with social, physical, and emotional skills as well."

PIONEER MONTESSORI. 400 N. Winchester, Santa Clara 95050. (408) 241-5077. Christine Hoerbelt, Educational Administrator. Est. 1979. Proprietary.

Preschool-gr. 6. $410/mo.; reg. fee $35; insurance $20. No scholarships. SDH: K, 8:30-2:30; gr. 1-6, 8:30-3. EDC: 7 a.m.-6 p.m. (study hall, art, & movement program part of afternoon day care.) Avg. class size 20, max. 23. Fully equipped Montessori program also includes gymnastics, dance. Applications accepted throughout the year. Observation required of parent and child. School is open year round. Field trips, special projects, and special unit studies during summer.

"At Pioneer we strive to provide an environment which encourages respect, self-motivation, self-discipline, and responsibility. Our program is self-paced with a minimum of competition within the mixed age classrooms."

RAINBOW MONTESSORI CHILD DEVELOPMENT CENTER. 790 E. Duane, Sunnyvale 94086. (408) 738-3261. Spyroula Rodenborn, Exec. Director. Est. 1975. Proprietary.

Infant care-gr. 6; 595 students. Morning K, $296/mo.; full day K-gr. 6, $432/mo. No scholarships. EDC: 6 a.m.-6 p.m.; cost included in tuition. School operates year round. Avg. & max. class size 36; student teacher ratio, 18-24:1. Extensive music & dance program includes music reading, music appreciation, improvisation, gymnastics. Spanish & German instruction. Summer program includes swimming. Apply anytime. Waiting list. Accredited by American Montessori.

"Montessori allows children freedom to select individual activities which correspond to their own periods of interest and readiness to progress at their own pace...At our school a foundation for learning in other subjects is also enhanced by the unique combination of both physical and mental skills in making music."

SIERRA ELEMENTARY AND HIGH SCHOOL. 220 Blake Ave. #B, Santa Clara 95051. (408) 247-4740. Linda Wesley, Director. Est. 1974. Non-profit.

K-gr. 12; 69 students. K-gr. 6, $4250; gr. 7-8, $5250; gr. 9-12, $6250. Inc. fees $175. Fin. aid for returning students only. SDH: 9-3. EDC: 7:15-9 a.m. (no charge); 3-5:30 p.m., $5/day, open on school holidays. Avg. class size 12-15, max. 16. Dress code. Wide variety of enrichment activities, computers, drama, Spanish, work experience. Private tutoring, off site consultant used to work with students with mild learning disabilities.
"The basis of the Sierra program lies in the belief that balance is the key to a successful academic career. Students are placed at a level at which they are comfortable and proficient, and their academic program for the coming year is set from that point forward. Sierra School offers individualized instruction

under a mastery system with an emphasis on high achievement. The curriculum focuses on a strong basic education, and through the mastery approach, students achieve thorough understanding of all material. Sierra offers a nurturing environment and focuses on building self-esteem."

Los Altos ◆ Mtn. View ◆ Palo Alto
CATHOLIC SCHOOLS

ST. ELIZABETH SETON. 1095 Channing Ave., Palo Alto 94301. (415) 326-9004. Melanie Maione, Principal. Est. 1978. Non-profit.

K-gr. 8; 260 students. $1500. $2250 for two or more children. Inc. fees $100. 30% receive fin. aid. SDH: 8:30-3. Avg. class size 26, max. 35. Uniforms. Early Intervention Literacy Program for children whose primary language is not English; remedial reading & math; challenge math in gr. 7-8; counseling; computers; library; gym; after-school sports. Applications for the coming school year are accepted in January. Applicants are admitted on the basis of entrance test scores and past school performance. Waiting list in some grades. Accredited by WCEA & WASC.

"St. Elizabeth Seton School is a Catholic Community School which serves a multicultural population. We provide a quality education for children regardless of their economic status, religious beliefs or language background."

ST. JOSEPH. 1120 Miramonte Ave., Mountain View 94040. (415) 967-1839. Miss Kay Ingalls, Principal. Est. 1952. Non-profit.

K-gr. 8; 300 students. $1800-$2400. Inc. fees $140. Fin. aid avail. SDH: 8:20-3. EDC: 6:30 a.m.-6 p.m., $2.50/hr. Avg. class size 32, max. 35. Uniforms. Music, art, band, after school sports. On-site LD specialist. Priority given to siblings. Others accepted according to registration date & entrance test. Classroom visits by appointment. Six week summer program and extended day-care. Accredited by WCEA & WASC.

"We, in partnership with the parents, are dedicated to guiding students toward a life centered in Jesus Christ. St. Joseph School assists students in achieving Christian maturity, enabling them to become more responsible for their own lives and those of others. We, therefore, commit ourselves to educating the whole child in an environment where spiritual growth, academic excellence and an appreciation of multi-cultural values are fostered ."

ST. NICHOLAS. 12816 El Monte Ave., Los Altos Hills 94022. (415) 941-4056. Stan Rose, Principal. Est. 1960. Non-profit.

K-gr. 8; 278 students. $2040-$3370. Reg. fee $175. 5% receive fin. aid. SDH: K, 8:30-12:30; gr. 1-8, 8:30-3. EDC: 12:30-6 p.m. Avg. class size 30, max.

35. Uniforms. Afterschool sports for gr. 5-8, computer room and large gymnasium. On site LD specialist. French & Spanish avail. after school. Electives in gr. 7 & 8: Spanish, journalism, theater arts. Initial inquiry should be made in Jan. Apply by early spring. Entrance test for placement. Waiting list for some grades. Accredited by WCEA & WASC.

"St. Nicholas is dedicated to providing a learning environment which fosters a commitment to Christian values. The Gospel message is the core of the educational process, enabling the students to develop as mature, articulate Christians."

ST. SIMON. 1840 Grant Rd., Los Altos 94024. (415) 968-9952. Sister Mary Glackin, IHM, Principal. Non-profit.

K-gr. 8; 540 students. Gr. 1-8: Parishioners $1850, out-of-parish Catholics $2100, non-Catholics $2400. Sibling discounts. SDH: K, 8:10-11:10 or 12-3; gr. 1-8, 8:10-2:40. EDC: 7 a.m.-6 p.m. Computer & science labs, library. Afterschool French & Spanish. Recognized nationally as an exemplary "Blue Ribbon School of Excellence." Accredited by WCEA & WASC.

"St. Simon Catholic School, in partnership with the family, strives to form a Community of Faith, dedicated to continuing the mission entrusted by Christ to His Church. We, therefore, commit ourselves to educating the whole child in an environment conducive to spiritual, intellectual, psychological, sociological and pysical growth. We strive to embue this environment with dedication and love that reflects the gospel message of Christ."

NON-CATHOLIC RELIGIOUS SCHOOLS

CANTERBURY CHRISTIAN. 101 N. El Monte, Los Altos 94022. (415) 949-0909. Norman R. Milbank, Administrator. Est. 1974. Non-profit.

K-gr. 6; 100 students. K, $2450; gr. 1-6, $2750. Reg. fee: K, $75; gr. 1-6, $100. 20-25% receive fin. aid. SDH: K, 8:30-12; gr. 1-6, 8:30-3. EDC: 7:30 a.m.-6 p.m., $2/hr. Avg. class size 11, max. 16. Uniforms. A Beka curriculum used. Special help for learning disabled students available. Students accepted regardless of family's religious beliefs. Waiting list in some grades. Accredited by CSI and ACSI.

The school "is designed as a missionary outreach to prepare children spiritually, mentally, and physically to be able to live effective, productive lives based upon the Bible."

LOS ALTOS CHRISTIAN. 625 Magdalena Ave., Los Altos 94024. (415) 948-3738. Debra Sammons, Director. Est. 1981. Non-profit.

K-gr. 6; 227 students. $2600; $4650 for learning disabilities program. Inc. fees, $112. No scholarships. SDH: 8:30-3. EDC: 7 a.m.-6 p.m. Avg. class size 22, max. 25. Self-contained learning disabilities classes for K-gr. 6. Separate teachers for art, PE, choir, computer. Gymnasium & cafeteria. Afterschool basketball program. Students must score in the 50th percentile or above on SAT. Student interview with principal required for admission. Waiting list in some grades. Summer enrichment program with full day care. Accredited by WASC .

"Scriptural values and Christian character training are integrated throughout entire curriculum, taking a non-denominational point of view. Particular emphasis is placed on positive reinforcement and building self-esteem."

MID-PENINSULA JEWISH DAY SCHOOL. (415) 424-8482. 655 Arastedero, Palo Alto 94306. Yaffa Tygiel, Director. Est. 1989. Non-profit.

K-gr. 5; 100 students. $5000. Fin. aid avail. SDH (for all grades): 8:30-3:30. EDC: available on site through Jewish Community Center. Avg. class size 18, max. 20. Modern Hebrew taught in all grades. Art, P.E., music, recorder instruction, special enrichment for all grades. Gym, pool, auditorium, playing fields available on site. The school integrates Judaica and general studies.

"Ours is a community based school with an equalitarian approach and a child-centered educational philosophy. The school offers an excellent education in general & Judaic studies."

MIRAMONTE. 1175 Altamead Dr., Los Altos 94022. (415) 967-2783. Gordon Swanson, Principal. Est. 1928. Non-profit.

K-gr. 8; 117 students. $1446, church members; $2457, non-church members. $115 reg. fee. No scholarships. SDH: 8-3. EDC until 6 p.m. Avg. class size 23, max. 32. Extensive music program including choir, band, hand bells, piano and instrumental music. Library program. Non-competitive physical education designed to develop individual skills. Parent and student interview required prior to admittance. Accredited by Central California Conference of Seventh-Day Adventists.

"The school is operated primarily for the education and training of the youth of the Seventh-Day Adventist Church; however, the school will consider applications from all youth who are in harmony with the philosophy and objectives of Christian education. We believe that all children are capable of growth; therefore we desire to promote the development of their full potential—mentally, physically, socially and spiritually—enabling them to achieve a worthwhile purpose."

SOUTHBAY CHRISTIAN. 1134 Miramonte Ave., Mt. View 94040. (415) 961-5781. Susan N. Torode, Principal. Est. 1964. Non-profit.

K-gr. 6, 155 students. K-gr. 2, $2790.; gr. 3-6, $2960. Reg. fee $100, testing $30. Fin. aid avail. SDH: 8:30-3. EDC: 6:30 a.m.-6 p.m., open on school holidays. Avg. class size 20, max. 25. Dress code. Cafeteria with full hot lunch, K-gr. 6 computer lab, extensive library, full gymnasium/auditorium. Weekly chapel services. Continuing admissions as long as space is available. Entrance test & interview with principal. Summer enrichment and daycare. Applicant for WASC accreditation.

"We strive to provide a safe nurturing Christian environment for children away from home with professionals who consistantly reflect the love of Jesus Christ; to educate the total child by providing a variety of activities and experiences that help the child develop socially, physically, emotionally, intellectually and spiritually."

SECULAR SCHOOLS

ANANDA SCHOOL. 4000 Middlefield Rd., Palo Alto 94036. (mailing address: 240 Monroe Dr., #101, Mtn. View 94040.) (415) 493-5270 or 948-7841. Paul Green, Director. Est. 1992. Non-profit.

K-gr. 3. $3500-$6000. Sliding tuition scale; fin. aid avail. SDH: 8:45-3. Holistic & thematic curriculum gives children age-appropriate experience in long-term projects, as well as skill development. Categories of curriculum include Our Earth-Our Universe, Personal Development, Self-Expression and Communication, Cooperation, and Wholeness. Admission based on interviews, school visits, reports by past teachers. Apply any time.

"For the past twenty years, Ananda Schools have provided California parents and their children an excellent and joyful alternative. Our Education for Life philosophy aims at providing children a *balanced* experience that not only trains the mind and strengthens the body, but also helps each child develop dynamic will power and an expansive, joyful spiritual life. We pay close attention to each individual child, while also helping him relate to others appropriately and with growing maturity."

THE DELPHI ACADEMY. 445 E. Charleston Rd., #7, Palo Alto 94306. (415) 493-3100. Hal Hawkins, Director. Est. 1986. Non-profit.

K-gr. 8, 65 students. $620/mo. No scholarships. Avg. class size 15, max. 22. SDH: 8:30-5. EDC: 8 a.m-5:30 p.m., no additional charge. Dress code. Full day program with extracurricular activities—sports, music, art, etc.—in the afternoon. Apply anytime of year. 9 wk. summer program with 4 wk. minimum sign-up.

"Delphi is designed to prepare students for a successful future and help them learn easily and fully comprehend their subjects. Each student is given a study program based on individual needs and abilities. Students also progress individually, with definite targets for completion. For bright students, the program is enriched. For slower students the problems are sorted out without that child falling behind the rest of the class. Attention is given to having the student use his education in life to ensure the student understands there is a use and purpose for education and to keep his enthusiasm for learning high. A major reason for the success of Delphi's academic programs rests on the study skills developed by L. Ron Hubbard."

KEYS. 2890 Middlefield Rd., Palo Alto 94306. (415) 328-1711. Est. 1971. Non-profit.

K-gr. 8; 180 students. $5750. Enrollment fee, $225. 16% receive fin. aid. SDH: 8:45-3. EDC: 7:30 a.m.-6 p.m.; $8/day. Avg. class size 18, max. 19. Outdoor education, drama, music, art, computer for all grades. Specialists teaching art, science, P.E. (includes ice-skating), Spanish, music, & computer. On site LD tutoring. Kindergartners must be five by Sept. Applicants visit Oct-Feb.; group screenings in March. Apply for gr. 1-8 by 3/1. Waiting list. 8 wk. summer program called "Interactive Experiences," an enrichment /recreation program built around weekly themes. Accredited by CAIS.

Keys provides "a demanding, creative, balanced program of academic excellence and social growth in a warm, supportive and nurturing environment. The Middle School, for grades 5-8, is designed to meet the needs of early adolescents while providing a strong academic program."

PENINSULA FRENCH-AMERICAN SCHOOL. 870 N. California Ave., Palo Alto 94303. (415) 328-2338. Beatrice De Elespp, Director. Est. 1979. Non-profit.

PreK-gr. 5; 215 students. $6400-$6650 (all inclusive). Fin. aid avail. SDH (for all grades): 8:30-3:15. EDC: 7:30-6 p.m., $4/hr. Avg. class size 15, max. 25. No admission of non-French speaking students after 1st grade. Waiting list. Summer program from 9 a.m.-noon during July. Accredited by CAIS & Ministry of French National Education.

"The aim of the P.F.A.S. is to provide an elementary education that combines the best of both French and American systems; the rigor of the French and the openness to experiment of the American. The school is committed to admitting students whose primary language is not French. Our goal is to maintain high standards of education so that, upon graduation, students may choose to follow a bilingual or international system and will also be qualified to continue in a purely American or purely French system."

PINEWOOD. 327 Fremont Ave., Los Altos 94022. (415) 941-2828. Mr. L. Victor Riches, Managing Director; Ms. Linda Mezgar, Principal. Est. 1959. Non-profit.

K-gr. 6 (gr. 7-12 on separate campus.) 295 students. K, $4300; gr. 1-6, $6600. Reg. fee $300; supplies $300, testing fee $50. Some fin. aid avail. SDH: K, 8:30-12:15; gr. 1-6, 8:30-3. EDC: 8-8:30 a.m.; 3-5 p.m.; $4/hr. (closed during school holidays.) Avg. class size: K- gr. 2, 16; gr. 3-6, 18. Max. class size 21. Drama, speech, music, very strong English program. Carden approach to language arts. Variety of summer programs. Applications taken from Nov.-Feb. Interview, audit, testing by March 1st. Notification of acceptance by March 15th. Classroom visits encouraged. Waiting list. Accredited by WASC.

We "create a learning climate wherein students may acquire academic stamina, intellectual vitality, and a high standard of behavior in order that they may live a life of purpose, dignity and concern for others."

WALDORF SCHOOL OF THE PENINSULA. 401 Rosita Ave., Los Altos 94022. (415) 948-8433. Est. 1983. Non-profit.

K-gr. 7; 106 students. Tuition guidelines: K, $4214; gr. 1-3, $5830; gr. 4-7, $6069. Fin. aid avail. SDH: 8:30-3. EDC until 6 pm. Avg. class size 14, max. 24. Dress code. Spanish, gardening, eurythmy (movement). Admissions procedure: interview to establish compatible goals and views between school and home; orientation mandatory for parents; classroom visit for gr. 2-8. We accept children within the normal to gifted range of physical and mental abilities. Summer gardening for ages 5-10. Accredited by the National Federation of Waldorf Schools.

"Waldorf School of the Peninsula is based on the philosophy and teachings of Rudof Steiner. The Waldorf approach is based on a profound understanding of the developmental stages of the child and is guided by a non-sectarian spiritual philosophy."

SANTA CLARA COUNTY
PRIVATE SECONDARY SCHOOLS

ARCHBISHOP MITTY. 5000 Mitty Ave., San Jose 95129. (408) 252-6610. Admissions office, 252-6610. Timothy Brosnan, Principal; Richard Robinson, Admissions Director. Est. 1964. Non-profit.

Gr. 9-12; 1150 students. $4250. Reg. fee $385. 10% receive fin. aid. SDH: 8-2:45. Avg. class size 27, max 35. Campus partially closed. Dress code. Honors-A.P. programs in all disciplines, state-of-the-art Technology Center, 8 period day, math & computer lab, broad offerings in art, art history, & performing arts. 19 team sports. Applicants must have grades and test scores that indicate they qualify for college prep. program. Feb. application deadline. Open house in November. School visitations by appointment. Waiting list. Full summer school program with many course offerings. Accredited by WASC.

"Archbishop Mitty High School is a college preparatory, coeducational, Catholic secondary school. The school accepts the challenge of enabling all students to grow spiritually, intellectually, physically and socially. The school seeks to engender in its students the dignity, grace, maturity and courage to become responsible members of society who contribute to their world through a keen use of intellect and decisions rooted in the Catholic tradition of faith and moral values. The school embraces the Catholic educational mission of developing community, teaching the message of the gospels, and promoting service and justice."

BELLARMINE COLLEGE PREPARATORY. 850 Elm St., San Jose 95126. (408) 294-9224. Father Edward Reese, Principal; Tim Petersen, Admissions. Est. 1851. Non-profit.

Boys, gr. 9-12; 1325 students. $4460. $35 application fee. 22% receive fin. aid. SDH: 8:35-2:15, Fridays out at noon. Closed campus for 9th & 10th graders. Avg. class size 28, max. 32. 40 clubs and organizations, many electives for juniors and seniors. 100 hrs. of community service required. Large athletic program. 6 wk. academic summer session. Apply before Jan. 22 for 9th grade, before May 13 for gr. 10-12. Students selected on basis of grades, test scores, recommendations, entrance exam. Waiting list. Accredited by WASC.

97% of grads. attend 4 yr. colleges; 2% attend 2 yr. colleges.

SAT's (99%): '93, V 522, M 594; 3 yr. avg.: V 515, M 594. 30 AP classes offered; 21 honors classes.

"We, the faculty, staff, and administration of Bellarmine College Preparatory, a Catholic school in the Jesuit tradition, commit ourselves to the task of helping young men develop both dynamic minds and bodies, and sensitive hearts so that their adult lives might contribute to the building of a more humane, more just, most godly world."

CASTILLEJA. 1310 Bryant St., Palo Alto 94301. (941) 328-3160. Joan Lonergan, Head; Jill Lee, Admissions Director. Est. 1907. Non-profit.

Girls, gr. 6-12; 325 students. Day students, $10,250; 5 day boarding, $18,650; 7 day boarding, $19,750. 13% receive fin. aid. Closed campus except for jr. & sen. privileges. Avg. class size 14. Uniforms. Olympic size swimming pool, tennis courts, language labs, music practice rooms, art studios, science and computer labs. Class retreats for every grade, school trips, A.P. & honors classes, long-standing traditions. Very competitive admissions. Feb. 1 priority deadline for admissions & financial aid. Waiting list. Summer camp for 7-13 yr. olds. Accredited by WASC & CAIS.

99% of grads. attend 4 yr. colleges. SAT scores (100%): '93: V 524, M 590.

"Castilleja School offers the acknowledged academic and personal advantages unique to an all-girls school through a non-sectarian day and residence program for motivated young women of diverse backgrounds and cultures. Now in its ninth decade, the school blends a contemporary global perspective with a challenging traditional curriculum which prepares students for college as well as for fulfilled, constructive lives."

CHRISTIAN COMMUNITY ACADEMY. See listing under San Jose Private Schools. Closed campus. SAT Scores(60%): '93, V 450, M 540; 3 yr. avg.: V 430, M 464.

DE YOUNG SCHOOL. See listing under San Jose Private Elementary Schools.

EAST VALLEY CHRISTIAN SCHOOL. See listing under San Jose Private Elementary Schools.

GAVILAN HILLS SCHOOL. See listing under Gilroy Private Elementary Schools.

LIBERTY BAPTIST. See listing under San Jose Private Elementary Schools.

THE KING'S ACADEMY. 560 Britton Ave., Sunnyvale 94086. (408) 481-9900. Jack McBirney, Principal. Est. 1991. Non-profit.

Gr. 7-12; 180 students. $3800/yr. Reg. & books $150. Fin. aid avail. Closed campus. Avg. class size 18; max. 20. Dress code. On site LD specialist avail. for LD students. Complete athletic facilities including swimming pool and theater. Inter-school league competition in major sports. Cooperation with home-school parents through students' part-time attendance.

"Ours is a non-denominational Christian school which teaches the Bible and builds Christian character. The school is college prep and wants students to excel academically."

MID-PENINSULA. 870 N. California Ave., Palo Alto 94303. (415) 493-5910. Philip Bliss, Director. Est. 1979. Non-profit.

Gr. 9-12; 150 students. $8000. Inc. fees, $150. 10-20% receive fin. aid. Avg. class size 11; max. 15. Closed campus. Counseling & guidance programs, computers, science. Special ed. program with L.D. specialist on site. Some students funded by P.L. 94-142. Art, drama, team sports, writing across the curriculum, active learning across the curriculum. Summer program for enrolled students. Accredited by WASC & CAIS, and a member of the Coalition of Essential Schools. Certified by the State of California.

70% of grads. attend 4 yr. colleges, 20% attend 2 yr. colleges. SAT scores (75%): Class of '92 (approx. scores): V 600, M 500.

"Our goal is to graduate literate, thoughtful & decent adults by making their high school education active and empowering."

MOUNTAIN VIEW ACADEMY. 360 S. Shoreline Blvd., Mtn. View 94041. (415) 967-2324. Milton Wheeler, Director. Lisa Ward, Admissions. Est. 1922. Non-profit.

Gr. 9-12; 100 students. $4500. Inc. fees $190; books extra. SDH: 8-3:20. Avg. class 18, max. 28. Closed campus. Dress code. Limited spaces for special needs students. College preparatory program. ESL, remedial math, honors English. 70% of grads. go to 4 yr. colleges; 30% to 2 yr. colleges. Accredited by WASC.

"The school is operated primarily for the education and training of the youth of the Seventh-Day Adventist Church; however, the school will consider applications from all youth who are in harmony with the philosophy and objectives of Christian education and who will cheerfully and sincerely endeavor to live according to its principles."

NOTRE DAME. 596 South 2nd St., San Jose 95112. (408) 294-1113. Patricia Cain, Principal. Karen De Monner, Admissions Director. Est. 1851. Non-profit.

Catholic, girls; gr. 9-12; 385 students. $4300. Reg. fee $200. 14% receive fin. aid. Avg. class size 22, max. 33. Uniforms. Small nurturing environment, strong fine arts program, many extracurricular programs, full range of honors courses. Location in downtown San Jose allows its students easy access to the Tech & Art Museums, Center for Performing Arts, Foreign Language Cinema, SJSU. Because of this location, field trips are an integral part of our curriculum and students experience a truly cosmopolitan education. Closed campus. Uniforms. Minimum requirements: "C" average, grade level on entrance test, positive recommendations from 7th & 8th grade teachers. Waiting list. Accredited by WASC.

68% of grads. go to 4 yr. colleges, 32% to 2 yr. colleges. SAT scores (95%): '93 V 431, M 461; 3 yr. avg. V 435, M 457.

"Notre Dame High School is committed to the development of the total person by offering a curriculum which stimulates the spiritual, academic, physical, aesthetic, and social dimensions of each student."

PALO ALTO PREPARATORY. 4000 Middlefield Rd., Palo Alto 94303. (415) 493-7071. Christopher Keck, Director. Est. 1984. Non-profit.

Gr. 8-12; 40 students, 8 teachers. $7500. 10% receive fin. aid. Open campus. Avg. class size 7, max. 12. 55% of grads. go to 4 yr. colleges; 40% to 2 yr. colleges. Classes in all subjects, tutoring, learning & study skills. Traditional core curriculum. Summer classes and seminars for transferable credit. On site L.D. specialist. Student Visas (I-20) avail. Annual field trips include but not limited to whale watching and deep sea fishing, Ropes Course through Pro-Action Assoc., river rafting and backpacking. Classroom visits encouraged for both students and parents. No application deadline. Mid-semester admissions. Applicant for WASC accreditation.

"Palo Alto Prep School believes that each student should experience success. By providing. . . personalized attention, we have created an environment that allows our students to regain respect for themselves and their abilities. We are here to help adolescents cope in a realistic, responsible and rewarding manner and to help them grow into mature, capable adults who will contribute to society. Our aim is to give students the necessary emotional and academic support to raise their self-esteem so that they can believe in themselves and become achievers in life...This positive learning experience leads to a desire to continue with higher educational goals."

PINEWOOD. 26800 Fremont Rd., Los Altos Hills 94022. (415) 941-1532. Victor L. Riches, Director; Mark Gardner, Admissions Director. Non-profit.

Gr. 7-12 (K-gr. 6 on separate campuses) 230 students. $8500. Inc. fees $500. Fin. aid avail. Closed campus. Avg. class size: 10-18, max. 20-23. Facilities include theater, gym, library, large sports field, tennis courts on 7 acre campus. Excellent sports program, computers (beginning to advanced), drama, art, speech. Apply March-May. Students selected according to interview, references, test scores. Waiting list for some grades. Summer programs in academics & enrichment. Accredited by WASC.

95% of grads. go to 4 yr. colleges, 5% to 2 yr. colleges. SAT scores (100%): '93 V 503, M 588; 3 yr. avg. V 501, M 580.

Pinewood offers "a learning climate wherein students may acquire academic stamina, intellectual vitality, and a high standard of behavior in order that they may live a life of purpose, dignity, and concern for others."

PRESENTATION. 2281 Plummer Ave., San Jose 95125. (408) 264-1664. Ms. Mary Miller, Principal. Mrs. Pauline Newton, Admissions Director. Est. 1962. Non-profit.

Catholic, girls; gr. 9-12; 600 students. $4300. 11% receive fin. aid. SDH: 8:20-2:10. Avg. class size 27, max. 32. Uniforms. Closed campus for gr. 9 & 10; open campus for gr. 11-12. Community involvement; 22 on-campus clubs and organizations; campus ministry; 11 sports; full range of honors courses. Full computer networking that brings library and other materials into each classroom; drama workshop taught by professionals of the San Jose Children's Musical Theater; academic, personal, and college counseling; full library with special collections and media collection staffed by full-time professional librarian. Feb. 1st application deadline for incoming 9th graders. Students accepted on basis of grades, recommendations, SRA scores, placement test. Range of students are accepted: 1/3 A level, 1/3 B level; 1/3 C level. Waiting list. Summer athletic training camp. Accredited by WASC.

85% of grads. go to 4 yr. colleges, 15% to 2 yr. colleges. 100% take SAT tests.

"Presentation High School is a secondary school for girls whose purpose and direction flow from the teaching mission of the Catholic Church and the educational ministry of the Sisters of the Presentation. As such, Presentation High School strives to permeate the entire educational process with the vision of life found in the Gospels. It endeavors to enable each student to integrate the acquisition of human knowledge and skills with her growing experience of life and the world and with her total development as a Christian person."

ST. FRANCIS. 1885 Miramonte Ave., Mountain View 94040. (415) 968-1213. James Bowler, Principal. Bill Delaney, Admissions. Est. 1954. Non-profit.

Gr. 9-12; 1350 students. $4400. 10% receive fin. aid. SDH: 7:50-2:30. Closed Campus. Dress code. AP classes: Eng. 4, U.S. History, Amer, Govt., Biology, Calculus. Avg. class size 33, max. 40. Summer academic and sports programs. Applications accepted from all qualified 8th grade students. Waiting list. Accredited by WASC.

80% of grads. go to 4 yr. colleges, 18% to 2 yr. colleges. SAT scores (99%): '92, V 464, M 515. 5 yr. avg.: V 469, M, 520.

"St. Francis is a private Catholic coeducational community which is established by the Brothers of the Holy Cross and the Diocese of San Jose. It is supported by involved families and individuals for the Catholic education of young people in Santa Clara and San Mateo counties."

ST. LAWRENCE ACADEMY. 2000 Lawrence Ct., Santa Clara 95051. (408) 296-3013. Ron Modeste, Principal. Dotty McCrea, Admissions. Est. 1960. Non-profit.

Catholic, gr. 7-12; 296 students. $4115. Reg fee $240, application fee $35. Fin. aid. avail. SDH: 8-2:30. Closed campus. Avg. class size 17, max. 31. AP classes in history, English, French, Spanish, biology, calculus, and computer science. 2 Limited English Proficiency classes for foreign students. Mid-Feb. application deadline for priority consideration; ongoing admissions as long as space available. Admission based on school records, recommendations, entrance exam, and interview when necessary. 6 wk. summer school. Accredited by WCEA & WASC.

60% of grads go to 4 yr. college, 40% to 2 yr. SAT scores (90%): Class of '93, V 430, M 450; 3 yr. avg.: V 427, M 447.

St. Lawrence Academy is "a safe co-ed, college prep school dedicated to personal attention and maximizing academic potential. 98% college admission record. We are small enough to care, large enough to count. "

SIERRA. See listing under Santa Clara Private Elementary Schools. 75% of grads go to 4 yr. colleges, 25% to 2 yr. colleges. SAT scores (95%) 3 yr. avg.: V 600, M 500.

VALLEY CHRISTIAN. 1570 Branham Lane, San Jose 95118. (408) 978-9955. Curt Willson, Principal. Dr. Clifford Daughtery, Superintendent. Est. 1969. Non-profit.

Gr. 6-12; 624 students. $4543, Fin. aid avail. Avg. class size 22, max. 28. Computer lab, theater, choir, band, interscholastic sports, art, photography with photo lab, student newspaper, 2 gyms and playing fields, stagecraft, string ensemble, choral ensemble, jazz band, associated student government, Bible classes, weekly chapel. On site L.D. specialist. Applicants must be recommended by educator & pastor of Evangelical, Bible-believing church, have a 2.0 G.P.A., and be at grade level in achievement tests. Interview required. Summer sports programs. Accredited by ACSI & WASC.

36% of grads. attend 4 yr. colleges, 54% attend 2 yr. colleges. Avg. SAT scores(55%): Class of '93: V 475, M 503; 3 yr. avg.: V 463, M 506.
Valley Christian High School "is a nurturing school, which supports ministry to Christian families attending Bible-believing, Evangelical Protestant churches."

WEST HEIGHTS CHRISTIAN. See listing under Los Gatos Private Elementary Schools.

SANTA CLARA COUNTY
SPECIAL EDUCATION SCHOOLS

THE ARK CENTER. 1570 Branham Lane, Box A, San Jose 95118. (408) 266-8600. Kathi McLaughlin, Director. Est. 1974. Non-profit.

For children 5 yrs.-22 yrs.; 13 students. All students paid through public school funds. Avg. class size 6, max. 8. Teacher student ratio 1:3. SDH: 8:30-2. Transportation provided by Santa Clara County. Dress code. School is designed for learning disabled, severely emotionally disturbed, communicatively handicapped, attention/hyperactivity problems, autism, other health impaired (e.g., Tourettes Syndrome). Specialized educational services for students whose emotional and learning problems require more intensive services than are available in the public schools. Our aim is to address those problems so students can return to public school as soon as possible. Strong whole language approach to academics, combined with individual, group, and family counseling to guide each child to reach his or her potential. Career education, social skills, and creative problem solving are infused into the total program to prepare students for productive adult lives. 6 wk. summer program. Students can be admitted at any time. Certified by State Department of Education.

"At the Ark Center we provide the kind of caring and nurturing academic and therapeutic programs necessary to ensure that the key to a better tomorrow doesn't remain locked inside of the mind of a child with special learning needs."

BEACON SCHOOL. 5670 Camden Ave., San Jose 95124. (408) 265-8611. John F. Font, PhD, Director. Est. 1970. Non-profit.

Serves students 7-21 yrs. 40 students. $131/day. 100% funded through public school funds. Avg. class size 6-8; max. 10. Teacher-student ratio 1:2.5. SDH: 8:30-2. Serves students categorized as SED. LH, & EH. 6 wk. summer program. Certified by State Dept. of Ed.

"The mission of Beacon School is to provide a safe, supportive environment that will help each student to develop independent thinking and living skills, academic achievement consistent with his or her potential, and the opportunity to gain sufficient maturity and judgement to succeed in an appropriate public educational program."

CAROLYN MITCHELL SCHOOL. 1718 Andover Lane, San Jose 95124. (408) 978-7120. Carolyn Mitchell and Katy Greenwalt, Directors. Est. 1981. Non-profit.

Serves students aged 9-22 yrs. $132.50/day. 100% funded through public schools. Avg. class size 6-8. Teacher student ratio 1:3. SDH: 8:45-1:45. EDC planned for the future. Serves severely emotionally disturbed and the learning handicapped. Individual & group therapy, parent counseling, art therapy, regular planned field trips, speech & language therapy, multi-sensory reading for A.D.D. School open year-round. Certified by State Dept. of Ed.

"Mitchell School offers students a therapeutic/academic program. Subjects are offered that meet state graduation requirements. Individual and small group instruction and counseling are integrated into total program. All staff members are trained in crisis intervention, behavior management and basic counseling as well as educational planning and teaching activities."

CASOLS—CALIFORNIA SCHOOL OF LEARNING SYSTEMS. 3800 Blackford Ave., San Jose 95117. (408) 246-2270. Carol Digardi, Director. Est. 1979. Non-profit.

Special day class for children 8-22 yrs; 14 students. Tuition paid by school districts or privately. SDH: 9-3. EDC: 7 a.m.-6 p.m. School operates year-round. Avg. class size 8, max. 12; teacher-student ratio: 1:2. Program designed primarily for learning handicapped and severely handicapped students. On site vocational ed, physical fitness, swimming, computer skills, specialized reading, survival in daily living skills, individualized academic program. Annual extended trip—"Learning by Doing." Tutoring, testing, consultations available. Intake interview and trial period required. Summer programs. Certified by State Dept. of Education.

"Casols structures curriculum around students' individual needs, emphasizing personal growth towards independence in a calm, supportive environment."

CHILDREN'S HEALTH COUNCIL. 700 Sand Hill Rd., Palo Alto 94304. (campus in Menlo Park) (415) 326-5530. Toni Perez, School Director. Est. 1953. Non-profit.

Ungraded, 4-1/2 yrs.-14 yrs. Tuition paid by school districts. Max. class size 8 (two teachers and one aide per class.) The school provides full day educationally and psychologically oriented classes for children with learning disabilities; developmental and language impairment; social, emotional and behavioral problems and/or neurological problems. Children may receive speech and language therapy, occupational therapy and counseling, or psychotherapy. Family counseling and day treatment component also available. 5 wk. summer program. Certified by State Department of Education.

MID-PENINSULA HIGH SCHOOL. 870 N. California Ave., Palo Alto 94303. See Santa Clara County Secondary Schools.

THE MORGAN CENTER. 201 Covington Rd., Los Altos 94024. (415) 948-6834. Louise Emerson, Director. Est. 1969. Non-profit.

Ungraded for ages four through 21; 34 students. Tuition funded by districts. SDH: 9-2:30. Avg. class size 7-9. Handicapped conditions include autism and brain injury. Accompanying handicaps include mental retardation, cerebral palsy, epilepsy and visual/hearing impairment. All of the children are affected by some degree of central nervous system dysfunction. New children are provided with a one-to-one ratio and are placed in small groups when they appear ready. Each child seen daily for work in speech, sensory-motor integration, gross and fine motor training, self-care, social skills, and pre-academic or academic work. The Morgan Adult Program provides a positive environment for neurologically impaired adults in a setting which addresses deficits in language, learning, and behavior while emphasizing training in independent living and vocational skills. School year extends through July. Waiting list. Certified by State Department of Education.

"The program at the Morgan Center is geared to the needs and learning style of the individual child...treatment is highly structured and is geared to teaching skills and developing potential. The availability of the one-to-one teaching ratio is critical to the effectiveness of the program, particularly in helping the child attend tasks, behave appropriately, and experience success."

PACIFIC AUTISM CENTER. 572 Dunhome Way, Sunnyvale, CA 94087. Dr. Linda Reese, Director. (408) 245-3400.

8-22 yrs. ; 14 students. 100% funded by public school districts. SDH: 9:30-2:30. Open all year. Staff/student ratio 1:1. "We serve children with autism and other related disorders."

PENINSULA CHILDREN'S CENTER (PCC.) 3860 Middlefield Rd., Palo Alto 94303. (415) 494-1200. Gail Switzer, LCSW, Director. Est. 1960. Non-profit.

Ungraded, 3 yrs.-22 yrs; 42 students. $117/day; 100% funded by public school districts. Limited fin. aid. SDH: 9-2:30; therapeutic recreation: 2:30-4:40 and during school holidays. $14.25/hr. Extended school year 217 days. Closed 1 wk. in June, 3 wks. in Aug., 2 wks. at Xmas, and 1 wk. in spring. Avg. class size 7, max. 12. Staff /student ratio ranges from 1:1 to 1:3. Transportation provided by public school districts. PCC accepts students for whom there is no appropriate public school program and the school feels it can provide an appropriate program. For admissions information contact "intake worker" between 9-5. Certified by State Department of Education.

PCC serves students with severe behavior and emotional problems who cannot be served in public school programs. This includes students with learning, language, and developmental disabilities from San Mateo, Santa Clara, & Alameda counties. Academics are provided by SH credentialed teachers through Individualized Education Plans. Program also includes speech & language therapy; vocational training on-site and in community sites; art and gross motor activities; individual, group & family therapy; case management services; and transition planning & services. "By combining the expertise of mental health and special education, by working in closely communicating staff teams, and by ongoing work with families, we meet the needs of each special child."

PINE HILL SCHOOL. 1975 Cambrianna Dr., San Jose 95124. (408) 371-5881. Betty Siemer, Director. Est. 1976. Non-profit.

Gr. 1-12, ages 5 to 22; 70 students. Tuition varies depending on grade level and program. 23% funded through public schools. Fin. aid avail. Avg. class size 15, max. 17; student teacher ratio 7:1. SDH: 8-2:30. EDC: 2-5 pm; $155/mo. Dress code. The school takes students with learning disabilities, learning differences, social-emotional difficulties and motivational problems. The school offers prescriptive academics, behavior consultation, computer lab, Slingerland, counseling, vocational job placement services. Applications accepted throughout the year. Admission procedure: intake interview, visitation, and multi-disciplinarian assessment. Summer programs: summer school, fun camp (EDC), tutoring, Slingerland instruction. Certified by Calif. State Dept. of Ed.

"We believe that children can achieve in a nurturing, structured, prescriptive school environment. Such a program enhances their self-esteem and academic and social development and assists them in fulfilling their potential. We consider parents to be experts concerning their own child and work collaboratively and supportively with them."

THE STANBRIDGE ACADEMY. 890 Pomeroy Ave., S, Santa Clara 95051-5200. (408) 261-6610. Andrea Jobe, Director. Est. 1982. Non-profit.

K-gr. 12; 90 students. $9500. Inc. fees $600. 5% receive public school funding. Fin. aid avail. SDH: 8:45-3:15. EDC: 3:15-5:30. Avg. class size 5, max. 8. Dress code. Programs are available for remedial through gifted learning levels and include instruction in basic and applied subjects, concept and perceptual development, critical thinking and communication, and music and art. Application process includes parent and student interviews, a minimum two day student visitation, and development of student learning style profile. Waiting list for some age groups. Summer program available.

"Stanbridge offers an Educational Management Program for children with verbal and non-verbal learning disabilities. We also take students without specific learning differences who need the kind of small, nurturing environment we offer. Our goal is to produce a balanced individual through the development of competency in physical, emotional and intellectual aspects of human behavior. Methods of instruction vary by the need of the student and match his/her individual style of learning."

ZONTA CHILDREN'S CENTER. 4300 Bucknall Rd., San Jose 95130. (408) 374-9050. Deirdre Cochran, Director. Est. 1964. Non-profit.

Special needs children age 3-22 yrs; 38-45 students. Tuition paid by school districts or on sliding scale by individuals. 32%-38% supported by public funds. SDH: Preschool 7:30-6; Other ages 9-2. Avg. class size 6, max. 10. Teacher student ratio 1:1 to 1:3. Programs designed for children with behavioral, emotional, and developmental problems. Preschool for developmentally normal children with behavior problems. Therapeutic emphasis. Extended school program in June & July. Year-round admissions. Certified by State Dept. of Education.

"We believe in treating the academic, social, emotional and behavioral needs of the child."

SAN MATEO COUNTY PRIVATE ELEMENTARY SCHOOLS

Atherton ◆ Menlo Park ◆ Portola Valley
CATHOLIC SCHOOLS

NATIVITY. 1250 Laurel St., Menlo Park 94025. (415) 325-7304. Sister Bernice Clifford, PBVM, Principal. Est. 1956. Non-profit.

K-gr. 8; 275 students. $2000; inc. fees $170. Fin. aid avail. SDH: K, 8:25-12 (enrichment program from 12-3 for no added cost); gr. 1-8, 8:25-3. EDC: 6:30 a.m.-5:30 p.m.; $110/mo. Avg. class size 30, max. 35. Uniforms. Computer program for K-gr. 8. Teacher with master's degree in Learning Disabilities, on site counselor. Applicants tested prior to April acceptance. Accredited by WASC & WCEA.

"Nativity School is a Catholic School dedicated to teaching our students the beauties and truths of our religion. Our task is to educate the whole person. Our goal is to provide quality education."

ST. JOSEPH'S. 50 Emilie Ave., Atherton 94027. (415) 322-9931. John Miller, Principal. Est. 1906. Non-profit.

Preschool-gr. 8, 500 students. (Preschool and kdg. are run as separate Montessori program.) $5200-$6950. Application fee $25; book fees vary by grade. Fin. aid avail. SDH: gr. 1-5, 8:15-2:45; gr. 6-8, 8:15-2:55. EDC: 2:40-5:30. Avg. & max. class size 22; max. in gr. 7-8, 25. Pick-up from Menlo train station. Uniforms. Challenging academic program — computer, math, and science labs; art studio; choral music instruction; athletic fields and regulation track. Test and interview for applicants. Priority given to siblings and alumni children. Waiting list. Summer programs: day camps for ages 3 yrs.-gr. 2 and gr. 2-5; drama and music conservatory; basketball; soccer, tennis, volleyball camps. Accredited by WASC and CAIS.

"St. Joseph's School is a member of a world-wide network of Sacred Heart Schools offering an education that is marked by a distinctive spirit. It is the essence of a Sacred Heart school that it be deeply concerned for each student's total development: spiritual, intellectual, emotional, and physical."

ST. RAYMOND'S SCHOOL. 1211 Arbor Rd., Menlo Park 94025. (415) 322-2312. Catherine Q. Thomson, Principal. Non-profit.

K-gr. 8, 265 students. K, $1220; gr. 1-8 $2600. $140 reg. fee. Some fin. aid. EDC: 7:15-6 pm, $2.50/hr. Avg. class size, 30, max. 32. Uniforms. Gym, computer lab & computers in each class, art specialist, science lab with full-time science teacher, advanced math program. Large afterschool sports program. Apply by March 1, but space may be available later. Admissions determined by entrance test and recommendations. Waiting list in some grades. Accredited by WCEA and WASC.

"The religious curriculum and opportunities provided for the students teach the values, heritage, and traditions of the Catholic Church. It is hoped that this dedication will lead to a personal conviction of his or her faith and a continual loving relationship with the total community."

NON-CATHOLIC RELIGIOUS SCHOOLS

TRINITY. 2650 Sand Hill Rd., Menlo Park 94025. (415) 854-0288. Kathy Hanley, Principal. Est. 1961. Non-profit.

Episcopal, Preschool-gr. 6; 100 students. $5970. 20% receive fin. aid . SDH: 8:20-3. EDC: 7:30-5:30. Avg. class size 17, max. 18. Uniforms. Daily chapel, P.E., music, art, Spanish, computers, Bible study, field trips, community outreach programs. Multi-day trips for gr. 4-6. Staff includes math, reading, & science specialists. High level of parent involvement. Families should apply by March 19. Priority given to siblings & members of parish. Accredited by CAIS & WASC.

"Emphasis is given to a strong, balanced academic program and a warm, kind community in which to grow. Our philosophy is to develop each child's skills in conjunction with his or her personal and physical stage of growth, thus making Trinity a 'child centered' educational program."

SECULAR SCHOOLS

BEECHWOOD SCHOOL. 50 Terminal Ave., Menlo Park 94025. (415) 327-5052. Operated by The California Family Foundation. Tim Willoughby, Principal. Non-profit.

K-gr. 8 $120/mo. Fin. aid avail. SDH: 8:30-3:15. EDC provided by the City of Menlo Park at the Onetta Harris Community Center from 3:15-5:30. Avg. class size 16, max. 17. Parent involvement required. Priority given to children who reside in East Palo Alto or eastern Menlo Park.

"Beechwood School was founded by the California Family Foundation for the purpose of providing educational opportunity to children of committed parents in the Bellehaven and East Palo Alto areas. The mission of Beechwood School is to help committed parents with the education of their children by providing a safe, secure, nurturing environment where dedicated, capable, and loving professional teachers will build solid foundations in basic educational skills, strengthen the children's self-esteem, and foster the development of important character traits and living skills, such as self reliance, self control, reverence for life and love of God and Country."

GERMAN-AMERICAN SCHOOL. 275 Elliott Dr., Menlo Park 94025. (415) 324-8617. Heinz J. Schmahl, Director. Est. 1988. Non-profit.

Preschool-gr. 8, 70 students. $400-$490/mo. Sibling discounts. Fin. aid. avail. Avg. class size 7, max. 11. SDH: (all grades) 8:45-2:10. EDC: 8 a.m.-5:30 p.m. Science & computer labs, large school grounds. Individual German and/or English tutoring when needed; French offered in gr. 7 & 8. Afterschool program organized by parents: flute, piano, dancing, sports. Students applying for gr. 1-8 must have knowledge of German language. Summer program offered in conjunction with local Saturday German-speaking school. Accredited by German Department of Education.

The German-American School is the "first full-time bilingual German/English elementary school on the West Coast accredited and supported by the West German government. It meets the high standards of the European educational system and covers a wide range of academic subjects taught in a small class, low-stress environment while emphasizing individual attention to maximize achievement."

PENINSULA SCHOOL. Peninsula Way, Menlo Park, CA 94025. (415) 325-1584. Carol Lou Young-Holt, Director. Est. 1925. Non-profit; parent-staff cooperative.

Preschool-grade 8; 250 students. $4600 for full day. $90 inc. fees. Approx. 33% of families receive fin. aid. SDH: K, 9-12:30; gr. 1-8, 9-3. EDC: 8-3:30 for nursery & kdg. Avg. class size 19, max. 21. Most classes staffed with parents as teaching assistants. In addition to classroom teachers, special teachers in physical education, music, art, science, weaving, woodshop, clay, library and Spanish. Class camping trips. Individual classroom buildings surrounded by six acres of wooded play areas. Victorian mansion is central location of library, studios and workshops. Six wk. summer session. Admissions procedures: parents visit and observe, child visits during classtime, school evaluates school records and recommendations, parents interviewed by director. Goal of admissions procedure is to promote understanding and assure support of school's philosophy. Parents should apply by Feb. 1. Waiting list for some classes.

"The school was founded by a group of parents...who sought an environment in which learning was joyful and exciting, where children were challenged to learn by doing, and where both independence and group cooperation were highly valued. Peninsula's mission has been to foster the development of the whole child by promoting creativity, independence, personal responsibility and self-esteem as well as academic excellence...Teachers and parents provide the guidance, trust, and unconditional support necessary for children to experiment and learn about themselves and their world."

PHILLIPS BROOKS SCHOOL. 2245 Avy Ave., Menlo Park 94025. (415) 854-4545. Elizabeth Root, Director. Est. 1961. Non-profit.

Preschool-gr. 6; 210 students. Gr. 1-3, $5975; gr. 4-6, $6225. $400 reg. fee. Fin. aid. avail. SDH: 8:15-3:15. EDC: for preschool and kindergarten students until 3:15. Avg. class size 22-24, max. 24. Teacher/student ratio 1:12. Uniforms. Strong academic program is enriched with music, art, computers, PE, foreign languages. Admissions based on interviews, class visits, tests. Priority given to siblings and students who demonstrate academic readiness. Needs of children with minimal learning disabilities addressed by teacher trained in L.D. Waiting list. Preschool and kindergarten summer programs. Accredited by CAIS.

Phillips Brooks is "a small caring community that seeks to educate the whole child in the areas of academic discipline, spiritual awareness, and physical and social aspects of growth."

WOODLAND SCHOOL. 360 La Cuesta Dr., Menlo Park 94025. (415) 854-9065. Mrs. Lynne A. Nelson, Director. Est. 1981. Non-profit.

Preschool-gr. 8; 200 students. K-gr. 4, $5300; gr. 5-8, $5600. $375 reg. fee. Fin. aid avail. SDH: K-gr. 8, 8:30-3. EDC: 7:30 a.m.-5:30 p.m.; $2/hr.; avail. year-round. Avg. class size 20, max. 23. Uniforms. Art, music, gymnastics, French, drama, sports. Feb. best time for initial inquiry. Required two day student visit. 5 wk. summer program, morning academics, summer camp activities. Waiting list in some classes.

"Students are evaluated on an individual basis. Our goal is to prepare students for the more select schools and create, by example and high expectations, a student who is well equipped academically and socially to continue life-long learning. We believe in rigorous academics without undue pressure or over-competitiveness."

East Palo Alto ◆ Redwood City ◆ San Carlos
CATHOLIC SCHOOLS

OUR LADY OF MT. CARMEL. 301 Grand St., Redwood City 94062. (415) 366-6127. Teresa Anthony, Principal. Non-profit.

Pre K-gr. 8; 295 students. $1835. Inc. fees, $135. Scholarships. SDH: 8:05-2:45; K, 8:05-11:45 or 9-1. EDC: 7 a.m.-6 p.m., not open on school holidays. Avg. class size 30, max. 35. Uniforms. Instrumental music. Apply in Jan. and Feb. Classroom visits welcome. Testing in March. Summer programs. Accredited by WCEA and WASC.

"Over one hundred years of Catholic tradition dedicated to learning, growing, and living."

ST. CHARLES. 850 Tamarack Ave., San Carlos 94070. (415) 593-1629. Stephen Farren, Principal. Est. 1950. Non-profit.

K-gr. 8, 300 students. $2000. 10% receive fin. aid. Inc. fees $200. SDH: 8:10-2:50. EDC: 7:15 a.m.-6 p.m., $2.75/hr. Avg. class size 33, max. 35. Uniforms. Computer literacy, Spanish, music, sports. Admissions test in March. Late applications accepted. Summer program for K-3, mornings only. Waiting list in some grades. Accredited by WASC and WCEA.

"Saint Charles School is committed to providing quality academic education in a strong Catholic environment. Through the combined efforts of parents, teachers, and administrators, Saint Charles provides a warm and caring environment where the needs of each child are actively searched out."

ST. PIUS. 1100 Woodside Rd., Redwood City 94061. (415) 368-8327. Rita Carroll, Principal. Est. 1953. Non-profit.

K-gr. 8; 344 students. $1950. Sibling discounts. Reg. fee $185. Fin. aid avail. Avg. & max. class size 35. SDH: 8:25-3. EDC: 7:30-6; closed during school holidays. Specialists teach art, science, computer and PE. Motor skills for K-gr. 2. Afterschool sports programs. Apply Feb.-March. Waiting list for some grades. Summer programs. Accredited by WASC & WCEA.

"St. Pius provides a strong academic curriculum integrated with Catholic values."

NON-CATHOLIC RELIGIOUS SCHOOLS

ALPHA BEACON CHRISTIAN. 750 Dartmouth Ave., San Carlos 94070. (415) 592-2811. Lillian G. Mark, Director. Sheri Lee, Admissions. Est. 1969. Non-profit.

Preschool-gr. 12; 265 students. $2800; gr. 7-12, $3800. Inc. fees $50-$200. Fin. aid avail. SDH: K, 8:30-11:30; gr. 1-3, 8:30-2:30; gr. 4-6, 8:30-2:45; gr. 7-12, 8:15-3:45. EDC: 7 am-6 pm. Avg. class size 20, max. 27. Uniforms. Classroom visits welcome. 20 acre campus leased from San Carlos School District; gymnasium. Interscholastic spelling, science, speech meets, drama, sports, music. 62% of h.s. grads go to 4 yr. colleges, 30% to 2 yr. Families must be open to Christian philosophy. Summer programs. Accredited by ACSI.

"The goal of Alpha Beacon Christian School is to train our students to be the godly leaders of tomorrow in our homes, in our community, in our nation, and in our world. Our school is an arm of the home and church, working together as a team. Our curriculum is Christ-centered, our faculty, born-again Christians and our mode of operation is based on biblical principles."

HERITAGE CHRISTIAN ACADEMY. 1305 Middlefield Rd., Redwood City 94063. (415) 366-3842. Dr. Gene Carper, Director. Est. 1971. Non-profit.

Preschool-gr. 8, 164 students. $325/mo., books $125, reg. fee $75. Fin. aid avail. SDH: 8:30-3. EDC: 7 a.m.-6 p.m. (no extra cost.) Music, art. Uniforms. Registration remains open until classes fill. Families must be open to Christian education. Summer program. Accredited by ACSI.

"While our sponsor church is affiliated with the Assemblies of God, we do not teach or require conformity to the creed or confession of any one particular denomination...The purpose of the school is to provide instruction of high academic quality in conformity with our Statement of Faith, so that the students may be prepared to take their place in the home, the church, the state, and their vocations or professions, in a manner that glorifies God."

REDEEMER LUTHERAN. 468 Grand St., Redwood City 94062. (415) 366-3466. Gary Behrens, Principal. Est. 1957. Non-profit.

K-gr. 8; 120 students. Church members $2050; non-members $2750; sibling discounts. Reg. fee: $250 SDH: K, 8:30-11:30; gr. 1-8, 8:30-3:00. EDC: 7 a.m.-5:45 p.m., $170/mo. for full time. Avg. class size 22, max. 25. Uniforms. Spanish, computer literacy, music appreciation, sports program. Participation in Lutheran Athletic League. Students need not be members of the Lutheran Church. Waiting list in some grades. Accredited by Lutheran Church Missouri Synod.

"RLS is a mission where teachers, parents, and congregation work together to share the Gospel with young people, nurturing them so they develp a positive view of the future and acquire the attitudes, knowledge and skills necessary to become successful, contributing Christian participants in a rapidly changing world."

REDWOOD BAPTIST CHRISTIAN ACADEMY. 435 5th Ave., Redwood City 94063. (415) 364-1606. Jerry Barge, Principal. Est. 1979. Non-profit.

K-gr. 12; 50 students. $1750. Application fee $100. No scholarships. SDH: 8:30-3. Two learning centers: one for K-1, one for gr. 2-12. Individualized instruction program uses Accelerated Christian Education materials. Computers, gym, strong PE program. Apply for kindergarten by opening of school; others may apply anytime. Families must be regularly attending members of a Bible-believing church.

"We feel it is our obligation to educate our children with Christ-centered curriculum."

SECULAR SCHOOLS

SHULE MANDALA ACADEMY. 321 Bell St., East Palo Alto 94303. (415) 327-5848. Nobantu Ankoanda, Director. Est. 1989. Non-profit.

K-gr. 8; 35 students maximum. $235/mo. Books $65; reg. $75. No scholarships. SDH: 8:15-3:30. EDC: 3:30-6, avail. year-round. Avg. class size 12, max. 15. Field trips. Uniforms. Test scores not used as criteria for admissions. Mandatory conference with parents & students.

"We believe that all children can learn and all children are gifted. We have high expectations regardless of ability or skills. We believe that by building self-esteem in educating students academically, socially, and psychologically they will survive in American society or anywhere in the world."

WHERRY ACADEMY. 820 Cassia St., Redwood City 94063. (415)367-6791. Janet Wherry, Director; Admissions, Martha Kay. Est. 1983. Non-profit.

K-gr. 12; 40 students. $3950; $75 testing & placement fee. 50% receive fin. aid. SDH: K, 9-1; gr. 1-12, 9-2:45. EDC avail. Avg. class size 6, max. 10; gr. 9-12, avg. class size 8, max. class size 25. Dress code. Advanced math & science, foreign language, field trips, voice, guitar, dance. Students accepted on basis of achievement test & interview. Applications accepted year-round if space available. On site LD specialist. 50% of h.s. grads. attend 4 yr. colleges; 40% attend 2 yr. colleges. SAT scores slightly above average. Summer program. Applicant for WASC accreditation.

"We offer an intense, broad academic program, full of enrichment. The high school is college preparatory and we use the University of California requirments for our graduation requirements."

Belmont ◆ Burlingame
Hillsborough ◆ San Mateo
CATHOLIC SCHOOLS

IMMACULATE HEART OF MARY. 1000 Alameda de las Pulgas, Belmont, 94002. (415) 593-4265. Dr. Margaret C. Purcell, Principal. Est. 1952. Non-profit.

K-gr. 8; 300 students. $1900. $175 reg. fee. No scholarships. SDH: 8:15-3. EDC: 7 a.m.-6 p.m.; closed on school holidays. Avg. class size 30, max. 35. Uniforms. Afterschool sports. Kdg. readiness screening in March, gr. 1-8 testing in April. Acceptance based on test scores. Waiting list for some grades. Accredited by WASC & WCEA.

"We believe in the three-fold purpose of Catholic education: to teach doctrine and proclaim gospel values, to build a community, and to foster service. Therefore, we emphasize the uniqueness of each child so that the total person may develop spiritually, morally, intellectually, socially, physically, and psychologically."

NOTRE DAME ELEMENTARY. 1500 Ralston Ave., Belmont, 94022. (415) 591-2209. Sister Dolores Quigg, Principal. Est. 1851. Non-profit.

Gr. 1-8; 268 students. $2300. Sibling discounts. Reg. fee $300. SDH: 8:20-3. EDC: 3-6 p.m. Avg. class size 30, max. 35. Extensive use of aides and parent volunteers creates a much lower student/instructor ratio. Uniforms. Music, lab science, T.V. studio, creative arts, computer program. Spanish or French in all grades. Extensive sports program. If parents cannot participate, extra donation requested. Apply Oct.-March; entrance exam in March. School tour every Wed. Waiting list. Accredited by WASC & WCEA.

"Notre Dame School endeavors to provide a warm and caring Christian learning environment in which the child, through the directed experiences of a personalized educational program, can grow spiritually, intellectually, emotionally, psychologically and physically as a child of God."

OUR LADY OF ANGELS. 1328 Cabrillo Ave., Burlingame 94010. (415) 343-9200. Joan Marino, Principal. Est. 1928. Non-profit.

Preschool-gr. 8; 304 students. $1830; $2406 for non-contributing families. Inc. fees $125. Fin. aid avail. SDH: K, 8:20-noon; gr. 1-8, 8:20-3. EDC: 7:15 a.m.-6 p.m. Avg. class size 30, max. 35. Uniforms. Computer literacy, science lab, spacious gym/multipurpose hall. Special community & family atmosphere, tremendous parent involvement. Waiting list for some grades. Accredited by WASC & WCEA.

"Our Lady of Angels School has for its purpose the Catholic, Christian education of its students, emphasizing the harmonious development of the spiritual, moral, intellectual, social, physical, and emotional endowments of young boys and girls."

ST. CATHERINE OF SIENNA. 1300 Bayswater Ave., Burlingame 94010. (415) 344-7176. Sister Antonella Manca, Principal. Est. 1938. Non-profit.

K-gr. 8; 315 students. $1780. Reg. fee $100. No scholarships but sibling discounts. SDH: 8:25-3. EDC: 3-6 p.m. $2.50/hr. Avg. & max. class size 35. Uniforms. Foreign language, computers, afterschool sports and music program, Montessori integrated kdg. Great parent involvement. Students are tested and interviewed before admission. Applications accepted throughout the year. Waiting list. Accredited by WASC & WCEA.

"St. Catherine of Sienna School is committed to the development of the whole child. The child's spiritual development is of primary importance. We proclaim Christ's life and teachings and try to live our faith in all our actions."

ST. GREGORY. 2701 Hacienda St., San Mateo 94403. (415) 573-0111. Michael Marshal, Principal. Est. 1951. Non-profit.

K-gr. 8; 317 students. $1850; in parish students eligible for tuition reduction from the Pastor. SDH: K, 8:10-11:30 or 10-1:30; gr. 1-8, 8:10-3. EDC: 7 a.m.-6 p.m. Avg. & max. class size 36. Uniforms. Computers, P.E., hands-on science. Four week summer program. Waiting list. Accredited by WASC & WCEA.

"St. Gregory is a parochial institution in the Catholic tradition which exists as an extension of the family and offers its students a quality education within a Christian community."

ST. MATTHEWS CATHOLIC SCHOOL. 900 S. El Camino Real, San Mateo 94402. (415) 343-1373. Thesea Canizzaro, Principal. Est. 1932. Non-profit.

K-gr. 8; 476 students. $1735-$2025. Reg. fee $165. Fin. aid avail. SDH: K, 8:20-11:30 or 12:30-3:30; gr. 1-8, 8:20-3. EDC: 3-6 pm; $2.75/hr. Avg. class size 28-30, max. 34-35. Choir; student government; Spanish K-gr. 8; piano, guitar lessons; computer lab gr. 1-8; Great Books Program; Outdoor Ed. for gr. 5; library staffed daily; personal counselor twice/wk.; on site LD specialist. Applications avail. in Jan. For kdg. must be 5 by fall; April applications for other grades. Some years summer enrichment programs. Accredited by WASC & WCEA.

"St. Matthew's Catholic School has an active parent involvement program which enables us to encourage a strong parent-student-teacher partnership."

ST. TIMOTHY. 1515 Dolan Ave., San Mateo. (415) 342-6567. Evelyn M. Nordberg, Principal. Est. 1961. Non-profit.

K-gr. 8; 253 students. $1934. Inc. fees $175. Fin. aid avail. SDH: 8:15-3:00. EDC: 7 a.m.-6 p.m. $35/wk. or $2.75/hr. Avg. class size 30, max. 35. Uniforms. Computer program/lab, P.E., library, gym, kitchen. Afterschool programs in art and instrumental music. Traditional academic curriculum with emphasis on religious education. Hot lunch 2 days/wk., annual school play, student curriculum fair. Kdg. testing in Feb. & March. Testing for other grades in March. Registration in April and May. Accredited by WASC & WCEA.

"St. Timothy School is a Catholic elementary school dedicated to the principles of Christian community, education of the whole child, and acknowlgement of the role of the parent as primary educator...We expect active participation from all members of our school family and encourage Christian service to the larger community. We strive to instill a sense of pride in who we are as children of God, respect for people of all cultures, and a concern for the needs of our world."

NON-CATHOLIC RELIGIOUS SCHOOLS

GLORIA DEI LUTHERAN. 2600 Ralston Ave., Belmont 94002. (415) 593-3361. Rev. Gerald E. Geiger, Director. Est. 1970. Non-profit.

K-gr. 8; 34 students. $1700. $100 inc. fees. No scholarships. SDH: 8:30-3. EDC. until 5. Avg. class size 4-6, max. 16. Christ-centered, Bible-focused basic curriculum with much personal attention. Primarily serves church members but accepts non-members if space available. No application deadline. Visits welcome anytime. Accredited by WELS.

"We offer a balanced program of education that permits the child to grow in knowledge of God's wisdom as revealed in the word and in the world. We seek to involve the parents in the program of education."

GRACE LUTHERAN. 2825 Alameda de las Pulgas, San Mateo 94403. (415) 345-9082. Mrs. Beth Landon, Director. Est. 1984. Non-profit.

K-gr. 8; 60 students. $2200 + inc. fees. Fin. aid avail. SDH: 8:30-3:15. EDC: 7 a.m.-6 p.m.; $2.50/hr. Avg. class size 14, max. 24. Uniforms. Music, choir. Admissions open to all children except those with severe learning and behavior problems.

"The purpose of Grace is to nurture children of the congregation and community. Through partnership with parents, the school will enable children to find identity, purpose and power for their lives. Grace strives to educate the whole child for successful and responsible citizenship."

NORTH PENINSULA JEWISH COMMUNITY DAY SCHOOL. 525 W. 42nd Ave., San Mateo 94403. (415) 345-8900. Rabbi Jim Rogozen, Director. Est. 1986. Non-profit.

K-gr. 5, 103 students. K, $4500; gr. 1-5, $5200. Fin. aid avail. SDH: K, 8:30-1:30; gr. 1-5, 8:30-3:30. EDC: 1:30-6:00. Avg. class size 16, max 22. Judaica, music, art, P.E., Young Authors Conference, science fair. Siblings given priority in admissions. Otherwise, acceptance based on order of application. Classroom visits welcome.

"We are dedicated to providing an outstanding General and Jewish education for students in the North Peninsula area. Our programs promote growth and development in the social, physical, intellectual, ethical and spiritual domains. We seek to develop and strengthen the Jewish identity of our students, as well as encourage their commitment to the Jewish Community at large."

ST. MATTHEWS EPISCOPAL. 16 Baldwin Ave., San Mateo 94401. (415) 342-5436. Douglas R. Ware, Head-of-School. Est. 1954. Non-profit.

Preschool-gr. 8 (including trans. kdg); 210 students. K, $5310; gr. 1-4, $6000; gr. 5-8, $6250. Application fee $50; reg. fee $250. Sibling discounts. Fin. aid. avail. SDH: K, 8:30-1:30; gr. 1-3, 8:30-3; gr. 4-8, 8:30-3:30. EDC: 7:15 a.m.-6 p.m. Avg. & max. class size 22. Dress code. French, art, drama, choir, music appreciation, computers. Siblings and parishioners given priority in admissions; otherwise students accepted on basis of test scores, class visit, evaluation and recommendation from current school. Waiting list for lower school. Summer enrichment program some summers. Accredited by CAIS.

The school's philosophy is "to foster an education which seeks not only to develop each student academically, but more importantly to prepare each student to live a creative, humane and compassionate life worthy of a child of God."

SECULAR SCHOOLS

ACACIA MONTESSORI. 2820 Ponce Ave., Belmont 94002. (415) 592-4725. Bob Kane, Director; Sophie McCarthy, Admissions. Est. 1981. Proprietary.

Preschool-gr. 5. $397/mo.; $100 materials fee. No scholarships. SDH: K, 9-2:30; gr. 1-5, 8:45-2:45. EDC: 7:15-6:15. Avg. class size 20, max. 24. Computers, piano, gymnastics & ballet. Summer programs. Apply anytime.

"We use Montessori principles to allow children to progress at their own natural pace within a rich, stimulating environment."

BELMONT OAKS ACADEMY. 2200 Carlmont Dr., Belmont 94002. (415) 593-6175. Pamela G. Clarke, Director. Est. 1948. Proprietary.

K-gr. 3; 160 students. $515/mo. Reg. fee $110; books & supplies, K $150, gr. 1-3 $175. No scholarships. SDH: K, 8:30-11:30; gr. 1-3, 8:30-3. EDC: 7 a.m.- 6 p.m, included in tuition. Year-round school. Uniforms. Avg. class size 15, max. 30 (with 2 teachers.) Hot lunches. Registration April-Aug. Admission based on space available, CAT scores. Summer day camp: field trips, academics, arts & crafts, cook-outs, swimming lessons.

Our goal is "to see that students have opportunities to build for themselves a foundation which will support the educational goals. To provide the best available methods which are structured to the students' individual patterns of learning."

THE CAREY SCHOOL. 2101 Alameda de las Pulgas, San Mateo 94403. (415) 345-8205. Robert W. Simpson, Headmaster. Est. 1928. Non-profit.

Preschool-gr. 5. $6100 7% receive fin. aid. SDH: K: 8:30-2; gr. 1-5, 8:30-3. EDC: 7:30-5:30. Avg. and max class size 22. Dress code. Computers, art, music, physical education, Spanish, Italian, French, field trips. Gr. 1-5 students selected on results of test scores and grades. Classroom visits required of perspective students. Waiting list. Provisional membership in CAIS.

"The Carey School philosphy recognizes that the best education takes place in a warm and accepting, yet challenging, environment...It offers a strong academic program which fosters a love of learning and encourages the student to work to his/her greatest potential..."

NUEVA LEARNING CENTER. 6565 Skyline Blvd., Hillsborough 94010. (415) 348-2272. Annabel L. Jensen, Ph.D., Executive Director. Est. 1967. Non-profit.

PreK-gr. 8; 305 students. K, $7105; gr. 1-2, $8115; gr. 3-6, $8440; gr. 7-8, $10,600. (Includes tuition insurance, field trips, activity fees and books.) Application & testing fee $165; fund development pledge $500 ($250 for siblings). 10% receive fin. aid. SDH: K, 8:45-12 (until March 1 when class extends to full day); gr. 1-6, 8:45-3:10; gr. 7-8, 8-3:10. EDC: 3:15-6; $3.50/hr.

Avg. class size 16-22, max. 22. Scheduling, specialists, teaching assistants & volunteers keep student-teacher ratio 8:1. SamTrans bus service to north & south. Vocal music program for all students, instrumental lessons available from private teachers on site; "hands-on" art and art history; activity centered science program; manipulatives based, problem solving approach to math; integrated, experiential social studies and language arts; extensive computer lab, Japanese. *Self-Science* life skills curriculum in gr. 3-8. Application procedure: parents visit, students take intelligence test, students visit for 2-3 days, parent interview. Child must be five years old by the beginning of kdg. Apply by Feb. 15 for March decision. Waiting list. Variety of summer programs. Accredited by CAIS & WASC.

"Nueva is an elementary and middle school serving gifted and talented young-sters. The program provides quality education with an integrated curriculum emphasizing problem solving, critical and creative thinking skills, independence in learning and personalized education."

TRUE LEARNING CENTER, INC. 2109 Broadway, Burlingame 94010. (Mailing address Box 1387, Redwood City 94064). Larry Kruesmark, Administrator. (415) 347-4311. K-gr. 8; 72 students.

Colma ◆ Half Moon Bay ◆ Pacifica
CATHOLIC SCHOOLS

GOOD SHEPHERD ELEMENTARY SCHOOL. 909 Oceana Blvd., Pacifica 94044. Patricia Volan, Principal. (415) 359-4544. Est. 1968. Non-profit.

K-gr. 8; 325 students. $2345. Inc. fees $175. Fin. aid avail. SDH: 8:15-2:45. EDC: 7 a.m.-6 p.m. Avg class size 36, max. 40. Uniforms. Computer lab for K-gr.8, instrumental band, choir, music instruction. No application deadline. Waiting list. Accredited by WASC & WCEA.

"Good Shepherd School exists to serve its students and their parents. The school provides a solid academic foundation in a Christian atmosphere. Good Shepherd School has for its purpose the Catholic education of its students, emphasizing the harmonious development of the spiritual, moral, intellectual, social, physical, and emotional endowments of young boys and girls."

HOLY ANGELS. 20 Reiner St., Colma 94014. (408) 755-0220. Sister Therese Improgo, OSF, Principal. Est. 1952. Non-profit.

K-gr. 8; 320 students. $185/mo. Books $100. No scholarships. SDH: 8:15-2:45. EDC: 7 a.m.-6 p.m. Avg. & max. class size 36. Uniforms. Computer lab. Afterschool photography club, sports. Slingerland testing & tutoring. LD specialist on site. Academic summer school. Registration in March. Entrance test. Accredited by WASC & WCEA.

"We educate the whole child spiritually, intellectually, physically and psycho-logically."

NON-CATHOLIC RELIGIOUS SCHOOLS

ALMA HEIGHTS CHRISTIAN ACADEMY. 1295 Seville Dr. Pacifica 94044. (415) 359-0555. Ronald Benton, Director. Est. 1955. Non-profit.

K-gr. 5; 150 students. (Gr. 6-12 at separate campus; see listing under San Mateo County Secondary Schools.) $180-$200/mo. Reg. fee $100; books & inc. fees

$115-$140. 10-15% receive fin. aid. SDH: K, 8:30-12; other grades 8:15-3:10. Avg. class size 23, max. 25. Uniforms. Speech meets, class plays & programs, track & field meets. Apply for kdg. 1 yr. in advance; as early as possible for other grades. Waiting list. Summer programs vary from year to year. Member of ASCI.

"Our school ministers to the whole child: spiritually, academically, emotionally, and socially. We gain our authority from the parent and seek to provide a Bible-centered philosophy of education to complement what is being done in the home. Our well-rounded program results in consistently high test scores and winning records in athletic and academic competition."

SECULAR SCHOOLS

WILKINSON SCHOOL. Box 1059, 130 Santa Ana, El Granada 94018. (415) 726-2990. Edward and Linda Wilkerson, Directors. Est. 1977. Non-profit.

Preschool-gr. 6; 120 students. K, $2700; gr. 1-6, $3700. SDH: K, 8:15-1:00; gr. 1-2, 8:15-2:15; gr. 3-6, 8:15-2:45. EDC: 7 a.m.-6 p.m.; closed only on legal holidays; $2000/yr. for K; $1000/yr. for gr. 1-6. Fin. aid avail. Avg. class size 20, max. 22. Trans. Kdg. Small classes, individualized approach. Gifted students move ahead at own rate. Slingerland method and tutorials used with dyslexic children. Suzuki violin offered to all students. Instrumental music, major drama production, field trips, career study with wide variety of professionals. One visitation day/mo. Academic summer program with day camp option.

"Head, hands, and heart are the three pillars in our program. We help children to think, create and feel to their fullest potential. Education, enrichment and nurturing are equally important in our small school with its family atmosphere."

Daly City ◆ San Bruno ◆ South San Francisco
CATHOLIC ELEMENTARY SCHOOLS

ALL SOULS. 479 Miller Ave., South San Francisco 94080. (415) 583-3562. Eileen Gorman, Principal. Non-profit.

K-gr. 8, 300 students. 1992 tuition: $1770. Inc. fees $150. Fin. aid avail. SDH: K, 8-12 or 9:30-1;15; Gr. 1-8, 8:15-2:55. EDC: 7:15 a.m.-6 p.m. Avg. & max. class size 39. Uniforms. Computer program. Algebra & introduction to foreign languages in 8th grade. Accredited by WASC & WCEA.

MATER DOLOROSA. 1040 Miller Ave., South San Francisco 94080. (415) 588-8175. William J. Kovacich, Principal. Est. 1961. Non-profit.

K-gr. 8; 295 students. $2515. Inc. fees $130.   SDH: 8:25-2:50. EDC: 7:10 -5:50 p.m. Avg. & max. class size, 35. Uniforms. Registration in Jan. & Feb. Waiting list.   Accredited by WASC & WCEA.

"Mater Dolorosa School provides quality education in a Catholic setting. Programs are designed to provide the academic and spiritual growth of each child. Students score above average on standardized tests of basic skills."

OUR LADY OF MERCY. 7 Elmwood Dr., Daly City 94015. (415) 756-3395. Ms. Arlene Fife, Principal. Est. 1955. Non-profit.

K-gr. 8; 550 students. K, $1,220; Gr. 1-8, supporting members of parish $1850; non-supporting members $2350. Sibling discounts. Reg. fee $190. SDH: K, 8-11 or 12-3; gr. 1-8, 8:15-2:50. EDC: 7 am-6 pm. Avg. class size 35, max. 40. Uniforms. Computer lab, music education, band, choir, instrumental music lessons, jazz band, drama, PE, afterschool sports. Boy and Girl Scout Programs available. Special ed. teacher on staff. Waiting list in some grades. Accredited by WASC & WCEA.

"Our Lady of Mercy School is a community of faith where we provide for the growth of the whole Christian person...We help children develop their distinctive abilities and prepare them to live effectively in the Church and the community. We support the role of parents as the primary religious educators."

OUR LADY OF PERPETUAL HELP. 80 Wellington Ave., Daly City 94014. (415) 755-4438. James Costello, Principal. Est. 1933. Non-profit.

K-gr. 8; 313 students. $180/mo. Fin. aid avail. SDH: 8:15-3. Avg. class size 35. All-day kdg., full time computer teacher, afterschool music program, full sports program. Apply by March 12. Waiting list. Accredited by WASC & WCEA.

"At OLPH, we believe eduation is a partnership of parents and teachers and dedicated to the creation of a Christian environment of care, encouragement, and love; the pursuit of academic excellence; and the joy of learning.

ST. DUNSTAN'S. 1150 Magnolia Ave., Millbrae 94030. (415) 697-8119. Ms. JoAnn Kozloski, Principal. Est. 1953. Non-profit.

K-gr. 8, 315 students. Parishioners, $2150; non-parishioners $2650. $125 reg. fee. Fin. aid avail. 30 hrs./yr. volunteer work required. SDH: K, 8:20-11:50 or 9:30-12:50; other grades, 8:20-2:45. EDC: 7:30 a.m.-6 p.m.; $3/hr. (not avail. during school holidays.) Avg. & max. class size 35. Uniforms. Computers, music program, Spanish for gr. 7-8. Admissions test. Waiting list. Accredited by WASC & WCEA.

"The school's goal is to provide a quality educational experience within a Catholic environment of peace, security, and love...to foster the religious, intellectual, social and physical growth of the student so that he may better serve himself, his family, his community, and his God."

ST. ROBERT'S. 345 Oak Ave., San Bruno 94066. (415) 583-5065. Sister Columba Galvin, Principal. Est. 1949. Non-profit.

K-gr. 8; 340 students. $1800-$2724. Inc. fees $150. No scholarships. SDH: K, 8:15-11:50 or 9:25-12:50; gr. 1-8, 8:15-2:45. EDC: 7:15-5:45. Avg. class size 35, max. 38. Uniforms. Entrance test. March registration. Accredited by WASC & WCEA.

ST. VERONICA'S. 434 Alida Way, South San Francisco, 94080. (415) 589-3909. Mrs. Joan Coleman, Principal. Est. 1957. Non-profit.

K-gr. 8; 340 students. $1728. No scholarships. SDH: 8:25-3. EDC: 7:10-5:45. Avg. & max. class size 38. Uniforms. Afterschool sports program, fully equipped computer lab, library. Registration first two weeks of Feb. Waiting list for some grades. Accredited by WASC & WCEA.

The school's goal is to "form well-educated Christians. We nourish students' spiritual, academic, physical, social & emotional growth."

NON-CATHOLIC RELIGIOUS SCHOOLS

HIGHLANDS CHRISTIAN. 1900 Monterey Dr. San Bruno 94066. (415) 873-4090. Vernita Sheley, Superintendent. Est. 1966. Non-profit.

Preschool-gr. 8; 800 students. K-gr. 5, $2750; gr. 6-8, $2850. Reg. fee, $70; supplies, $70-$110. No scholarships. SDH: 8:20-3. EDC: 7 a.m.-6 p.m., (not avail. on school holidays.) Avg. class size 26, max. 30. Uniforms. Computer training and Spanish in gr. 2-8. Classroom music and physical education classes. Afterschool vocal and instrumental music available. Science fair, fine arts programs, speech meets, other enrichment programs. Waiting list in some grades. Summer programs for students enrolled during school year. Accredited by WASC & ACSI.

"We are sponsored by Church of the Highlands, a non-denomination Protestant church. We believe each child is unique, endowed with special gifts, and has a God-ordained purpose in life. We endeavor to supplement the educational process in the home to 'train up a child in the way he should go' (Proverbs 22:6) and to meet his/her needs in all areas: academically, physically, spiritually and socially."

SECULAR SCHOOLS

HILLDALE. 79 Florence St., Daly City 94014. (415) 756-4737. Mary Ann von Rosen, Director. Est. 1962. Proprietary.

K-gr. 8. $3850. Inc. fees $110. Reg. fee $25. No scholarships. SDH: 9-3:30. EDC: 7 a.m.-6 p.m. (included in tuition.) Avg. class size 15-20. Uniforms. Variety of afterschool enrichment programs. On campus heated pool, Red Cross swim program. Summer program includes swimming instruction and academics. Entrance test and interview in May. Summer day camp.

"Our goal is to provide an educational environment which builds upon the child's natural curiosity and desire for learning and to encourage each child to progress as rapidly as possible in all academic areas."

YOUNG WORLD LEARNING CENTER. 699 Serramonte Blvd., Daly City 94015. (415) 994-6599. Becky Hanvey, Director. Est. 1978. Proprietary.

Preschool-gr. 6. $400/mo. One scholarship a year. SDH (all grades): 9-3:30. EDC: 7 a.m.-6 p.m. (no extra fee). Avg. class size 15, max. 20. Music, aerobics, & Spanish. Dance & computers for extra fee. Admissions begin May 1, ongoing until full. The school is closed only 4 wks./yr.

Young World "respects each child's individual differences and creates an environment that provides and demands skills necessary for learning."

SAN MATEO COUNTY
PRIVATE SECONDARY SCHOOLS

ALMA HEIGHTS CHRISTIAN ACADEMY. 1030 Linda Mar Blvd., Pacifica 94044. (415) 355-1935. Joseph Gross, Director. Est. 1955. Non-profit.

Gr. 6-12. $210-230/mo. Reg. fee $100; book & lab fee $155-$175. 10-15% receive fin. aid. Closed campus. Avg. class size 22, max. 25. Dress Code. Essay contests, speech meets, science fairs, track & field meets. Summer school varies year to year. Applicants accepted on basis of test scores and behavior. Waiting list.

90% of grads. go to 4 yr. colleges, 10% to 2 yr. SAT scores (100%): '93: V 550, M 600. 3 yr. avg.: V 550, M 597.

ALPHA BEACON CHRISTIAN. See listing under San Carlos Private Elementary Schools.

CRYSTAL SPRINGS UPLANDS. 400 Uplands Dr., Hillsborough 94010. (415) 342-4175. Richard A. Drew, Headmaster. John Draper, Admissions. Est. 1952. Non-profit.

Gr. 6-12; 350 students. $10,150; inc. fees $875. 15% receive fin. aid. SDH: 8:30-3:15 (2:30 on Fri.). Avg. class size 14, max. 18. Special bus connection to train station. Closed campus. Advanced placement courses in major subjects, area-wide humanities festival, math contests, science days, all-school overnight trips, athletic play days. Facilities: theater, dance studio. Fall of '93 school will have a new student center and commons, biology lab, photography lab, computer center and three interactive classes. Summer programs in sports, theater, science, English, & math, computers, video, marine biology, Mandarin, Japanese and Spanish. Admissions based on test scores, personal interviews, teacher recommendations, and grades from previous schools. Take entrance test by January for March decision. 95-100% of grads. go to 4 yr. colleges. Waiting list. Accredited by WASC & CAIS.

The school believes "students learn best in an atmosphere of rigorous demand balanced by sensitive support and trust. The school provides a challenging traditional academic program along with significant opportunities in athletics and the arts. We believe that stimulation of the mind and encouragement of a desire for lifelong learning should be among the prime goals of any teaching program."

MENLO SCHOOL. 50 Valparaiso Ave., Atherton 94027. (415) 688-3856. Norman Colb, Headmaster. Glen Pritzker, Director of Admissions, 688-3866. Est. 1915. Non-profit.

Gr. 6-12, 525 students. Gr. 6-8, $9500; gr. 9-12, $10,995. Inc. fees $300. 15% receive fin. aid. SDH: 8-3, sports 3-5. Avg. class size 16, max. 20. Van service avail. from some areas. Strong college preparatory program. Library with 56,000 volumes, computer center, theater. Extensive athletic facilities include gym, track, tennis courts, football, baseball and soccer fields, pool. Elective courses in all programs. Extensive arts program focusing on drama, studio art, and music. Many extracurricular activities and clubs. Closed campus for gr. 6-9. Apply by Feb.15. Students selected on the basis of entrance exam, transcripts, and recommendations. Waiting list. Academic summer school. Accredited by WASC,WAIS, CAIS.

95-100% of graduates go on to 4 yr. colleges. SAT scores (100%): Class of '93, V 542, M 615; 3 yr. avg.: V 545, M 624.

"Menlo is an outwardly informal but inwardly rigorous school. It provides an environment that values participation not only in the classroom but also in extracurricular activities such as sports, the arts, clubs, community service, and student activities. At Menlo the individual is important."

MERCY HIGH SCHOOL. 2750 Adeline Dr., Burlingame 94010. (415) 343-3631. Sister Rosann Fraher, Principal. Est. 1931. Non-profit.

Catholic, girls, gr. 9-12; 325 students. $4675; books & uniforms $300; reg. fee $300. Fin. aid. avail. SDH: 8:00-2:45. Closed Campus. Avg. class size 19, max. 30. Uniforms. College prep curriculum with wide variety of course offerings. Many clubs and activities. Campus Ministry program. Tennis courts, swimming pool. Intramural sports. Placement test in Jan. Parent Open House in Nov. Students accepted on basis of placement test, grades & recommendations. Accredited by WASC.

"Believing that the message of Jesus can be taught only when deed matches word, the goal of educators at Mercy High School is not simply academics, but an overall service of compassion, respect and justice. The curriculum offered at Mercy reflects this goal."

NOTRE DAME HIGH SCHOOL. 1540 Ralston Ave., Belmont 94002. (415) 595-1913. Rita Gleason, Principal. Sr, Angele Lewis, Admissions Director. Est. 1923. Non-profit.

Girls, gr. 9-12; 350 students. $5414. Books $300. 22% receive fin. aid. SDH: 9-4. Closed Campus. Avg. class size 22, max. 28. Uniforms. Performing Arts Center: drama, dance, chorus. 8 varsity sports including swimming & tennis. Apply in Jan. for Sept. placement. Students accepted on basis of entrance tests, grades, recommendations. Summer programs in academics, enrichment, sports camps, middle school program. Accredited by WASC.

65% of grads attend 4 yr. colleges, 35% attend 2 yr. colleges.
SAT's(100%): Class of '92, V 530, M 570.

"Notre Dame High School is an independent Catholic girls school owned and sponsored by the Sisters of Notre Dama whose mission is to provide a quality college preparatory education for young women within a Christian community environment."

REDWOOD BAPTIST CHRISTIAN ACADEMY. See listing under Redwood City Private Elementary Schools.

SACRED HEART PREPARATORY. 150 Valparaiso Ave., Atherton 94027. Richard A. Dioli, Headmaster; John A. Stephensen, Admissions. (415) 322-1866. Est. 1898. Non-profit.

Catholic, gr. 9-12; 285 students. $9600. Books $250. 30% receive fin. aid. Avg. class size 17, max. 20. Vans meet students at Menlo Park Train Station. Closed campus for gr. 9 & 10. Dress code. Drama, music, yearbook, newspaper, student council, model U.N., Interact Club (Rotary), Campus Ministry. 100 hrs. of community service required for graduation. Facilities: three science labs including state-of-the art physics/chem. lab, computer lab, sports center, pool, 11 tennis courts, track, playing field, gym, theater. Full-time college counselor. J.V., varsity and some frosh sports teams; 80% of students play at least one sport. Unusually diverse student body. Students accepted on basis of academic record, student statement, teacher recommendations, entrance exam., full day campus visit. Waiting list. Summer programs: chamber music; drama conservatory; soccer, tennis, basketball and tennis camps. Accredited by WASC, CAIS & Religious of Sacred Heart NCOG.

98% of grads. attend 4 yr. colleges; 2% attend 2 yr. colleges.
Avg. SAT scores (100%): '93, V 530, M 540; 3 yr. avg., V 530, M 540.

"SHP, a member of a world-wide network of nineteen Sacred Heart Schools, is deeply concerned for each student's total development: spiritual, intellectual, emotional & physical....A Sacred Heart Education is distinguished by its commitment to the following five goals: a personal and active faith in God; a deep respect for intellectual values; a social awareness which impels to action; the building of community as a Christian value; personal growth in an atmosphere of wise freedom."

SERRA HIGH SCHOOL. 451 W. 20th Ave., San Mateo 94403. (415) 345-8207. Mr. Michael Peterson, Principal. Mr. Randy Vogel, Admissions. Est. 1944. Non-profit.

Catholic, boys gr. 9-12; 820 students. $4725, books extra. 22% receive fin. aid; 2.5% on academic scholarships.. Closed campus for everyone except seniors. Avg. class size 28, max. 40. Dress code. College preparatory program with many electives and extracurricular activities. Credentialed guidance counselors. Annual Mini-Course Week between semesters. Academic summer school for gr. 7-12; summer sports camp for gr. K-6. Application period: Dec.1 through mid-Feb. Acceptance based on standardized test scores, grades, interview and letters of recommendation. 85% of grads. go to 4 yr. colleges, 15% to 2 yr. colleges. Waiting list. Accredited by WASC.

"Our approach is holistic and unique, since the educational process is rooted in a Christian faith experience. In striving for excellence, we place emphasis not only on the development of intellectual and physical skills, but also on the spiritual, psychological and social growth of each student...We ask the student to make choices not only for his own good, but also for the good of the community."

WEST BAY HIGH SCHOOL. 1482 Laurel, San Carlos 94070. Mailing address: Box 1387, Redwood City 94064. 595-5022. Larry Krusemark, Administrator. Gr. 9-12; 57 students.

WHERRY ACADEMIC SCHOOL. See listing under Redwood City Private Elementary Schools.

WOODSIDE PRIORY. 302 Portola Rd., Portola Valley 94028-7897. (415) 851-8221. Bro. Joachim W. Froehlich, OSB, Headmaster; Al D. Zappeli, Admissions. Est. 1957. Non-profit.

Catholic (Benedictine), Coed, gr. 6-12; 175 students. Day students $9470; boarders $19,510. Inc. fees $960. 28% receive fin. aid. Closed Campus. Dress Code. Avg. class size 15, max. 20. Student-teacher ratio 10:1. 90% of grads. attend 4 yr. colleges; 10% attend 2 yr. colleges. Approx. 15% of the students are international; others mostly from SF Bay Area. 7 day boarding program. High school applicants must take SSAT or STS exam. Make initial inquiry in fall; application deadline in mid-Feb., notification in March. Accredited by WASC & CAIS.

"The aim of the curriculum is to achieve academic excellence and to prepare the student for college and for an enriched personal and social life. The school is founded on principles that value diversity in individuals, a commitment to hard work and a deep understanding of the importance of spirituality. Non-Christian students are welcomed, but it is the responsibility of each person at the Priory to enhance the genuinely human and recognizably Christian character of the school. The Priory gives emphasis to the sound development of the whole person, physical as well as intellectual and moral aspects."

SAN MATEO COUNTY PRIVATE SPECIAL EDUCATION SCHOOLS

BELMONT HILLS SCHOOL. 1301 Ralston Ave., Belmont 94002. (415) 593-2143. Diane Fornasier, Director. Est. 1968. Proprietary. Non-profit.

K-Gr.12, 30 students. Belmont Hills School is a year-round school program that is part of an inpatient program for emotionally troubled adolescents. It also offers day treatment for youths who can benefit from additional classroom structure. No scholarships. SDH: 8:30-2:30. EDC: 8-5. Avg. class size 8, max. 12; teacher student ratio 1:10. Summer day treatment program.

"Belmont Hills strives to provide a structured school program in which both the emotional and academic needs of adolescents are addressed."

BRIDGE SCHOOL. 545 Eucalyptus, Bldg. B., Rm. 5, Hillsborough 94010. (415) 342-7317. Est. 1987. Non-profit.

Ungraded, serves children 5-15 yrs. 12 students. $150/day. 75% of students funded by public school districts. 15-25% receive fin. aid. Avg. & max. class size 6. Teacher/student ratio 2:6. Referrals accepted throughout the year. The school admits students who are severely speech impaired and physically challenged. Team teaching approach is utilized in which a special education teacher and a speech pathologist develop and implement a communication based curriculum. The school is located on an integrated site and students are involved in social and academic mainstreaming. Open house twice yearly. Parent visitation encouraged. 20 day summer session, 4 hrs./day.

"The mission of Bridge School is to enable physically challenged, severely speech impaired students to achieve full participation using Augmentative / Alternative Communication and technology, so that they may achieve their educational potential."

CHARLES ARMSTRONG SCHOOL. 1405 Solana Dr., Belmont 94002. (415) 592-7570. Stephen Waters, Director. Est. 1968. Non-profit.

Grades 1-8; 185 students. $9200; 35% receive fin. aid; 7% funded by public school districts. EDC: 2:30-5:30, $5/hr. Avg. class size 13, max. 15; student teacher ratio 8:1. Students come from as far north as San Francisco and as far south as Gilroy. The school uses Slingerland — a simultaneous multi-sensory instructional approach which integrates the three main sensory modalities (visual, auditory, and kinesthetic) in the presentation of language. Summer school programs for teachers and students. Year-long tutoring. Students accepted on basis of screening procedure, previous records and performance in summer school. Certified by State Department of Education.

"Armstrong serves the dylexic learner by providing an appropriate educational environment in which basic language skills are learned. We seek to instill a joy of learning, enhance self-esteem, and allow each student the right to know, understand, and fulfill personal potential."

HART DAY SCHOOL. 1151 Vancouver, Burlingame 94010. (415) 348-0921. George Hart, Director. Est. 1980. Proprietary.

Gr. 5-12 (ages 12-18 yrs.); 6 students. $44/day. 99% paid for by public school districts. Sliding scale fees. Avg. class size 8, max. 12; teacher/student ratio 1:6. SDH: 8:30-2:30. Dress code. Program for learning handicapped students & underachievers. Application procedure: social, psychological, and academic history reviewed; formal intake meeting with student and parents. Six wk. half day summer program, $600. Certified by State Dept. of Education.

"The school offers a very structured LH program with the goal of returning students to the public school system. The school's primary emphasis is on education. Behavior modification is used to improve classroom behavior. Teacher-directed peer groups support individual needs."

MARY STONE SCHOOL. 2145 Bunker Hill Dr., San Mateo 94402. (415) 574-5005. Mary & Charles Stone, Co-Directors. Est. 1974. Proprietary.

K-gr. 12; 10 students.. $65/day. 90% funded through public funds. No scholarships but occasional tuition reduction. SDH: 8:15-3. Avg. class size 8, max. 12. Teacher/student ratio 1:8-12. The school serves students with language, learning, speech & hearing handicaps The school accepts students with language disabilities who have difficulty achieving at their ability level or who have poor study habits. When appropriate, students are mainstreamed in regular classes with aide assistance. Rural atmosphere. 5 wk. summer session. No application deadline. Certified by State Department of Education.

"Mary Stone School attempts to help students realize their full potential by utilizing special methods and materials, resolving and/or helping students compensate for disabilities, and filling in other gaps."

RUSSELL BEDE SCHOOL. 446 Turner Terrace, San Mateo 94401. (415) 579-4400. Helen Myers, Director; Warren Hagberg, Principal. Est. 1983. Nonprofit.

K-gr. 6; 12 students. $6000. Inc. fees $200. 10% receive public school funding. No scholarships. SDH: 8:45-2:30. Avg. class size 4, max. 8. Teacher/student ratio 1:4. School serves students with learning handicaps, specific learning disabilities & speech difficulties. Individualized program where students receive individual attention and small group instruction. For admissions must be parent/school consensus of appropriate program. New students apply by June 1. 20 day summer academic skills program 9-noon.

"The school was founded on the principle of a relaxed atmosphere but a strictly structured program in which attention is given to individual academic needs, social behavior and basic motor skills. Our four goals are to build positive self-esteem, to remediate/accommodate the specific disabilities, to work closely with parents, and to mainstream the students as soon as they are ready. This last goal is usually achieved within two to three years."

FOUR FAMILIES

The following experiences of four Bay Area families illustrate important aspects of the school selection process. The names of the families and schools involved have been changed.

Sally Adams becomes livid when anyone mentions Greer, a prestigious school in her affluent suburban community. Sally's daughter Anne attended Greer her first three years of school, and Sally is convinced that the experience was damaging to her child's emotional and academic development.

Sally is embarrassed to admit that she selected Greer without visiting other private or public schools. "My father was willing to pay for the best education for his granddaughter, and although I had grown up here and gone to the public schools, I had heard that they were now terrible. I didn't look at other private schools because Greer was close, had been there a long time, and looked so impressive."

In the first grade, Anne began to have real problems. "She was nervous and acting out in school. She had hours of homework, and the work was just too hard. When I tried to talk to the principal or teachers, they dismissed her problems as stemming from laziness "

Sally is most angry at Greer because she feels that it was dishonest about Anne's progress. "The school inflates grades and misrepresents test scores so parents will be happy and keep their kids in the school. Despite all her problems, Anne's grades were always good at Greer. When I finally took Anne out because of her anxiety and unhappiness, Greer had me convinced that she would be way ahead of most of the public school kids. I thought her third grade year at public school would be a real breeze."

Sally had a real shock when she discovered that Anne was, in fact, way behind most of her public school classmates. "Anne didn't know the number facts, didn't understand basic math concepts, and her reading and phonics skills were weak. When the public school gave achievement tests, Anne's scores were dismal compared to those of the other children in her class. Greer had shown parents only the grade equivalencies and had us believe that only its students scored above grade level. I discovered that almost all Anne's public school classmates score substantially above grade level. Unlike the public schools, Greer doesn't show parents percentages, which are the best indicators of where a child stands."

Sally admits that her daughter's problems didn't miraculously disappear once she changed schools. "Because she has some serious gaps in her basic skills, she still needs a private tutor. But we are both much happier. Anne's teacher is very supportive and understands that Anne has learning disabilities. That is something Greer never cared to recognize because it won't make allowances for individual difficulties, and, besides, most of its teachers aren't trained to recognize learning problems. Anne is now happier socially because there isn't just one tight little clique of girls like there was at Greer. After a year and a half at the public school, Anne's anxiety, which was so acute at Greer, is almost gone. Naturally, because Anne is happier, my husband and I are happier."

Sally, who is on numerous parent committees and serves as a volunteer aide, also enjoys feeling like an important part of the school community. "At Greer, we were expected to drop the kids off, pick them up, and not ask too many questions. I like knowing more about Anne's day, and I feel our relationship is more complete because I'm involved in her education."

Despite her experience at Greer, Sally does not condemn all private schools. She merely recognizes that she didn't spend enough time evaluating Greer's program and philosophy and realizes that many public schools are better than their reputations. Sally may send Anne to a private junior high and high school. But she knows that her approach will be far different the second time around. "I would look for one appropriate to my child's needs and one which has open channels of communication with parents. That may be hard to find, but it's well worth the effort."

Jim and Pat Stark learned six years ago the importance of matching a child with the appropriate school. Their older son Dave decided when he was in the eighth grade that he wanted to attend St. Mark's, a boys' prep school known for its strict discipline, rigorous academic demands, and competitive sports program. Although his family is not Catholic and had always been public school oriented, Dave chose to go to St. Mark's because he wanted the academic challenge and because several of his public school friends were also going.

Dave worked hard and did well, so when his brother Phil, two years younger, completed junior high, he too decided to leave the public school system and enter St. Mark's. Reflecting back on that decision, Phil states, "I wanted to succeed and be admired. My brother was successful there, and so I figured I would be too. My parents left the decision to me, but I knew they were pleased when I decided to follow Dave."

Jim and Pat acknowledge that the two boys had always been different. "Dave was much more self-motivated academically and things came easily to him. Phil was more social and athletic. He was always more interested in girls than his brother was, but he was also more sensitive."

Despite these differences, the Starks assumed that St. Mark's would offer Phil the same positive experience it had given Dave. However, several months into Phil's freshman year, the family began to realize that Phil was having a difficult time. Pat recalls, "He was so anxious to please us. He studied with intense diligence, but with a joylessness that gave us the feeling he was doing it for us rather than himself. That year he had a terrific amount of work and just seemed overwhelmed." Despite the effort he expended, Phil's grades the first semester hovered in the low C range, a real shock since he had always earned A's and B's in public school.

As Phil struggled with his studies, his family witnessed a troubling personality change. "Phil had always been a real charmer, very open and easy to be with. But he began to lose his self-confidence. He became very quiet and withdrawn. He would stay hunched over his desk for hours, until we called him for dinner. As soon as he finished eating, he would go right back up to study."

Phil and his parents now realize that academic pressure was not the sole cause of his unhappiness. While Dave's best friends had joined him at St. Mark's, Phil's had remained at Pierce, the public school across the street from his house. However, his inability to participate in St. Mark's highly competitive athletic program was probably the most demoralizing aspect of Phil's freshman year. "I loved basketball, but I didn't make the team. That was tough for me. I really needed that outlet. By the spring my grades had improved, and I knew I could make it through academically. I was proud of that, but, overall, I had a bad feeling about myself and school. I knew St. Mark's was teaching me good study habits, and the teachers were dedicated and caring, but all that didn't make up for what was missing for me."

The summer after his ninth grade year, Phil saw a family counselor who specializes in working with troubled adolescents. Phil's parents feel those visits helped him make the decision to return to public school. His mother recalls, "Once he made that decision, he could relax again."

Both parents note, somewhat sadly, that Phil never worked very hard at Pierce and maintained a B average with minimum effort. Despite their realization that Phil wasn't being academically challenged in the public school, Pat stresses, "I felt much better about the whole Phil. He played basketball, had girlfriends, and was much easier to get along with." Jim adds, "He had more time to hunt and spend time at our ranch, activities he'd always loved but had little time for that year at St. Mark's."

Phil, now a hard-working sophomore at a state university, knows that college might be easier for him had he stayed at St. Mark's. But he also believes that public school offered him broader educational experiences that were not available at a private school. "Because Pierce's student body was predominantly minority, I was exposed to other cultures and backgrounds. St. Mark's was just too narrow for me. I wasn't comfortable with academics taking over my whole life. When I tried to go that route, I just moved inside myself and was a pretty miserable human being."

Like the Starks, Mimi Cohn also has two very different children. Her older child Jenny has always been a bright, self-motivated student, and school choice for her was never a problem. "Adams, our public high school, was perfect for her. She was in all the honors classes, had fabulous teachers, and received an excellent education. Even if we were very wealthy, I never would have considered a private school because I can't imagine her getting a better education anywhere else."

Jenny's younger brother Bruce is also bright and was placed in the gifted program in junior high school. "But," notes Mimi with a sigh, "he was a gifted child who didn't want to work. His teachers, recognizing his laziness, did not recommend him for the honors classes at Adams." Bruce's grades were good his first year of high school, but his parents were displeased with how little effort he expended. "The school just doesn't challenge the kids much if they're not in the honors group. However, Bruce seemed happy enough that first year so we accepted his lack of academic motivation with resignation."

At the end of Bruce's freshman year, the Cohn's school district closed one of its three high schools. Mimi describes that year as traumatic for everyone. "There was a huge influx of new students and staff, and the transition was tough on everyone." Because Bruce had always been shy and overly sensitive, his mother believes he was especially affected by the confusion. "Bruce sat in the back of his very large classes and did nothing. He became less social and wasn't involved in any extra-curricular activities — even sports, which he had always loved." Bruce's parents became most concerned when they discovered he had been cutting history, and the school never let them know. "He was getting an A just by copying his friends' notes. When I contacted the school about his cutting classes, the teachers and counselors kept telling me they would do something, but they never did."

By the end of his sophomore year, Bruce's parents realized their son needed a different school. "At home we were having constant battles, and the tensions created by Bruce's problems affected us all." The private day schools in the area were either full or didn't seem right for Bruce. At that point, Bruce told his parents he was willing to try a boarding school, and so Mimi contacted an educational consultant. After interviewing the Cohns and Bruce, the consultant recommended three schools that still had openings and would serve Bruce's needs. In retrospect, Mimi is very glad that they spent several hundred dollars to get professional advice. "I had no idea how to start looking for a good boarding school. We would have dragged Bruce around for weeks and spent far more money trying to find the right school on our own."

The Cohns selected Shannon School, a small prep school in Southern California, which, according to the consultant, did a good job of motivating underachievers. The school, impressed by Bruce's test scores, accepted him for the eleventh grade and gave him a partial scholarship. Even with financial assistance, the Cohns had to dip into savings intended for Bruce's college education. "But," Mimi says, "we realized that if he stayed in public school, he might never even make it to college."

Bruce's performance his first year at Shannon surpassed his parents' expectations. He received all As and Bs, partly his mother admits because "as a new student that first grading period, he was required to spend his evenings in a supervised study hall." But Bruce and his parents were also pleased that attending a small school allowed him to star in athletics. At Adams, he hadn't even tried out for a team, but at Shannon he made varsity soccer, basketball, and baseball. The most unexpected dividend of Bruce's boarding school experience was his involvement in the arts. Bruce had taken a little piano and trumpet when he was younger but hadn't done anything musically for years. He had a free period, so the school put him in the band. Then, on his own, he started taking piano lessons from the music teacher, who soon had him composing his own music. "Music," states his mother, obviously pleased, "has now become an important part of his life. He still composes music to relax. What's even more remarkable," continues Mimi, "is that Bruce was in a play his senior year. That would never have happened at Adams."

Mimi feels one of Shannon's greatest strengths was its college counseling. "If Bruce had still been at home, I would have gone mad trying to get him through his applications. The public school counselors just have too many students to give much individual aid. Shannon's counselor not only made sure the students completed their applications correctly and promptly but also did a good job recommending appropriate colleges. Knowing Bruce's past, the school steered him towards small schools where he would have a chance to shine."

Mimi acknowledges that her son did have some difficulties during his two years at Shannon. "Despite his success that first year, he almost didn't return for his senior year because he missed the freedom and social life of home. But he went back because he wanted to go to a good college and knew returning to public high school would be a real risk." During that second year, some of Bruce's old habits re-appeared. "When he had a teacher he didn't like, he just refused to work, and his grades dropped. However, the staff helped him pull through, and he was accepted to all the colleges he applied to."

In trying to assess why Shannon was so good for Bruce, Mimi attributes much of its success to size. "Because he had an opportunity to succeed in several activities, his self-esteem naturally improved. And with small classes, students couldn't get away with cutting or slacking off without the teachers knowing." Mimi doesn't think Shannon's teachers are necessarily better than those at Adams, although they tend to be younger and more energetic. "Small classes allow the faculty to be more effective with kids like Bruce. It's easier to be a better teacher with only 15 students, instead of 30 or 35, in a class. The public school teachers have so many students that they, quite understandably, focus on the ones like my daughter who want to learn." Mimi also believes that boarding school was good for Bruce because it allowed him to get away from his achieving sister. "It was healthy for all of us to be off his back. When he came home for vacations, we were all more relaxed, and he and Jenny began to get along for the first time in years."

Mimi is still grateful that the public high school gave her daughter such an excellent education. But she knows that Bruce's experience there was not unique. "Our public school serves two levels well — the top and the bottom. But not enough is done for the average or unmotivated kids. I'm not sure what the answer is, but I'm afraid a lot of them fall through the cracks as Bruce was doing."

When Nick and Jan Ryan went house hunting, their first priority was to find a house within walking distance of a neighborhood public school. Nick explains, "Education has always had a high priority in our family. We had heard from friends that the public schools were a mess, but we really wanted our children to receive a public education." Jan adds, "I didn't plan to work until the children were older, and I was willing to work very hard to help improve the schools." Despite their determination, the Ryans' experience with Grant, their "friendly little neighborhood school," turned out to be a nightmare.

The Ryans believe Grant's biggest problem was its principal. "He was politically ambitious — eager to move on to a more powerful position in the district office. Consequently, he was never around and rarely considered the children's interests when he made decisions." The Ryans were also dismayed by the incompetency of the kindergarten and first grade teachers. Jan recalls with a sigh, "The kindergarten teacher was obsessively neat. She was most comfortable when the kids huddled quietly in the corner watching Captain Kangaroo. When children became too noisy, she taped their mouths shut. She didn't like equipment with a lot of pieces which might mess up the room. And when she did art projects, she wanted the finished products to be all the same."

The Ryan children remember the first grade teacher as being even worse. Sam, the younger son, relates, "We were terrified of her. She really seemed to hate kids."

Despite her dissatisfaction with the principal's indifference and the teachers' unprofessionalism, Jan remained determined to help improve the school. Her husband recounts his wife's efforts. "Jan put all her energy into that school. She became the P.T.A. president and organized a parent volunteer program. She even took a class at her own expense so she could start a motor fitness program for the children, something the staff had no interest in doing themselves."

All that determination to stick with Grant dissolved in the Ryans' third year at the school. Sam, now in the seventh grade, recalls the incident that drove the family to surrender. "I was in the first grade. The class troublemaker was acting out again, so the teacher phoned the mother to come get the child. The woman arrived with a belt, and in front of the whole class the teacher let the mother whip the kid. We were supposed to close our eyes, but we could hear him screaming. The teacher told us not to tell our parents about what had happened, but some of us did." Within several weeks, the Ryans, along with two other families, had found a new school for their children.

The Ryans decided to take advantage of their district's open enrollment policy, and they were also determined to use their painful lessons from Grant to set up criteria for what they were looking for in a school. "We wanted a dedicated, harmonious faculty and an active parents' group. But most of all, we wanted a warm, involved principal who was tending the ship." After several weeks of talking to friends and visiting schools, the Ryans enrolled their children in Brodie, a racially mixed school in another middle class neighborhood.

The entire Ryan family is convinced that Brodie's principal, Mr. Peters, is responsible for making his school as good as Grant was bad. Nick succinctly summarizes Mr. Peters' kindness and dedication with the comment, "That man walks on water." The children describe in more detail the wonderful Mr. Peters.

"Sometimes he substitutes; he tutors kids having difficulties; he is always on the playground at lunch." Jan is most impressed by "this man's ability to stand up for his faculty while also keeping the kids' interests his top priority. He knows how to work with his staff and help them become better teachers."

According to the Ryans, Mr. Peters' concern and warmth permeate the entire school, creating a true feeling of community. "The school's parent group is active and enthusiastic, constantly raising money and bringing special programs to the school. The teachers spend free periods and lunch hours offering help sessions, and they constantly take classes to improve their teaching skills." Jan acknowledges, "Certainly not every teacher there is fabulous, but there is the expectation that everyone will be good, so even the average teacher rises to those standards. At Grant the feeling had been that a good teacher threatened the others by making them look bad."

Once Mark, the Ryan's older child, reached the sixth grade, the family found itself facing another dilemma — where to send the children for junior and senior high school. Although the district claimed that all its schools were equally good, the Ryans knew that their assigned junior high was very weak academically. Jan, who tutors university students lacking basic skills, did not want to take the chance that her own children would need similar help when they entered college.

Many of the children at Brodie go on to what Nick describes as "a very good public junior high school, but that option was not available to us because the school already had its quota of Caucasian families." Nick adds, "perhaps we could have clawed our way into that good junior high; we knew a few families who did that. But we were reluctant to go through the uncertainties of that process. We didn't want to be bouncing the children around from school to school. Besides, at the time that school was changing principals, and there were a lot of politics going on in the district office. We didn't want to go through another Grant experience."

During Mark's last year at Brodie, the Ryans very methodically compared their private and public school options. The family made a list of what they wanted in a school. "First of all, we wanted a well-balanced school, a place that would offer the children lots of opportunities in the arts, sports, and academics. We also wanted a school that did a thorough job of teaching writing skills and had strong science and history programs." After six months of visiting schools and talking to parents, the Ryans enrolled Mark in Duff, a well-established K-12 independent school.

Nick states that leaving the public school system caused them a lot of anguish. "But Duff could serve our children's needs and our expectations as parents. Our public school choices just couldn't do that." The Ryans, now in their third year at Duff, cite many factors that convince them that they made the right decision. Many of these factors stem from the class size (16-20 students) and the relative smallness of the school. Jan believes that small classes have been especially important to Sam. "He is shy, and in a large class he could get away with never participating. But at Duff no one is anonymous, and the kids participate in everything." Sam adds, "In a public school I never would have made the team, but at Duff I'm on the J.V. basketball team. I'm not very good, but the better players help me out." Both Mark and Sam also like the feeling of knowing almost everyone in the school and participating in activities with students of all grade levels.

The Ryans are also delighted that Duff's teachers are not tenured. "Most of the teachers are excellent, but it's reassuring to know that when incompetent ones do turn up, they aren't around very long." The Ryans' list of Duff's advantages is lengthy and includes excellent college counseling, school trips, caring staff, and the wide participation of students in all aspects of school life. But all agree that they most value Duff's atmosphere of trust. Nick explains, "The public schools, understandably, must run on rules and regulations. At Duff a love of learning and respect for each individual pervades the whole school. The children rarely abuse that trust."

The Ryan children also point out some not-so-obvious advantages. Mark believes that "at Duff, it's easier to be yourself. The pressure to conform, to be and dress like everyone else, was stronger at Brodie." Sam sees less racism among the students. "Our public schools had a lot of minority students, but there wasn't much real mixing. The racial groups remained pretty separate. At Duff, race isn't important in determining who your friends will be."

The Ryans have changed their feeling about the role of private education. Jan states, "When the kids were young, we saw private schools as elitist institutions and an unnecessary expense. Now, although I have had to go back to work to pay for the tuition, we are very grateful for Duff's existence." Nick adds, "We still support public schools and hope that they get the financial and moral support that they need to solve some of their problems. At Brodie, we saw how good a public school can be, but we've also seen how important private schools are in serving children's needs when the public schools can't do that."

APPENDIX

CALIFORNIA DISTINGUISHED SCHOOL AWARDS

Since 1986 the State Department of Education has annually recognized schools as a reward for achievement and as a motivation for other schools to strive for excellence. Awards are given in alternate years to elementary and secondary schools. Because of budget cuts and the resulting suspension of statewide testing, no awards were given in 1991.

Schools are usually selected for the award on the basis of statewide "quality indicators" which are derived from information collected by the state for all schools and reported in the *Performance Report for California Schools*. Schools are recognized for either high achievement (performance) or for significant improvement. Some schools are recognized in both categories. At all levels, this award is based upon a school's performance or improvement in CAP (California Assessment Program) scores and attendance rate. Instructional time (length of school day) is also considered in awards to elementary and middle schools. Middle schools are also judged by course enrollment in science and algebra classes. High schools are evaluated by an even wider range of criteria: dropout rate, enrollment in specified academic courses, and performance on SAT, ACT, and College Board Advanced Placement exams. Schools are nominated for the award on the basis of their composite scores on these quality indicators. They are then evaluated on the basis of a written application and a site visit to validate that the school's educational program realistically supports the data on which the nomination is based.

Because CAP testing had not been administered to elementary schools since 1990, the 1993 awards to elementary schools were based on assessment of other factors: e.g., curriculum reform, community involvement, and the extent of collaborative learning incorporated into the curriculum. The 1993 winners of the award won for their "competitive application."

Not all schools, including many excellent ones, choose to apply for the award because the application is ten pages long and many schools choose not to expend their efforts on winning this kind of recognition. Schools cannot win in successive cycles. For example, a "1993 Distinguished Elementary School" cannot compete in the next cycle (1995) for elementary schools. However, schools that have won in the previous cycle can be recognized for "Sustained Achievement." Once recognized as a "Distinguished School," no school loses the award.

SAN MATEO COUNTY
DISTINGUISHED SCHOOLS

DISTRICT	SCHOOL	YEAR	CLASS
Burlingame	Burlingame Int.	87-88	perf.
Burlingame	Lincoln Elem.	88-89	perf.
Cabrillo Unified	Kings Mountain	88-89	imp.
Cabrillo Unified	Farallone	92-93	com. ap.
Hillsborough	Crocker Mid.	87-88	perf.
Hillsborough	Crocker Mid.	91-92	perf.
Hillsborough	South Elem.	86-87	perf.
Hillsborough	South Elem.	92-93	com. ap.
Hillsborough	West Elem.	86-87	both
Hillsborough	West Elem.	92-93	com. ap.
Jefferson	Colma Elem.	88-89	imp.
Jefferson	Kennedy Elem.	88-89	imp.
Jefferson	Westlake Elem.	88-89	both
Jefferson High	Terra Nova	89-90	imp.
Las Lomitas	La Entrada Mid.	87-88	perf.
Las Lomitas	La Entrada Mid.	89-90	sust.
Las Lomitas	La Entrada Mid.	92-93	perf.
Las Lomitas	Las Lomitas Elem.	88-89	perf
Menlo Park	Hillview Mid.	85-86	N.A.
Menlo Park	Hillview Mid.	89-90	perf.
Menlo Park	Hillview Mid.	91-92	sust.
Menlo Park	Hillview Elem.	86-87	perf.
Menlo Park	Encinal Mid.	89-90	perf.
Millbrae	Lomita Park Elem.	86-87	perf.
Millbrae	Taylor Int.	85-86	N.A.
Portola Valley	Corte Madera (El)	86-87	perf.
Portola Valley	Corte Madera (Mid)	87-88	perf.
Portola Valley	Corte Madera (Mid)	91-92	perf.
Portola Valley	Ormondale	86-87	perf.
Ravenswood	James Flood Science	92-93	com. ap.
Cabrillo Unified	Kings Mountain	88-89	imp.
San Bruno Park	Crestmoor Elem.	86-87	perf.
San Mateo-F.C.	Abbott Mid.	87-88	imp.
San Mateo-F.C.	Baywood Elem.	86-87	both
San Mateo-F.C.	Highlands	86-88	both
San Mateo-F.C.	Parkside	86-87	both
San Mateo Un. Hi.	Aragon H.S.	87-88	perf.
San Mateo Un. Hi	Mills H.S.	87-88	perf.

DISTRICT	SCHOOL	YEAR	CLASS
Sequoia Un. Hi.	Carlmont H.S.	87-88	imp.
Sequoia Un. Hi.	Carlmont H.S.	89-90	sust.
Sequoia Un. Hi.	Menlo Atherton H.S.	85-86	N.A.
Sequoia Un. Hi.	Sequoia H.S.	85-86	N.A.
So. San Francisco	El Camino	89-90	imp.
Woodside	Woodside Elem.	86-87	perf.
Woodside	Woodside Elem.	92-93	both

SANTA CLARA COUNTY
DISTINGUISHED SCHOOLS

DISTRICT	SCHOOL	YEAR	CLASS
Alum Rock	George Mid.	87-88	perf.
Alum rock	George Mid.	91-92	perf.
Berryessa	Northwood	86-87	perf.
Berryessa	Ruskin Elem.	86-87	perf.
Cambrian	Ida Price Mid.	89-90	perf.
Campbell	Blackford	89-90	perf.
Campbell	Campbell Mid.	89-90	perf.
Campbell	Hazelwood	88-89	perf.
Campbell	Lynhaven Elem.	86-87	perf.
Campbell	Marshall Lane	92-93	com. ap.
Campbell	Rolling Hills Mid.	87-88	imp.
Campbell	Rosemary Elem.	86-87	perf.
Cupertino	Nimitz	92-93	com. ap.
Cupertino	Blue Hills	88-89	perf.
Cupertino	Collins Elem.	86-87	perf.
Cupertino	Cupertino Int.	89-90	perf.
Cupertino	Eisenhower	88-89	imp.
Cupertino	Faria Elem.	88-89	perf.
Cupertino	Kennedy Jr. High	89-90	perf.
Cupertino	Kennedy Jr. High	91-92	sust.
Cupertino	Lincoln Elem.	86-87	perf.
Cupertino	McAuliffe	92-92	com. ap.
Cupertino	Miller Mid.	85-86	N.A.
Cupertino	Miller Int.	89-90	Perf.
Cupertino	Miller Int.	91-92	sust.
Cupertino	Montclaire Elem.	86-87	both
Cupertino	Muir Elem.	88-89	imp.
Cupertino	Regnart Elem.	86-87	perf.
Cupertino	Stevens Creek Elem.	86-87	both
Cupertino	West Valley	88-89	perf.
East Side Union H.S.	Overfelt H.S.	87-88	imp.
Evergreen	Cedar Grove	92-93	com. ap.
Evergreen	Leyva Int.	89-90	perf.
Evergreen	Millbrook	92-93	com. ap.
Evergreen	Norwood Creek	88-89	perf.
Evergreen	Norwood Creek	92-93	com. ap.

DISTRICT	SCHOOL	YEAR	CLASS
Evergreen	O.B. Whaley	88-89	both
Evergreen	Quimby Oak Int.	91-92	imp.
Evergreen	Smith Elem.	86-87	perf.
Franklin-McKinley	Meadows	92-93	com. ap.
Fremont Union H.S.	Cupertino	89-90	perf.
Fremont Union H.S.	Homestead	89-90	perf.
Fremont Union H.S.	Lynbrook	89-90	perf.
Fremont Union H.S.	Monte Vista H.S.	87-88	both
Fremont Union H.S.	Monte Vista H.S.	89-90	sust.
Loma Prieta	English Mid.	87-88	perf.
Loma Prieta	English Mid.	89-90	sust.
Loma Prieta	English Mid.	91-92	perf.
Los Altos	Almond Elem.	88-89	perf.
Los Altos	Blach Int.	89-90	perf.
Los Altos	Blach Int.	91-92	sust
Los Altos	Bullis-Purisima	88-89	perf.
Los Altos	Egan Mid.	87-88	perf.
Los Altos	Egan Mid.	89-90	sust.
Los Altos	Loyola Elem.	88-89	perf.
Los Altos	Oak Ave. Elem.	88-89	perf.
Los Altos	Santa Rita Elem.	88-89	perf.
Los Altos	Springer Elem.	88-89	perf.
Los Gatos	Louise Van Meter	88-89	perf.
Los Gatos	Fisher J.H.	87-88	perf.
Los Gatos	Fisher J.H.	89-90	sust.
Los Gatos-Sar. H.S.	Los Gatos H.S.	85-86	N.A.
Los Gatos-Sar. H.S.	Los Gatos H.S.	89-90	perf.
Los Gatos-Sar. H.S.	Saratoga H.S.	85-86	N.A.
Los Gatos-Sar. H.S.	Saratoga H.S.	89-90	perf.
Los Gatos-Sar. H.S.	Saratoga H.S.	91-92	sust.
Milpitas	Joseph Weller	88-89	imp.
Moreland	Anderson Elem.	86-87	perf.
Moreland	Baker Elem.	86-87	both
Moreland	Castro Mid.	87-88	perf.
Moreland	Castro Mid.	89-90	sust.
Moreland	Country Lane	88-89	perf,
Moreland	Easterbrook Elem.	86-87	both
Moreland	Latimer Elem.	88-89	both
Moreland	Latimer Elem.	92-93	com. ap.
Moreland	Payne	92-93	com. ap.
Moreland	Rogers Mid.	87-88	perf.
Moreland	Rogers Mid.	89-90	sust.
Moreland	Rogers Mid.	91-92	perf.
Morgan Hill	Encinal Mid.	88-89	imp.
Morgan Hill	Walsh	92-93	com. ap.

DISTRICT	SCHOOL	YEAR	CLASS
Mountain View	Bubb Elem.	86-87	perf.
Mountain View	Graham Mid.	85-86	N.A.
Mountain View	Graham Mid.	89-90	perf.
Mountain View	Graham Mid.	91-92	sust.
Mountain View	Landels Elem.	86-87	perf.
Mt. View- Los Altos	Los Altos H.S.	85-86	N.A.
Mt. View-Los Altos	Mountain View H.S.	87-88	both
Oak Grove	Baldwin	88-89	imp.
Oak Grove	Bernal	89-90	perf.
Oak Grove	Davis Int.	89-90	perf.
Oak Grove	Hayes Elem.	86-87	perf.
Oak Grove	Parkview Elem.	88-89	both
Palo Alto Unified	Gunn H.S.	87-88	perf.
Palo Alto Unified	Gunn H.S.	89-90	perf.
Palo Alto Unified	Gunn H.S.	91-92	perf.
Palo Alto Unified	Palo Alto H.S.	85-86	N.A.
Palo Alto Unified	Palo Alto H.S.	89-90	perf.
Palo Alto Unified	Palo Alto H.S.	91-92	sus.
Palo Alto Unified	Stanford Mid.	87-88	perf.
Palo Alto Unified	Stanford Mid.	89-90	sus.
Palo Alto Unified	Stanford Mid.	91-92	perf.
Santa Clara Unified	Milliken	88-89	perf.
Santa Clara Unified	Santa Clara H.S.	87-88	perf.
Santa Clara Unified	Westwood Elem.	86-87	perf.
Santa Clara Unified	Westwood Elem.	92-93	com. ap.
Saratoga	Argonaut Elem.	86-87	perf.
Saratoga	Argonaut Elem.	92-93	com. ap.
Saratoga	Foothill	88-89	perf.
Saratoga	Redwood Mid.	89-90	perf.
Saratoga	Redwood Mid.	91-92	sus.
Saratoga	Saratoga Elem.	86-87	perf.
Saratoga	Saratoga Elem.	92-93	sus.
Sunnyvale	Bishop	88-89	imp
Sunnyvale	Cherry Chase	88-89	perf.
Sunnyvale	Columbia Com.	88-89	both
Sunnyvale	Cumberland Elem.	86-87	perf.
Sunnyvale	Hollenbeck Elem.	86-87	perf.
Sunnyvale	Sunnyvale Mid.	91-92	perf.
Union	Guadalupe Elem.	86-87	perf.
Union	Lietz Elem.	86-87	both
Union	Lone Hill Elem.	86-87	both
Whisman	Crittenden Mid.	89-90	imp
Whisman	Crittenden Mid.	91-92	both
Whisman	Monte Loma Elem.	86-87	perf.
Whisman	Theuerkauf Elem.	86-87	imp.

NATIONAL SCHOOL RECOGNITION PROGRAM

During the 1982-83 school year, the U.S. Department of Education established the Secondary School Recognition Program to identify private and public secondary schools that are exceptionally good at educating students. In the 1985-86 school year, the program was extended to include elementary schools and now alternates the awards between secondary and elementary schools each year.

The Chief School Officers of each state nominate public schools based on common criteria and guidelines developed by the U.S. Department of Education. The number of schools that may be nominated is equal to the size of the state's congressional delegation. The Council for American Private Education nominates private schools. A review panel screens the nominations and chooses the most promising schools for site visits. Site visitors observe the school and submit a report to the review panel which then makes recommendations to the U.S. Secretary of Education. Schools are evaluated on the basis of organization, leadership, curriculum, student achievement, character development, relations with the community, and efforts to maintain high quality programs. Secondary schools are also evaluated on student performance on standard achievement tests, a safe and drug free climate, success of students in post-secondary endeavors, number of disciplinary referrals, and dropout rates. The program looks for schools with an established record of sustained achievement and schools that have overcome obstacles and problems and are continuing to concentrate on improvement. Schools cannot receive the award in two consecutive cycles.

While winning a National Blue Ribbon award from the Department of Education is a great honor for a school, parents should realize that many excellent schools don't bother to apply. The application is 35 pages long and some districts feel that their energies and resources are better spent focusing on improving their students' education rather than getting recognition for what they do.

WINNERS OF NATIONAL SCHOOL RECOGNITION PROGRAM

SAN MATEO COUNTY SCHOOLS

DISTRICT	SCHOOL	YEAR
Hillsborough	Crocker Mid.	1983, 1989
San Mateo-Foster City	Borel Mid.	1984
Sequoia	Menlo Atherton H.S.	1987
Private school	Nueva Learning Center	1988
San Mateo Union High	San Mateo	1991
San Mateo-Foster-City	Bowditch Middle	1993
San Mateo Union High	Hillsdale H.S.	1993

SANTA CLARA COUNTY SCHOOLS

Evergreen	Levya Jr. High	1983
Cupertino	Garden Gate Elem.	1986
Cupertino	West Valley Elem.	1986
Cupertino	Miller Jr. High	1987
Fremont	Homestead H.S.	1987
Los Gatos-Saratoga	Los Gatos H.S.	1987, 1991
Palo Alto	Palo Alto H.S.	1987
Berryessa	Ruskin Elem.	1988
Cupertino	Collins Elem.	1988
Cupertino	Regnart Elem.	1988
Cupertino	Stevens Creek Elem.	1988
Evergreen	K.R. Smith Elem.	1988
Moreland	Anderson Elem.	1988
Campbell	Rolling Hills Mid.	1989
Cupertino	Hyde Jr. High	1989
Los Gatos	Fischer Jr. High	1989
Los Gatos-Saratoga	Saratoga H.S.	1989
Mountain View-Los Altos	Mountain View H.S.	1989
Evergreen	O.B. Whaley	1990
Los Gatos-Saratoga	Los Gatos	1991

DISTRICT	SCHOOL	YEAR
Private School	St. Francis	1991
Los Altos	Bullis-Purissima	1992
Los Altos	Santa Rita	1992
Private School	St. Simon	1992
San Jose	Graystone	1992
Saratoga	Foothill	1992
Campbell	Rolling Hills	1993
Cupertino	Kennedy Jr. High	1993
Moreland	Rogers Mid.	1993
Oak Grove	Davis Int.	1993

EXPLANATORY NOTES FOR CALIFORNIA ASSESSMENT PROGRAM SCORES

The following appendix contains public school CAP scores for 1989 and 1990 and eighth grade scores for 1992. The statewide rank (SR) is similar to a percentile rank and indicates how a school compares with every other school in the state. To allow for more equitable comparisons, the state has organized schools into comparison groups composed of schools serving students with similar backgrounds. These relative ranks (RR) compare a school's scores with those of schools most similar to it in such factors as socioeconomic level, student mobility, number of LEP (limited English proficiency) students, and percentage of families receiving public assistance. Parents wishing to determine how well a school is teaching basic skills should pay more attention to the Relative Ranking than the Statewide Rank.

Since schools tend to teach to the student norm, those which consistently score in the 90th percentiles are apt to have a more accelerated and demanding program than those with much lower scores. However, parents should not choose a school purely on the basis of high CAP scores. In many cases, high test scores tell more about the socioeconomic make-up of a school than the quality of teaching. Schools with high test scores do not necessarily have superior teachers and programs; furthermore, the CAP tests may not reflect how well schools teach higher thinking skills, encourage creativity, instill intellectual curiosity, or motivate students. Many schools with relatively low test scores have skilled teachers and challenging programs.

Parents should also realize that fluctuations in test scores do not necessarily mean a decline or improvement in the caliber of teaching. All schools experience years when they are blessed with especially gifted classes and years with students of more average abilities.

Having a child in a high-testing school district can be a mixed blessing. While these schools are apt to be filled with many gifted students and offer a challenging curriculum, children of average intelligence or those with learning disabilities often have difficulty keeping up with their peers and thus can suffer from poor academic self-esteem.

Because of the budget crisis of the early 1990's, CAP testing was suspended in 1991, and in 1992 the test was given only to eighth graders. When statewide testing resumed in the spring of 1993, the state had begun to implement a five year plan to alter the assessment system so that the tests would more accurately reflect the new state-wide curriculum frameworks. The CAP tests contained virtually all multiple-choice questions (with the exception of the writing sample given to 8th graders in 1992) and emphasized knowledge of facts. The new California Learning Assessment System (CLAS) tests assess analytical thinking, problem-solving, and the ability to work in groups—skills emphasized in the new curriculum. Supporters of the new assessment program argue that it will speed up reform in instruction and recognize a broader range of abilities; critics contend that performance-based testing— with its emphasis on open-ended questions, written, oral and artistic responses, collaborative work among students, and the inclusion of portfolios of student work— will prove to be prohibitively expensive to administer and score. Unlike the old multiple-choice tests, performance-based tests cannot be scored by computers. Consequently, there is concern that without right or wrong answers, scores assigned by individual raters will be subjective and therefore inconsistent.

At the time of publication of this book, the results of the 1993 CLAS scores were not yet available. Those wishing to receive the most recent test scores or the 1992 history and science CAP scores for eighth graders should phone (408) 453-6877 for Santa Clara County schools or (415) 802-5322 for San Mateo County schools.

SANTA CLARA COUNTY
CAP SCORES

School	Gr.	Yr.	Reading		Writing		Math	
			SR	RR	SR	RR	SR	RR

ALUM ROCK SCHOOL DISTRICT

School	Gr.	Yr.	SR	RR	SR	RR	SR	RR
Arbuckle	3	88-89	17	63	16	56	35	78
		89-90	5	24	4	21	14	52
Cassell	3	88-89	32	72	31	69	28	60
		89-90	25	53	32	64	31	66
Cureton	3	88-89	54	71	41	50	33	37
		89-90	23	19	41	49	47	64
Dorsa	3	88-89	19	49	27	61	24	51
		89-90	19	44	16	36	15	36
Fischer	6	88-89	13	na	13	na	14	na
		89-90	18	61	22	65	20	58
	8	89-90	21	59	23	58	36	86
		91-92	31	69	51	93	26	78
George	6	88-89	28	50	31	52	20	27
		89-90	31	47	37	53	29	42
	8	89-90	50	87	55	91	47	90
		91-92	30	48	50	84	28	72
Goss	3	88-89	39	75	42	77	21	41
		89-90	18	17	32	39	11	11
Hubbard	3	88-89	20	65	14	47	9	25
		89-90	14	47	24	66	22	64
LindaVista	3	88-89	55	40	70	62	50	35
		89-90	60	46	54	35	32	21
Lyndale	3	88-89	34	64	29	53	15	24
		89-90	26	48	30	52	13	24
	6	88-89	28	53	29	53	21	32
		89-90	11	27	18	39	23	51
Mathson	6	88-89	18	71	17	65	15	55
		89-90	11	49	13	48	12	48
	8	89-90	13	45	16	52	14	63
		91-92	21	51	15	40	20	67
Mayfair	3	88-89	7	26	13	42	21	53
		89-90	4	3	14	23	6	10

School	Gr.	Yr.	Reading		Writing		Math	
			SR	RR	SR	RR	SR	RR
McCollam	3	88-89	42	47	39	43	50	58
		89-90	47	62	36	47	28	41
	3	88-89	51	68	39	51	24	25
		89-90	46	53	46	54	41	55
Miller	3	88-89	39	83	42	84	61	91
		89-90	31	82	31	79	47	89
Ocala	6	88-89	33	56	42	68	36	55
		89-90	20	21	23	23	19	20
	8	89-90	24	36	16	20	21	54
		91-92	34	39	46	64	29	63
Painter	3	88-89	26	32	33	40	21	22
		89-90	29	56	45	76	22	46
Pala	6	88-89	16	41	33	68	19	39
		89-90	5	13	15	32	7	17
	8	89-90	8	10	6	6	10	29
		91-92	14	23	19	36	23	64
Rogers	3	88-89	18	26	24	32	17	20
		89-90	40	58	44	65	36	58
Ryan	3	88-89	26	57	39	72	34	60
		89-90	25	60	26	61	26	64
San Antonio	3	88-89	31	83	30	80	10	34
		89-90	19	48	16	38	9	20
	6	88-89	42	93	42	91	55	93
		89-90	30	80	57	93	65	96
Sheppard	6	88-89	39	64	34	55	29	40
		89-90	21	54	28	66	17	43
	8	89-90	19	30	16	19	31	70
		91-92	30	34	37	49	22	49
Shields	3	88-89	22	46	47	78	28	47
		89-90	19	22	18	16	27	43
Slonaker	3	88-89	48	60	66	82	50	62
		89-90	8	14	23	46	20	44

BERRYESSA UNION ELEMENTARY

School	Gr.	Yr.	Reading		Writing		Math	
Brooktree	3	88-89	44	19	44	17	40	18
		89-90	50	39	60	55	66	70
Cherrywood	3	88-89	62	48	76	69	66	57
		89-90	68	48	62	34	64	53

School	Gr.	Yr.	Reading		Writing		Math	
			SR	RR	SR	RR	SR	RR
Laneview	3	88-89	60	38	72	56	43	19
		89-90	73	57	72	55	47	32
	6	88-89	66	29	74	41	60	21
		89-90	90	78	83	63	85	71
Majestic Wy.	3	88-89	41	18	62	46	41	21
		89-90	62	20	67	27	60	31
Morrill Mid	6	88-89	53	34	41	16	60	43
		89-90	50	33	50	28	50	35
	8	89-90	61	61	61	46	55	67
		91-92	65	59	57	39	65	80
Noble	3	88-89	82	68	64	33	73	56
		89-90	65	22	63	19	74	46
Northwood	3	88-89	58	51	53	41	51	43
		89-90	77	58	70	44	57	40
Piedmont	6	88-89	66	45	71	55	74	51
		89-90	56	34	60	38	62	44
	8	89-90	73	61	83	71	76	74
		91-92	56	34	71	60	71	83
Ruskin	3	88-89	86	79	81	69	89	82
		89-90	82	65	87	74	81	70
Sierramont	6	88-89	75	71	70	67	70	60
		89-90	50	31	50	28	59	47
	8	89-90	74	78	58	34	59	68
		91-92	83	87	73	84	77	93
Summerdale	3	88-89	62	59	70	69	76	76
		89-90	34	20	35	19	27	21
Toyon	3	88-89	73	42	78	51	61	30
		89-90	91	72	91	71	75	47
Vinci Park	3	88-89	74	64	84	78	76	67
		89-90	43	9	55	19	42	17

CAMBRIAN ELEMENTARY

School	Gr.	Yr.	Reading		Writing		Math	
Bagby	3	88-89	78	45	87	61	65	30
		89-90	89	71	86	63	79	59
Fammatre	3	88-89	85	59	68	28	69	36
		89-90	88	74	87	72	85	76
Farnham	3	88-89	88	89	81	82	91	90
		89-90	85	79	80	69	92	89

School	Gr.	Yr.	Reading		Writing		Math	
			SR	RR	SR	RR	SR	RR
Ida Price	6	88-89	56	47	79	83	62	55
		89-90	63	48	90	89	69	57
	8	89-90	84	90	58	35	86	95
		91-92	61	54	61	52	65	81
Sartorette	3	88-89	80	87	67	74	66	72
		89-90	97	98	96	97	95	97

CAMPBELL UNION ELEMENTARY

School	Gr.	Yr.	Reading		Writing		Math	
Blackford	3	88-89	55	56	63	65	52	51
		89-90	46	49	72	84	52	68
Campbl. Md.	6	88-89	58	60	78	86	53	48
		89-90	45	61	50	67	44	59
	8	89-90	72	81	76	82	72	89
		91-92	61	53	49	26	58	73
Capri	3	88-89	64	50	78	71	74	67
		89-90	82	76	82	75	90	88
Castlemont	3	88-89	89	71	91	74	91	77
		89-90	76	37	75	35	77	51
Forest Hill	3	88-89	59	41	74	63	79	71
		89-90	65	46	72	55	69	61
Hazelwood	3	88-89	87	95	82	92	79	89
		89-90	82	89	74	84	82	90
Lynhaven	3	88-89	39	7	50	14	57	24
		89-90	39	37	49	54	34	40
MarshallLn	3	88-89	92	76	95	81	80	52
		89-90	59	16	71	29	63	31
Monroe	6	88-89	67	63	86	88	68	59
		89-90	64	76	74	83	57	66
	8	89-90	83	89	73	73	72	88
		91-92	51	41	65	65	57	76
Rolling Hls.	6	88-89	87	80	87	83	86	75
		89-90	75	51	84	68	81	63
	8	89-90	90	91	73	53	91	95
		91-92	89	83	91	86	92	93
Rosemary	3	88-89	67	89	74	93	79	92
		89-90	53	78	58	82	58	82

School	Gr.	Yr.	Reading		Writing		Math	
			SR	RR	SR	RR	SR	RR

CAMPBELL UNION HIGH SCHOOL DISTRICT

School	Gr.	Yr.	SR	RR	SR	RR	SR	RR
Blackford	12	88-89	50	23	46	25	66	76
		89-90	67	57	38	10	68	74
Branham	12	88-89	74	43	54	16	66	43
		89-90	70	40	50	7	50	16
Del Mar	12	88-89	42	14	31	12	58	67
		89-90	50	29	42	22	66	83
Leigh	12	88-89	90	62	80	35	83	57
		89-90	87	74	82	53	86	86
Prospect	12	88-89	89	61	86	54	92	83
		89-90	89	84	71	36	89	94
Westmont	12	88-89	95	92	94	88	90	84
		89-90	75	41	67	20	81	73

CUPERTINO UNION ELEMENTARY

School	Gr.	Yr.	SR	RR	SR	RR	SR	RR
Blue Hills	3	88-89	87	64	97	88	96	82
		89-90	98	92	99	94	98	94
	6	88-89	97	94	99	97	99	98
		89-90	97	90	94	84	99	97
Collins	3	88-89	99	97	99	98	99	97
		89-90	91	71	97	86	94	80
	6	88-89	98	97	99	99	99	98
		89-90	98	95	98	97	98	96
Cupertino	8	89-90	89	76	94	75	97	91
		91-92	94	87	97	95	97	96
Devargas	3	88-89	93	77	92	75	91	75
		89-90	95	88	88	70	95	88
	6	88-89	51	44	49	37	53	41
		89-90	82	85	82	82	73	71
Dilworth	3	88-89	96	85	91	73	98	94
		89-90	98	93	99	97	99	96
	6	88-89	96	87	95	85	99	98
		89-90	98	96	97	90	99	98
Eisenhower	3	88-89	82	54	87	61	78	48
		89-90	95	81	88	61	83	61
	6	88-89	88	66	93	82	92	74
		89-90	70	35	79	48	88	70

School	Gr.	Yr.	Reading		Writing		Math	
			SR	**RR**	**SR**	**RR**	**SR**	**RR**
Faria	3	88-89	98	96	98	94	96	84
		89-90	98	95	97	88	99	96
	6	88-89	98	96	98	97	99	97
		89-90	98	94	97	90	98	96
Gate	3	88-89	75	39	78	44	75	45
		89-90	83	52	85	55	91	77
	6	88-89	77	68	67	53	84	75
		89-90	88	65	92	78	84	60
Hyde Inter.	8	89-90	95	88	91	65	95	87
		91-92	93	76	93	74	94	82
Kennedy	8	89-90	98	93	97	90	98	95
		91-92	98	93	98	95	98	95
Lincoln	3	88-89	98	95	92	75	94	79
		89-90	93	76	83	51	87	69
	6	88-89	93	80	97	91	96	89
		89-90	92	78	93	79	97	89
McCauliffe	3	88-89	96	85	96	83	98	81
		89-90	95	79	95	80	93	79
	6	88-89	99	99	84	61	98	94
		89-90	99	98	98	92	98	94
Meyerholz	3	88-89	95	81	95	82	86	63
		89-90	94	77	90	67	93	79
	6	88-89	74	84	84	91	79	83
		89-90	96	98	94	96	95	96
Miller Int.	8	89-90	97	92	98	91	97	93
		91-92	97	91	97	87	98	95
Montclaire	3	88-89	96	84	96	83	88	66
		89-90	99	97	98	93	97	90
	6	88-89	95	85	98	94	99	96
		89-90	99	98	98	92	99	96
Muir	3	88-89	96	95	95	91	92	87
		89-90	99	96	97	86	95	83
	6	88-89	96	86	90	75	95	83
		89-90	91	73	95	85	95	86
Nimitz	3	88-89	75	44	61	22	85	63
		89-90	71	90	71	90	79	93
	6	88-89	50	40	76	80	76	72
		89-90	57	70	49	58	84	92
Older	3	88-89	95	93	98	97	96	92
		89-90	93	83	98	92	98	94
	6	88-89	93	94	95	97	80	76
		89-90	92	76	82	54	92	79

School	Gr.	Yr.	Reading		Writing		Math	
			SR	RR	SR	RR	SR	RR
Regnart	3	88-89	97	88	94	77	98	90
		89-90	93	76	97	88	98	91
	6	88-89	97	94	97	92	98	93
		89-90	96	88	98	96	99	97
Stevens Crk.	3	88-89	88	65	92	75	87	65
		89-90	94	78	96	84	96	85
	6	88-89	98	95	98	94	99	96
		89-90	99	97	98	93	98	94
Stocklmeir-	3	88-89	88	65	80	46	96	82
Ortega		89-90	97	89	96	83	98	95
	6	88-89	96	89	92	78	96	87
		89-90	77	45	90	73	91	75
West Valley	3	88-89	97	92	97	88	96	83
		89-90	97	88	94	77	98	92
	6	88-89	98	95	99	97	98	92
		89-90	95	84	94	82	98	92

EAST SIDE UNION HIGH SCHOOL DISTRICT

School	Gr.	Yr.	Reading		Writing		Math	
Hill, And.	12	88-89	31	77	25	65	28	79
		89-90	26	65	34	74	36	90
Independence	12	88-89	30	38	29	40	38	74
		89-90	33	39	29	29	43	84
Lick, James	12	88-89	35	32	45	47	38	55
		89-90	31	39	40	54	32	65
Mt. Pleasant	12	88-89	38	59	43	67	21	37
		89-90	40	54	33	46	27	60
Oak Grove	12	88-89	57	35	57	45	65	74
		89-90	60	52	46	29	54	66
Overfelt	12	88-89	16	51	15	48	18	64
		89-89	20	68	19	58	20	79
Piedmont Hls	12	88-89	42	5	47	21	40	14
		89-90	52	22	51	21	54	53
Santa Teresa	12	88-89	71	48	73	61	61	43
		89-90	65	35	56	17	50	18
Silver Creek	12	88-89	38	82	40	83	42	92
		89-90	23	36	27	47	41	89
Yerba Buena	12	88-89	14	48	16	51	24	82
		89-90	8	32	7	21	16	69

School	Gr.	Yr.	Reading		Writing		Math	
			SR	RR	SR	RR	SR	RR

EVERGREEN ELEMENTARY DISTRICT

School	Gr.	Yr.	Reading		Writing		Math	
			SR	RR	SR	RR	SR	RR
Cadwallader	3	88-89	57	45	75	70	87	84
		89-90	41	32	40	28	49	54
	6	88-89	70	80	77	86	60	63
		89-90	38	33	78	85	72	79
Cedar Grove	3	88-89	83	76	85	76	89	82
		89-90	59	38	70	54	72	66
	6	88-89	77	83	70	74	82	82
		89-90	56	42	84	83	74	71
Chaboya	8	91-92	70	66	65	57	59	74
Dove Hill	3	88-89	37	64	59	85	45	66
		89-90	39	49	65	81	41	58
	6	88-89	70	88	67	89	58	75
		89-90	35	64	59	88	48	79
Evergreen	3	88-89	72	42	81	59	52	20
		89-90	94	85	81	52	89	78
	6	88-89	93	84	93	85	92	80
		89-90	80	79	83	81	78	76
Holly Oak	3	88-89	78	90	89	95	92	95
		89-90	29	44	32	47	41	65
	6	88-89	82	97	86	98	86	97
		89-90	66	89	91	98	68	89
Laurelwood	3	88-89	84	81	85	81	86	81
		89-90	83	70	90	81	68	54
	6	88-89	96	99	89	94	82	85
		89-90	57	35	70	52	64	46
Leyva Inter.	6	88-89	56	80	43	67	35	50
		89-90	30	42	42	61	40	59
	8	89-90	39	62	39	56	59	90
		91-92	63	82	69	91	65	94
Millbrook	3	88-89	87	85	81	76	68	58
		89-90	65	69	81	86	80	87
	6	88-89	79	89	85	91	79	83
		89-90	76	80	89	91	74	74
Montgomery	3	88-89	63	86	72	91	71	89
		89-90	49	65	58	75	50	73
	6	88-89	72	91	75	94	72	89
		89-90	38	64	54	80	40	66
Norwood Crk	3	88-89	93	91	93	89	90	85
		89-90	93	77	95	80	85	64

School	Gr.	Yr.	Reading		Writing		Math	
			SR	**RR**	**SR**	**RR**	**SR**	**RR**
Quimby Oak	6	88-89	89	84	91	90	89	82
		89-90	83	67	93	89	88	81
	8	89-90	72	76	74	72	65	76
		91-92	58	63	58	73	66	89
Smith	3	88-89	42	67	48	73	52	74
		89-90	49	82	40	75	45	80
	6	88-89	37	81	46	84	66	93
		89-90	40	86	83	98	73	97
Whaley	3	88-89	58	93	58	92	83	97
		89-90	68	95	64	94	69	93

FRANKLIN-MCKINLEY ELEMENTARY DISTRICT

School	Gr.	Yr.	Reading		Writing		Math	
Fair Jr. High	6	88-89	5	42	11	51	23	70
		89-90	15	53	15	50	19	57
	8	89-90	24	67	32	78	32	85
		91-92	25	58	44	86	31	82
Franklin	3	88-89	15	62	18	64	17	52
		89-90	10	46	18	62	24	75
	6	88-89	16	69	15	62	8	40
		89-90	26	83	48	93	23	73
Hellyer	3	88-89	24	32	38	53	34	44
		89-90	24	20	35	39	29	39
Hillsdale	3	88-89	34	57	45	69	30	44
		89-90	17	19	23	27	16	24
	6	88-89	31	59	32	58	12	15
		89-90	20	16	24	22	25	26
Kennedy	3	88-89	13	46	13	42	23	58
		89-90	14	54	19	65	18	63
	6	88-89	23	75	29	79	35	80
		89-90	28	85	42	90	43	91
Los Arboles	3	88-89	17	47	18	45	15	30
		89-90	10	27	18	44	16	41
McKinley	3	88-89	6	36	6	33	7	22
		89-90	15	58	13	50	24	75
Santee	3	88-89	6	35	13	52	27	73
		89-90	1	9	3	17	6	26
Seven Trees	3	88-89	15	28	28	49	31	50
		89-90	23	54	25	57	11	24
	6	88-89	11	19	21	37	14	21
		89-90	8	27	14	36	15	40

School	Gr.	Yr.	Reading		Writing		Math	
			SR	RR	SR	RR	SR	RR
Stonegate	3	88-89	50	58	35	35	44	49
		89-90	39	40	33	31	41	54
	6	88-89	41	50	36	41	41	44
		89-90	40	43	44	48	35	36
Sylvandale	6	88-89	32	65	38	71	49	78
		89-90	21	38	29	52	38	68
	8	89-90	49	90	35	81	50	94
		91-92	26	46	42	80	39	85
Windmill Sp	3	88-89	30	28	29	25	44	48
		89-90	17	9	21	13	30	37
	6	88-89	35	62	33	56	43	66
		89-90	36	60	35	53	25	38

FREMONT UNION HIGH SCHOOL DISTRICT

School	Gr.	Yr.	Reading		Writing		Math	
Cupertino	12	88-89	95	93	82	69	95	99
		89-90	97	97	79	33	96	99
Fremont	12	88-89	62	36	58	41	82	94
		89-90	72	71	62	42	83	98
Homestead	12	88-89	95	79	90	63	97	97
		89-90	95	88	87	50	97	97
Lynbrook	12	88-89	97	94	97	90	97	97
		89-90	92	70	87	50	96	96
Monta Vista	12	88-89	97	95	97	92	98	99
		89-90	95	88	84	42	98	99

GILROY UNIFIED SCHOOL DISTRICT

School	Gr.	Yr.	Reading		Writing		Math	
Brownell	3	88-89	84	82	86	84	81	74
		89-90	90	86	87	77	68	55
	6	88-89	84	84	82	80	83	79
		89-90	77	72	69	54	81	76
El Roble	3	88-89	61	77	51	66	51	64
		89-90	60	77	51	67	54	74
	6	89-90	59	83	42	66	47	70
Eliot	3	88-89	50	25	64	44	36	14
		89-90	65	52	57	37	38	26
	6	88-89	62	42	47	20	24	4
		89-90	52	16	26	1	18	1
Gilroy High	12	88-89	34	16	38	22	30	21
		89-90	55	48	62	62	42	48

School	Gr.	Yr.	Reading		Writing		Math	
			SR	RR	SR	RR	SR	RR
Glen View	3	88-89	60	67	72	82	65	71
		89-90	56	66	61	72	41	52
	6	88-89	69	85	78	91	55	64
		89-90	81	87	79	84	66	64
Jordan	3	88-89	50	86	34	69	39	68
		89-90	41	51	37	44	30	42
	6	88-89	20	38	25	42	22	33
		89-90	47	80	40	72	23	45
Las Animas	3	88-89	42	45	35	33	41	43
		89-90	30	34	25	23	26	36
	6	88-89	28	47	26	39	18	22
		89-90	44	63	37	50	46	65
Rod Kelley	3	88-89	40	56	50	69	49	64
		89-90	70	61	50	32	69	68
	6	88-89	80	89	93	97	88	92
		89-90	70	82	44	40	69	76
Rucker	3	88-89	93	98	89	96	72	86
		89-90	83	87	83	88	60	67
	6	88-89	58	58	58	57	58	55
		89-90	64	61	54	38	43	30
San Ysidro	3	88-89	57	69	64	77	46	50
		89-90	52	51	39	27	46	50
	6	88-89	71	90	64	88	70	87
		89-90	61	85	60	85	61	83
South Valley	8	89-90	55	67	62	72	39	54
		91-92	70	75	50	55	44	67

LAKESIDE JOINT ELEMENTARY SCHOOL DISTRICT

School	Gr.	Yr.	Reading		Writing		Math	
Lakeside	3	88-89	97	91	92	74	91	73
		89-90	99	98	97	86	98	95
	6	88-89	97	94	98	96	97	89
		89-90	95	85	92	78	97	92

LOMA PRIETA JOINT UNION SCHOOL DISTRICT

School	Gr.	Yr.	Reading		Writing		Math	
English Mid.	6	88-89	91	90	93	94	94	93
		89-90	93	79	83	56	91	76
	8	89-90	98	95	92	67	94	86
		91-92	96	86	98	94	96	88

School	Gr.	Yr.	Reading		Writing		Math	
			SR	RR	SR	RR	SR	RR
Loma Prieta	3	88-89	84	58	74	36	79	49
		89-90	93	76	75	35	80	56

LOS ALTOS ELEMENTARY SCHOOL DISTRICT

School	Gr.	Yr.	SR	RR	SR	RR	SR	RR
Almond	3	88-89	96	85	98	93	97	87
		89-90	99	96	97	88	97	91
	6	88-89	98	96	98	96	98	96
		89-90	98	97	98	94	97	91
Blach	8	89-90	98	95	98	94	98	96
		91-92	98	93	96	85	98	94
Bullis-Puris	3	88-89	99	97	99	95	98	92
		89-90	98	92	98	94	99	98
	6	88-89	98	97	99	99	99	98
		89-90	99	98	99	99	99	99
Egan	8	89-90	98	96	98	91	98	96
		91-92	98	91	92	70	97	92
Loyola	3	88-89	98	95	98	90	97	89
		89-90	97	88	97	86	97	88
	6	88-89	99	98	99	97	99	98
		89-90	96	88	99	99	99	98
Oak	3	88-89	98	94	98	90	94	78
		89-90	98	94	97	85	99	97
	6	88-89	99	98	99	99	99	99
		89-90	98	94	96	88	99	96
Santa Rita	3	88-89	78	46	94	79	90	72
		89-90	99	97	99	94	98	95
	6	88-89	94	82	98	94	98	95
		89-90	98	94	99	98	99	96
Springer	3	88-89	99	97	98	90	97	90
		89-90	98	91	98	94	97	89
	6	88-89	99	98	99	98	98	95
		89-90	92	76	96	86	97	91

LOS GATOS UNION ELEMENTARY DISTRICT

School	Gr.	Yr.	SR	RR	SR	RR	SR	RR
Blossom Hill	3	88-89	94	79	98	90	95	81
		89-90	96	82	91	71	94	81
Daves Ave	3	88-89	88	66	87	62	91	75
		89-90	90	68	88	62	70	41

School	Gr.	Yr.	Reading		Writing		Math	
			SR	RR	SR	RR	SR	RR
Lexington	3	88-89	97	91	97	91	73	45
		89-90	96	84	98	94	95	83
Louise	3	88-89	96	85	93	75	94	80
Van Meter		89-90	90	68	95	79	69	40
Raymond	6	89-90	94	82	91	77	93	82
Fisher	8	89-90	94	87	87	52	96	90
		91-92	95	80	93	74	96	88

LOS GATOS-SARATOGA UNION HIGH SCHOOL DISTRICT

School	Gr.	Yr.	Reading		Writing		Math	
Los Gatos	12	88-89	97	93	96	87	96	94
		89-90	98	96	98	95	96	96
Saratoga	12	88-89	98	96	99	98	98	99
		89-90	99	97	99	98	98	99

LUTHER BURBANK ELEMENTARY SCHOOL DISTRICT

School	Gr.	Yr.	Reading		Writing		Math	
Lthr Burbank	3	88-89	21	24	18	16	15	13
		89-90	6	2	12	3	12	10
	6	88-89	25	71	25	68	13	38
		89-90	39	71	17	30	21	38
	8	89-90	28	53	4	4	45	87
		91-92	37	73	10	23	15	56

MILPITAS UNIFIED SCHOOL DISTRICT

School	Gr.	Yr.	Reading		Writing		Math	
Burnett	3	88-89	72	51	62	33	60	36
		89-90	67	58	40	17	43	34
	6	88-89	64	64	58	55	77	76
		89-90	49	45	40	29	56	58
Curtner	3	88-89	87	70	62	26	62	31
		89-90	92	82	76	43	71	51
	6	88-89	68	75	57	58	67	68
		89-90	84	90	70	69	85	88
Milpitas High	12	88-89	61	53	50	43	70	91
		89-90	58	36	52	23	60	66
Pomeroy	3	88-89	97	88	74	36	52	16
		89-90	80	45	68	26	75	47
	6	88-89	89	69	87	70	85	59
		89-90	93	93	89	89	82	79

School	Gr.	Yr.	Reading		Writing		Math	
			SR	RR	SR	RR	SR	RR
Rancho	8	89-90	57	69	61	74	58	82
		91-92	50	31	65	54	50	54
Randall	3	88-89	54	65	60	72	63	75
		89-90	75	80	73	80	71	80
	6	88-89	58	67	52	61	55	59
		89-90	69	86	31	32	50	66
Rose	3	88-89	36	20	43	28	41	30
		89-90	69	70	58	54	70	77
	6	88-89	50	48	39	28	34	21
		89-90	60	91	29	60	25	51
Russell	8	89-90	68	70	77	80	78	90
		91-92	69	47	80	70	63	58
Sinnott	3	88-89	90	72	76	39	53	16
		89-90	58	20	43	8	52	24
	6	88-89	92	85	85	75	81	61
		89-90	80	56	81	58	85	69
Spangler	3	88-89	54	54	55	50	37	26
		89-90	69	60	78	71	72	70
	6	88-89	83	74	88	83	88	79
		89-90	48	38	42	26	10	2
Weller	3	88-89	59	46	50	28	37	18
		89-90	60	54	37	19	36	32
	6	88-89	60	63	59	62	58	57
		89-90	92	94	82	83	91	94
Zanker	3	88-89	56	23	45	11	22	3
		89-90	67	46	77	61	81	75
	6	88-89	74	85	48	51	74	77
		89-90	85	88	78	79	90	93

MONTEBELLO ELEMENTARY SCHOOL DISTRICT

School	Gr.	Yr.	Reading		Writing		Math	
Montebello	3	88-89	70	60	59	38	88	83
		89-90	96	94	91	86	81	76
	6	88-89	68	58	61	50	53	32
		89-90	93	81	13	1	93	81

MORELAND ELEMENTARY SCHOOL DISTRICT

School	Gr.	Yr.	Reading		Writing		Math	
Anderson	3	88-89	82	62	79	54	88	74
		89-90	67	86	68	86	91	96

School	Gr.	Yr.	Reading		Writing		Math	
			SR	RR	SR	RR	SR	RR
Baker	3	88-89	93	88	94	86	89	80
		89-90	85	57	95	80	95	82
Castro Mid.	6	88-89	95	94	96	96	93	90
		89-90	94	89	82	65	86	78
	8	89-90	82	88	75	76	69	84
		91-92	72	45	66	31	75	74
Country Lane	3	88-89	97	92	98	90	98	95
		89-90	99	96	99	94	99	97
Easterbrook	3	88-89	75	57	81	66	73	57
		89-90	88	75	74	45	78	65
Latimer	3	88-89	98	98	98	97	98	98
		89-90	95	94	95	90	95	92
Payne	3	88-89	71	34	78	43	72	40
		89-90	74	56	77	61	64	54
Rogers	6	88-89	83	86	84	84	84	83
		89-90	81	83	72	68	76	75
	8	89-90	84	91	71	79	92	98
		91-92	91	93	84	93	89	98

MORGAN HILL UNIFIED SCHOOL DISTRICT

School	Gr.	Yr.	Reading		Writing		Math	
Britton	8	89-90	70	47	74	43	77	37
		91-92	89	89	90	92	81	90
Burnett	3	88-89	52	65	44	50	45	52
		89-90	62	63	60	58	62	68
	6	88-89	89	96	79	87	86	89
		89-90	48	43	36	21	28	17
Encinal	6	88-89	81	67	78	64	80	62
		89-90	77	73	87	86	92	92
Gwinn	6	88-89	64	61	59	54	42	27
		89-90	50	59	79	89	39	42
Jackson	3	88-89	84	58	77	41	84	58
		89-90	70	28	59	16	81	58
	6	88-89	91	84	82	69	86	72
		89-90	86	65	82	56	86	69
Live Oak	12	88-89	65	30	67	34	65	40
		89-90	81	49	67	17	80	65
Los Paseos	3	88-89	71	34	59	17	73	42
		89-90	80	45	80	43	82	58

School	Gr.	Yr.	Reading		Writing		Math	
			SR	RR	SR	RR	SR	RR
Murphy	8	89-90	80	82	88	89	84	90
		91-92	72	63	85	86	75	85
Nordstrom	3	88-89	65	64	76	77	72	72
		89-90	60	57	45	33	43	41
	6	88-89	64	63	58	53	46	33
		89-90	84	87	68	60	78	77
Paradise	3	88-89	73	35	84	54	66	31
		89-90	80	46	73	33	44	13
	6	88-89	82	68	81	67	79	58
		89-90	79	58	71	42	62	32
San Martin	3	88-89	55	57	53	50	51	51
		89-90	66	76	57	65	58	74
Walsh	3	88-89	63	51	54	34	38	20
		89-90	40	27	37	21	36	34
	6	88-89	64	66	69	72	60	56
		89-90	69	78	64	65	57	61

MOUNTAIN VIEW ELEMENTARY SCHOOL DISTRICT

Bubb	3	88-89	93	76	96	85	88	66
		89-90	95	81	98	91	98	92
Castro	3	88-89	59	87	48	77	62	83
		89-90	32	57	46	73	69	89
Graham	6	88-89	86	91	84	88	76	74
		89-90	88	92	91	94	78	79
	8	89-90	81	89	91	96	74	92
		91-92	69	63	92	96	79	91
Landels	3	88-89	92	75	96	83	87	65
		89-90	90	68	94	76	97	89
Slater	3	88-89	80	78	74	68	75	71
		89-90	40	41	54	63	29	33

MOUNTAIN VIEW-LOS ALTOS UNION HIGH SCHOOL DISTRICT

Los Altos	12	88-89	87	51	88	57	95	92
		89-90	86	57	77	28	83	78
Mnt.View	12	88-89	84	42	91	66	95	92
		89-90	88	56	82	36	93	86

School	Gr.	Yr.	Reading		Writing		Math	
			SR	**RR**	**SR**	**RR**	**SR**	**RR**

MT. PLEASANT ELEMENTARY SCHOOL DISTRICT

School	Gr.	Yr.	SR	RR	SR	RR	SR	RR
Boeger Mid	8	89-90	35	67	28	47	38	84
		91-92	51	80	26	36	41	84
Marten	3	88-89	32	62	28	54	21	38
		89-90	50	79	38	66	29	56
Marten	6	88-89	33	86	43	89	36	82
		89-90	33	72	29	64	34	71
Mt. Pleasant	3	88-89	39	68	32	55	32	51
		89-90	56	86	49	80	49	80
	6	88-89	60	82	51	73	52	69
		89-90	26	56	44	76	22	43
Sanders Trad	3	88-89	86	91	84	88	73	78
		89-90	69	40	79	56	90	83
	6	88-89	59	76	66	86	39	46
		89-90	75	86	65	71	54	60
Valle Vista	3	88-89	59	74	72	88	50	61
		89-90	60	24	72	41	40	15
	6	88-89	58	59	29	16	46	37
		89-90	91	94	75	76	77	78

OAK GROVE ELEMENTARY SCHOOL DISTRICT

School	Gr.	Yr.	SR	RR	SR	RR	SR	RR
Anderson	3	88-89	75	88	91	96	69	82
		89-90	76	67	79	70	60	54
	6	88-89	92	97	91	96	81	85
		89-90	54	47	53	39	56	51
Baldwin	3	88-89	67	62	86	86	73	70
		89-90	84	64	82	57	96	90
	6	88-89	80	91	87	94	87	92
		89-90	84	93	89	94	89	95
Bernal Int.	8	89-90	76	71	63	31	83	87
		91-92	80	77	86	88	80	90
Blossom Vly.	3	88-89	83	82	79	74	74	69
		89-90	84	67	82	60	75	59
	6	88-89	91	86	75	62	97	96
		89-90	67	52	83	75	94	93
Christopher	3	88-89	37	28	26	13	21	12
		89-90	31	18	27	12	13	7
	6	88-89	59	78	72	91	45	55
		89-90	33	36	72	86	33	36

School	Gr.	Yr.	Reading		Writing		Math	
			SR	**RR**	**SR**	**RR**	**SR**	**RR**
Davis	8	89-90	71	84	75	89	58	82
		91-92	68	72	75	88	71	90
Del Roble	3	88-89	57	51	79	80	58	53
		89-90	75	64	63	42	46	34
	6	88-89	66	86	57	79	62	79
		89-90	52	75	55	75	26	34
Edenvale	3	88-89	49	87	41	81	57	86
		89-90	57	82	51	76	54	79
	6	88-89	26	78	50	92	32	77
		89-90	34	80	58	93	30	74
Frost	3	88-89	91	94	86	88	64	64
		89-90	75	70	86	85	65	65
	6	88-89	62	73	73	85	76	82
		89-90	72	85	89	94	85	90
Glider	3	88-89	85	86	86	86	74	73
		89-90	71	63	75	67	86	84
	6	88-89	74	81	66	72	68	69
		89-90	80	88	91	94	75	80
Hayes	3	88-89	81	93	85	93	78	88
		89-90	84	87	82	84	73	78
	6	88-89	78	77	82	82	69	58
		89-90	86	91	68	64	83	85
Herman Int.	8	89-90	81	85	55	26	78	85
		91-92	83	86	61	62	68	88
Miner	3	88-89	58	57	66	66	49	41
		89-90	41	23	49	33	42	35
	6	88-89	77	89	76	88	74	80
		89-90	55	75	69	87	62	80
Oak Ridge	3	88-89	87	85	82	79	72	65
		89-90	73	58	62	38	72	65
	6	88-89	76	77	78	82	64	55
		89-90	59	75	62	79	70	86
Parkview	3	88-89	71	52	90	85	81	69
		89-90	53	33	77	69	41	29
	6	88-89	95	97	92	96	81	80
		89-90	90	95	84	88	73	76
Sakamoto	3	88-89	79	61	82	64	69	47
		89-90	91	74	92	75	87	72
	6	88-89	88	90	90	93	80	77
		89-90	45	32	76	78	44	33

School	Gr.	Yr.	Reading		Writing		Math	
			SR	RR	SR	RR	SR	RR
San Anselmo	3	88-89	83	87	82	86	75	78
		89-90	50	39	62	57	33	28
	6	88-89	82	88	91	94	90	91
		89-90	81	94	83	93	83	93
Santa Teresa	3	88-89	87	90	75	79	83	85
		89-90	52	32	69	56	64	59
	6	88-89	82	91	82	88	79	82
		89-90	81	89	91	94	78	82
Stipe	3	88-89	34	68	39	74	24	45
		89-90	53	73	52	72	24	39
	6	88-89	70	93	84	97	60	85
		89-90	36	68	70	93	37	69
Taylor	3	88-89	68	35	76	46	82	61
		89-90	84	75	85	76	62	51
	6	88-89	95	84	95	85	91	72
		89-90	78	60	87	78	74	51

ORCHARD ELEMENTARY SCHOOOL DISTRICT

School	Gr.	Yr.	Reading		Writing		Math	
Orchard	3	88-89	22	8	27	10	34	21
		89-90	76	37	64	21	61	29
	6	88-89	33	47	53	74	53	70
		89-90	45	9	42	6	27	3
	8	89-90	71	82	72	85	70	89
		91-92	91	90	37	5	56	60

PALO ALTO UNIFIED SCHOOL DISTRICT

School	Gr.	Yr.	Reading		Writing		Math	
Addison	3	88-89	91	73	85	57	69	36
		89-90	94	77	80	43	87	69
	6	88-89	97	93	96	89	91	71
		89-90	90	71	93	81	88	69
Briones	3	88-89	73	39	50	12	48	13
		89-90	48	15	33	5	42	21
	6	88-89	69	58	81	79	92	91
		89-90	64	71	75	79	75	80
Duveneck	3	88-89	97	91	94	79	97	85
		89-90	97	88	94	78	99	96
	6	88-89	99	98	99	98	99	97
		89-90	99	98	98	94	99	98
El Carmelo	3	88-89	95	83	95	82	97	85
		89-90	84	54	89	64	90	76

School	Gr.	Yr.	Reading		Writing		Math	
			SR	RR	SR	RR	SR	RR
	6	88-89	99	99	91	94	91	92
		89-90	98	97	99	98	95	93
Escondido	3	88-89	98	96	96	83	99	95
		89-90	96	82	91	70	87	69
	6	88-89	86	82	86	83	97	96
		89-90	97	91	95	85	98	95
Fairmeadow	3	88-89	83	55	77	41	86	64
		89-90	81	48	92	73	98	92
	6	88-89	98	95	97	89	98	91
		89-90	94	83	92	78	94	84
Gunn	12	88-89	97	94	97	92	98	99
		89-90	98	96	97	89	98	99
Hays	3	88-89	97	92	95	82	99	95
		89-90	89	66	96	83	84	63
	6	88-89	96	87	92	78	98	94
		89-90	98	95	98	96	98	96
Hoover	3	88-89	98	96	99	95	99	96
		89-90	99	99	99	99	99	99
	6	88-89	99	99	99	99	99	99
		89-90	99	96	99	96	98	95
Jordan	8	91-92	99	95	99	97	99	98
Nixon	3	88-89	97	91	99	96	98	91
		89-90	98	91	96	84	99	96
	6	88-89	98	97	96	89	98	93
		89-90	98	96	99	98	98	93
Ohlone	3	88-89	85	59	59	17	78	48
		89-90	89	66	78	39	87	69
	6	88-89	98	97	97	91	98	93
		89-90	98	95	98	95	98	94
Palo Alto High	12	88-89	98	96	96	85	98	99
		89-90	98	96	96	87	98	99
Palo Verde	3	88-89	92	75	90	68	79	51
		89-90	97	85	93	74	95	82
	6	88-89	97	94	94	85	98	93
		89-90	91	74	92	78	97	90
Stanford Md.	8	89-90	98	94	99	96	99	98
		91-92	98	91	96	85	99	98

School	Gr.	Yr.	Reading		Writing		Math	
			SR	**RR**	**SR**	**RR**	**SR**	**RR**

SAN JOSE UNIFIED SCHOOL DISTRICT

School	Gr.	Yr.	SR	RR	SR	RR	SR	RR
Allen	3	88-89	40	46	33	31	22	19
		89-90	49	57	46	54	29	36
Almaden	3	88-89	35	69	42	76	46	74
		89-90	19	54	27	67	29	73
Bachrodt	3	88-89	50	48	68	75	58	60
		89-90	39	53	47	64	64	84
Booksin	3	88-89	62	54	72	68	50	37
		89-90	77	50	74	43	71	53
Burnett Mid.	6	88-89	18	52	25	61	14	34
		89-90	23	45	35	62	15	26
	8	89-90	23	43	37	67	31	77
		91-92	43	71	57	90	19	52
Carson	3	88-89	89	94	91	94	86	89
		89-90	63	79	66	82	69	87
Castillero	6	88-89	59	28	61	35	65	34
		89-90	63	51	61	45	62	50
	8	89-90	42	18	81	77	65	72
		91-92	70	54	66	42	75	84
Darling	3	88-89	13	25	16	26	15	23
		89-90	24	46	26	46	16	30
Empire Grdns	3	88-89	31	57	31	54	20	30
		89-90	19	14	30	30	26	35
Erickson	3	89-90	84	93	66	79	69	84
Gardner	3	88-89	36	50	33	44	35	45
		89-90	32	34	41	48	48	64
Grant	3	88-89	9	22	12	27	10	18
		89-90	16	10	23	17	11	8
Graystone	3	88-89	95	82	84	55	87	65
		89-90	98	91	92	73	93	79
Gunderson	12	88-89	65	27	74	43	70	45
		89-90	56	25	63	36	72	84
Hacienda Snc	3	88-89	48	10	69	29	59	22
		89-90	39	7	46	12	43	19
Harte Mid	6	88-89	92	78	93	82	95	82
		89-90	85	61	88	69	88	69
	8	89-90	96	89	94	75	98	96
		91-92	94	78	91	68	94	82

School	Gr.	Yr.	Reading		Writing		Math	
			SR	RR	SR	RR	SR	RR
Hester	3	88-89	25	41	33	50	29	41
		89-90	29	44	23	30	22	36
Hoover Mid	6	88-89	37	44	52	64	36	37
		89-90	42	36	50	44	29	19
	8	89-90	42	54	53	71	43	68
		91-92	43	33	50	51	47	64
Horace Mann	3	88-89	15	19	12	9	21	26
		89-90	67	86	42	60	53	76
Leland	12	88-89	97	94	83	45	96	93
		89-90	96	93	91	63	96	96
Lincoln	12	88-89	61	84	83	98	54	90
		89-90	59	73	77	95	54	85
Los Alamitos	3	88-89	93	77	91	71	74	43
		89-90	71	29	79	42	69	40
Lowell	3	88-89	30	72	16	44	39	73
		89-90	19	58	16	50	25	70
Muir Middle	6	88-89	39	56	44	64	44	58
		89-90	41	62	54	76	44	65
	8	89-90	65	78	88	97	61	84
		91-92	49	41	32	16	51	70
Olinder	3	88-89	31	52	41	65	46	65
		89-90	37	70	41	74	24	53
Pioneer	12	88-89	78	53	61	26	83	84
		89-90	82	88	81	82	87	99
Randol	3	88-89	55	38	72	63	59	46
		89-90	65	39	69	44	55	38
Reed	3	88-89	50	33	65	54	57	44
		89-90	88	83	88	84	86	84
San Jose Ac.	12	88-89	7	28	24	73	8	37
		89-90	15	52	14	43	38	95
Schallenbrgr	3	88-89	52	58	49	49	38	32
		89-90	23	15	31	25	17	16
Simonds	3	88-89	90	72	94	78	69	36
		89-90	89	66	89	64	73	45
Steinbeck	6	88-89	48	57	50	59	49	53
		89-90	45	41	51	46	42	37
	8	89-90	61	64	69	70	59	77
		91-92	53	44	52	46	59	78
Terrell	3	88-89	62	59	75	76	59	55
		89-90	51	38	70	66	43	37

School	Gr.	Yr.	Reading		Writing		Math	
			SR	**RR**	**SR**	**RR**	**SR**	**RR**
Trace	3	88-89	33	24	41	34	20	12
		89-90	42	61	41	60	29	48
Washington	3	88-89	20	47	18	40	8	14
		89-90	11	17	7	7	15	27
Willow Glen	3	88-89	62	62	66	66	62	62
Elem.		89-90	50	39	53	45	41	38
Willow Glen	6	88-89	30	28	34	34	35	31
South Ed.		89-90	25	15	24	12	16	7
	8	89-90	20	10	16	8	33	40
		91-92	27	25	8	5	34	67
Willow Glen	12	88-89	76	61	47	16	76	81
		91-92	42	6	35	7	57	55

SANTA CLARA UNIFIED

School	Gr.	Yr.	Reading		Writing		Math	
Bowers	3	88-89	55	59	72	79	71	77
		89-90	34	22	42	34	40	41
Bracher	3	88-89	25	26	31	33	50	61
		89-90	36	32	50	54	23	24
Briarwood	3	88-89	43	25	47	29	48	33
		89-90	50	51	56	59	78	87
Buchser Mid.	6	88-89	70	72	76	82	75	71
		89-90	74	78	83	86	73	73
	8	89-90	70	79	69	66	64	81
		91-92	80	81	76	81	65	81
Haman	3	88-89	56	61	58	63	55	59
		89-90	56	54	79	82	39	38
Hughes	3	88-89	60	72	81	91	93	95
		89-90	66	67	71	73	89	92
Laurelwood	3	88-89	79	83	81	84	91	92
		89-90	74	55	80	66	73	63
Mayne	3	88-89	14	21	14	16	24	34
		89-90	12	5	19	11	13	11
Milliken	3	88-89	93	76	98	94	96	83
		89-90	99	97	98	92	96	85
Montague	3	88-89	33	14	60	50	54	44
		89-90	28	4	64	36	45	25
Peterson	6	88-89	48	52	50	55	58	62
		89-90	52	54	65	70	60	66

School	Gr.	Yr.	Reading		Writing		Math	
			SR	RR	SR	RR	SR	RR
	8	89-90	49	50	56	56	72	91
		91-92	52	50	57	62	61	80
Pomeroy	3	88-89	42	24	66	58	50	36
		89-90	66	64	49	36	62	65
Ponderosa	3	88-89	77	52	79	53	81	62
		89-90	89	81	82	65	84	77
Santa Clara	12	88-89	50	55	57	66	60	90
		89-90	44	37	76	92	54	78
Scott Lane	3	88-89	54	67	59	73	52	63
		89-90	50	59	70	83	51	68
Sutter	3	88-89	88	76	88	73	95	88
		89-90	90	89	96	94	94	91
Westwood	3	88-89	78	46	80	46	87	65
		89-90	65	21	60	17	69	40
Wilcox High	12	88-89	50	48	53	51	71	94
		89-90	41	27	54	53	52	78

SARATOGA UNION ELEMENTARY SCHOOL DISTRICT

School	Gr.	Yr.	Reading		Writing		Math	
Argonaut	3	88-89	98	96	98	91	98	91
		89-90	98	91	96	84	97	89
	6	88-89	98	94	98	93	98	92
		89-90	98	95	97	90	98	94
Foothill	3	88-89	99	98	98	94	99	96
		89-90	99	96	94	76	96	86
	6	88-89	98	95	97	91	98	96
		89-90	98	95	98	92	99	97
Redwood Int.	8	89-90	98	94	96	84	97	91
		91-92	99	96	99	96	99	97
Saratoga	3	88-89	95	82	90	68	92	76
		89-90	98	94	97	89	98	91
	6	88-89	98	94	98	94	99	98
		89-90	95	85	98	92	99	96

SUNNYVALE ELEMENTARY SCHOOL DISTRICT

School	Gr.	Yr.	Reading		Writing		Math	
Bishop	3	88-89	66	77	84	92	94	96
		89-90	91	94	80	82	80	85
	6	88-89	40	65	43	69	42	61
		89-90	55	75	72	90	78	92

School	Gr.	Yr.	Reading		Writing		Math	
			SR	**RR**	**SR**	**RR**	**SR**	**RR**
Cherry Chse	3	88-89	83	61	84	60	81	60
		89-90	61	17	63	19	57	25
	6	88-89	58	74	78	92	64	78
		89-90	69	66	60	49	66	60
Columbia	3	88-89	70	71	76	77	58	54
		89-90	62	55	68	63	60	60
	6	88-89	53	62	59	70	53	57
		89-90	52	53	57	57	62	67
Cumberland	3	88-89	92	75	78	44	91	75
		89-90	92	74	83	50	85	65
	6	88-89	92	81	91	81	87	66
		89-90	86	73	91	83	70	44
Ellis	3	88-89	50	44	55	47	47	37
		89-90	84	77	83	77	52	40
	6	88-89	33	42	41	54	44	52
		89-90	50	46	55	49	29	19
Hollenbeck	3	88-89	85	83	94	90	89	84
		89-90	99	99	96	98	96	98
	6	88-89	89	97	79	90	93	96
		89-90	81	90	81	86	83	87
Lakewood	3	88-89	84	94	88	95	69	82
		89-90	80	86	77	84	69	78
	6	88-89	80	94	78	94	65	83
		89-90	57	71	54	64	59	72
Sunnyvale	8	89-90	83	90	84	92	68	88
		91-92	75	77	71	74	61	78

UNION ELEMENTARY SCHOOL DISTRICT

School	Gr.	Yr.	Reading		Writing		Math	
Alta Vista	3	88-89	95	83	94	79	92	76
		89-90	95	79	98	91	94	81
Althenour	3	88-89	90	89	86	83	88	83
		89-90	80	62	84	69	86	78
Carleton	3	88-89	88	66	96	83	94	80
		89-90	85	57	93	75	86	67
Dartmouth	6	88-89	86	70	81	59	81	56
		89-90	68	62	78	76	78	78
	8	89-90	85	83	57	19	80	75
		91-92	85	84	82	78	83	91
Guadalupe	3	88-89	92	74	96	83	95	82
		89-90	79	42	87	60	85	64

School	Gr.	Yr.	Reading		Writing		Math	
			SR	**RR**	**SR**	**RR**	**SR**	**RR**
Lietz	3	88-89	87	84	87	84	79	72
		89-90	98	96	99	99	99	98
Lone Hill	3	88-89	87	75	78	53	82	66
		89-90	63	20	70	28	52	19
Noddin	3	88-89	78	46	92	74	89	70
		89-90	85	55	83	51	71	42
Oster	3	88-89	73	49	77	55	58	31
		89-90	95	93	87	82	90	87
Union Mid.	6	88-89	83	56	82	56	79	43
		89-90	81	60	89	79	83	67
	8	89-90	91	80	74	31	87	74
		91-92	81	51	75	40	90	86

WHISMAN ELEMENTARY SCHOOL DISTRICT

School	Gr.	Yr.	Reading		Writing		Math	
Crittenden	6	88-89	65	82	66	84	66	78
		89-90	72	86	87	93	69	79
	8	89-90	72	81	87	94	73	91
		91-92	73	72	50	26	55	65
Monta Loma	3	88-89	69	62	80	77	73	68
		89-90	77	68	80	72	56	48
Theuerkauf	3	88-89	47	10	55	15	59	23
		89-90	73	65	82	78	67	65
Whisman	3	88-89	78	75	74	68	68	62
		89-90	77	60	88	80	62	50

SAN MATEO COUNTY
CAP SCORES

School	Gr.	Yr.	Reading		Writing		Math	
			SR	RR	SR	RR	SR	RR

BAYSHORE ELEMENTARY SCHOOL DISTRICT

School	Gr.	Yr.	Reading SR	Reading RR	Writing SR	Writing RR	Math SR	Math RR
Bayshore	3	88-89	20	18	15	8	29	32
		89-90	45	45	38	34	14	10
Robertson	6	88-89	22	38	27	44	10	9
		89-90	19	13	42	49	16	10
	8	89-90	39	53	44	57	19	31
		91-92	53	56	47	48	29	34

BELMONT ELEMENTARY SCHOOL DISTRICT

School	Gr.	Yr.	Reading SR	Reading RR	Writing SR	Writing RR	Math SR	Math RR
Central	3	88-89	83	70	86	73	90	81
		89-90	85	55	85	56	75	48
Fox	3	88-89	90	70	93	76	65	30
		89-90	88	64	87	60	79	55
Nesbit	3	88-89	73	44	73	42	86	72
		89-90	44	16	58	30	82	77
Ralston Int.	6	88-89	87	68	84	64	89	71
		89-90	87	64	84	59	89	72
	8	89-90	89	76	75	31	93	75
		91-92	93	75	92	70	95	86

BRISBANE ELEMENTARY SCHOOL DISTRICT

School	Gr.	Yr.	Reading SR	Reading RR	Writing SR	Writing RR	Math SR	Math RR
Brisbane	3	88-89	79	78	60	45	79	74
		89-90	53	48	39	23	35	32
Lipman Int.	6	88-89	77	82	64	63	86	86
		89-90	68	85	60	74	49	63
	8	89-89	66	75	66	75	56	78
		91-92	41	22	41	22	80	95
Panorama	3	88-89	64	71	63	70	42	39
		89-90	49	37	52	43	70	75
	6	88-89	49	69	70	91	62	80
		89-90	52	64	48	57	68	82

School	Gr.	Yr.	Reading		Writing		Math	
			SR	RR	SR	RR	SR	RR

BURLINGAME ELEMENTARY SCHOOL DISTRICT

School	Gr.	Yr.	SR	RR	SR	RR	SR	RR
Burling Int.	6	88-89	86	73	87	77	67	34
		89-90	43	9	30	3	78	51
	8	89-90	90	77	97	92	92	79
		91-92	94	82	84	53	88	78
Franklin	3	88-89	95	81	89	67	92	76
		89-90	97	85	97	85	93	79
Lincoln	3	88-89	83	55	89	65	80	52
		89-90	88	61	79	41	89	72
McKinley	3	88-89	50	11	49	10	24	2
		89-90	91	84	84	67	70	54
Washington	3	88-89	27	7	24	5	31	12
		89-90	77	64	61	36	76	68

CABRILLO UNIFIED SCHOOL DISTRICT

School	Gr.	Yr.	SR	RR	SR	RR	SR	RR
Cunha Int.	6	88-89	48	35	53	39	58	47
		89-90	50	50	46	43	61	67
	8	89-90	81	86	92	92	84	92
		91-92	73	35	63	21	73	58
El Granada	3	88-89	83	76	84	76	76	63
		89-90	67	25	54	13	52	19
Farallone	3	88-89	90	71	89	65	68	34
		89-90	85	57	71	29	58	26
H.M.B. High	12	88-89	84	78	59	29	75	73
		89-90	65	42	56	21	70	69
Hatch	3	88-89	47	57	53	66	42	48
		89-90	33	20	19	6	30	26
Kings Mtn.	3	88-89	98	94	81	50	59	22
		89-90	71	29	63	19	29	5

HILLSBOROUGH CITY ELEMENTARY SCHOOL DISTRICT

School	Gr.	Yr.	SR	RR	SR	RR	SR	RR
Crocker Mid.	6	88-89	90	72	91	78	96	87
		89-90	97	91	98	93	98	92
	8	89-90	98	95	98	93	94	84
		91-92	99	96	99	97	97	90

School	Gr.	Yr.	Reading		Writing		Math	
			SR	RR	SR	RR	SR	RR
South Elem.	3	88-89	80	51	81	50	94	78
		89-90	80	45	83	51	87	69
West Elem.	3	88-89	99	97	95	80	98	93
		89-90	92	73	91	69	95	83

JEFFERSON ELEMENTARY SCHOOL DISTRICT

School	Gr.	Yr.	Reading		Writing		Math	
Brown	3	88-89	35	20	37	21	21	10
		89-90	75	72	68	63	61	62
	6	88-89	32	55	31	49	59	81
		89-90	63	88	49	73	64	86
Colma	3	88-89	46	52	38	38	64	77
		89-90	57	76	47	64	53	75
Columbus	3	88-89	67	58	69	59	50	33
		89-90	39	22	39	19	35	29
	6	88-89	57	71	57	72	49	56
		89-90	49	56	64	74	57	68
Edison	3	88-89	57	35	42	14	37	15
		89-90	66	35	68	37	52	28
	6	88-89	77	85	85	91	61	62
		89-90	77	79	71	67	82	82
Franklin	8	89-90	50	47	50	41	50	59
		91-92	67	62	80	87	50	58
Garden Vlg.	3	88-89	73	69	88	87	82	79
		89-90	85	87	94	94	86	89
	6	88-89	87	95	71	80	46	41
		89-90	74	89	76	89	62	77
Kennedy	3	88-89	44	66	51	74	38	52
		89-90	50	60	65	79	69	85
Pollicita	6	88-89	19	29	25	37	26	37
		89-90	44	50	48	54	42	47
	8	89-90	45	71	45	66	34	72
		91-92	38	47	73	93	38	75
Rivera	8	89-90	65	65	72	65	44	38
		91-92	72	72	54	39	62	78
Roosevelt	3	88-89	70	59	59	37	52	35
		89-90	81	94	88	97	78	92
	6	88-89	37	15	37	12	39	17
		89-90	64	91	74	95	76	94

School	Gr.	Yr.	Reading		Writing		Math	
			SR	RR	SR	RR	SR	RR
Tobias	3	88-89	78	47	89	68	88	69
		89-90	83	74	88	81	85	81
	6	88-89	88	95	57	61	85	89
		89-90	84	72	76	58	84	72
Washington	3	88-89	56	78	49	69	29	39
		89-90	52	70	53	71	35	53
Webster	3	88-89	50	35	54	37	76	72
		89-90	82	78	95	93	91	90
	6	88-89	90	94	89	92	88	89
		89-90	80	94	72	91	86	96
Westlake	3	88-89	86	96	93	97	96	98
		89-90	58	71	69	83	68	83
	6	88-89	95	98	99	99	97	98
		89-90	47	74	78	95	78	95
Wilson	3	88-89	64	65	67	68	57	52
		89-90	44	43	52	58	50	64
	6	88-89	32	61	34	62	43	70
		89-90	60	76	68	82	68	83

JEFFERSON UNION HIGH SCHOOL DISTRICT

School	Gr.	Yr.	Reading		Writing		Math	
Jefferson	12	88-89	12	4	17	22	9	8
		89-90	18	38	22	46	13	39
Oceana	12	88-89	42	36	65	82	28	27
		89-90	63	71	77	93	41	57
Terra Nova	12	88-89	83	87	84	90	76	87
		89-90	72	69	77	73	63	70
Westmoor	12	88-89	42	14	42	22	35	17
		89-90	47	39	35	24	39	53

LA HONDA-PESCADERO UNION SCHOOL DISTRICT

School	Gr.	Yr.	Reading		Writing		Math	
La Honda	3	88-89	68	29	53	13	45	9
		89-90	63	19	41	5	25	3
Pescadero	3	88-89	83	78	60	37	89	84
		89-90	23	8	12	2	49	48
	6	88-89	41	66	37	60	86	97
		89-90	27	21	44	45	82	88
Pescadero Hi	8	89-90	60	86	15	19	39	79
		91-92	35	17	65	74	80	95

School	Gr.	Yr.	Reading		Writing		Math	
			SR	**RR**	**SR**	**RR**	**SR**	**RR**
	12	88-89	26	7	69	80	12	3
		89-90	28	38	3	2	26	63

LAGUNA SALADA UNION SCHOOL DISTRICT

School	Gr.	Yr.	Reading		Writing		Math	
			SR	**RR**	**SR**	**RR**	**SR**	**RR**
Cabrillo	3	88-89	80	57	84	62	69	43
		89-90	75	35	72	31	65	34
	6	88-89	75	66	54	35	56	36
		89-90	84	78	75	61	67	49
Fairmont	3	88-89	45	15	57	27	29	7
		89-90	42	6	30	3	20	2
	6	88-89	71	85	44	52	34	31
		89-90	61	57	42	23	66	62
Linda Mar	3	88-89	76	64	78	65	79	65
		89-90	65	37	72	47	85	79
	6	88-89	77	82	69	73	69	67
		89-90	89	91	61	48	70	64
Oddstad	3	88-89	82	53	67	26	51	15
		89-90	78	40	73	32	52	19
	6	88-89	66	47	59	39	41	15
		89-90	74	39	92	78	56	20
Ortega	6	88-89	84	60	78	51	88	69
		89-90	66	32	86	66	91	79
	8	89-90	84	81	98	98	70	57
		91-92	74	59	89	90	70	74
Pacific Hgts.	6	88-89	75	56	81	69	53	22
		89-90	84	91	68	69	42	36
	8	89-90	72	81	93	97	49	57
		91-92	51	46	41	25	43	53
Pacific Manr.	3	88-89	71	73	77	78	80	81
		89-90	71	47	78	57	75	64
	6	88-89	70	72	72	76	60	53
		89-90	96	96	69	54	57	41
Portola	3	88-89	63	22	62	21	66	31
		89-90	38	4	48	9	49	16
	6	88-89	95	97	53	46	91	92
		89-90	87	80	89	83	88	82
Sharp Park	3	88-89	68	60	60	44	62	51
		89-90	34	22	38	25	53	59
	6	88-89	77	85	52	49	52	44
		89-90	59	72	59	69	36	38

School	Gr.	Yr.	Reading		Writing		Math	
			SR	RR	SR	RR	SR	RR
	8	89-90	27	25	47	58	37	60
		91-92	89	66	98	94	80	58
Vallemar	3	88-89	85	61	84	55	86	64
		89-90	95	89	95	86	94	86
	6	88-89	88	78	82	68	76	49
		89-90	89	95	57	57	59	64
	8	89-90	82	81	67	36	50	30
		91-92	71	43	95	95	78	77
Westview	3	88-89	76	92	71	88	44	54
		89-90	32	29	45	49	15	12
	6	88-89	80	92	81	93	77	88
		89-90	70	88	79	93	35	45

LAS LOMITAS ELEMENTARY SCHOOL DISTRICT

School	Gr.	Yr.	Reading		Writing		Math	
La Entrada	6	88-89	96	88	96	88	94	81
		89-90	96	87	96	89	97	90
	8	89-90	99	97	99	98	97	93
		91-92	98	91	99	99	99	96
Las Lomitas	3	88-89	99	97	96	85	96	85
		89-90	98	92	93	74	96	86

MENLO PARK CITY ELEMENTARY SCHOOL DISTRICT

School	Gr.	Yr.	Reading		Writing		Math	
Encinal	3	89-90	96	82	85	54	89	73
Hillview	6	88-89	92	77	92	78	96	87
		89-90	95	86	97	91	97	91
	8	89-90	99	97	99	97	97	92
		91-92	97	91	97	87	97	92
Oak Knoll	3	88-89	89	68	85	56	89	69
		89-90	95	80	93	75	94	80

MILLBRAE ELEMENTARY SCHOOL DISTRICT

School	Gr.	Yr.	Reading		Writing		Math	
Green Hills	3	88-89	75	65	70	54	62	49
		89-90	91	90	83	78	77	72
Lomita Park	3	88-89	42	36	36	24	41	35
		89-90	62	78	55	70	37	52
Meadows	3	88-89	98	96	98	97	95	87
		89-90	96	83	91	70	95	82

School	Gr.	Yr.	Reading		Writing		Math	
			SR	**RR**	**SR**	**RR**	**SR**	**RR**
Spring Vly.	3	88-89	55	14	44	6	39	7
		89-90	49	10	55	14	53	20
Taylor Int.	6	88-89	64	35	72	50	79	54
		89-90	66	54	69	54	82	78
	8	89-90	75	75	93	93	80	88
		91-92	72	50	93	93	91	94

PORTOLA VALLEY ELEMENTARY SCHOOL DISTRICT

School	Gr.	Yr.	Reading		Writing		Math	
Corte Mdra.	6	88-89	97	94	99	97	96	85
		89-90	98	95	97	90	98	93
	8	89-90	95	88	99	99	97	93
		91-92	99	96	99	98	98	94
Ormondale	3	88-89	98	96	97	86	98	94
		89-90	99	98	98	93	96	85

RAVENSWOOD CITY ELEMENTARY SCHOOL DISTRICT

School	Gr.	Yr.	Reading		Writing		Math	
Belle Haven	3	88-89	16	46	42	80	26	55
		89-90	20	67	37	85	18	63
	6	88-89	1	7	7	18	8	17
		89-90	8	50	15	60	6	36
	8	91-92	10	27	10	26	4	29
Brentwood	3	88-89	7	38	9	42	7	25
		89-90	11	33	16	44	8	22
Costano	6	88-89	5	20	13	39	12	31
		89-90	16	67	22	73	43	91
	8	91-92	1	3	47	86	2	11
Flood	3	88-89	74	86	84	92	90	93
		89-90	98	98	95	90	97	95
	6	88-89	69	84	64	78	37	37
		89-90	78	98	70	97	63	96
	8	91-92	95	95	80	86	71	88
McNair	6	88-89	12	34	25	59	9	21
		89-90	2	28	10	46	8	45
	8	91-92	1	2	5	8	3	22
Menlo Oaks	6	88-89	13	29	18	40	12	22
		89-90	10	55	7	40	9	46
	8	89-90	8	15	13	21	3	9
		91-92	1	3	35	71	4	20

School	Gr.	Yr.	Reading		Writing		Math	
			SR	**RR**	**SR**	**RR**	**SR**	**RR**
Ravenswood	8	89-90	9	22	14	30	4	18
New Elem.		91-92	14	18	7	8	11	33
Willow Oaks	3	88-89	12	25	18	35	15	24
		89-90	18	64	23	72	8	33

REDWOOD CITY ELEMENTARY SCHOOL DISTRICT

School	Gr.	Yr.	Reading		Writing		Math	
Clifford	3	88-89	77	58	67	36	57	28
		89-90	74	50	78	57	80	71
	6	88-89	63	46	77	73	90	87
		89-90	70	65	84	84	65	57
Cloud, Roy	3	88-89	71	34	82	51	60	24
		89-90	65	22	56	15	76	49
	6	88-89	90	72	97	90	97	89
		89-90	92	76	96	89	97	89
Fair Oaks	3	88-89	1	7	2	10	1	4
		89-90	5	26	3	12	7	27
Ford, Henry	3	88-89	71	34	65	24	62	27
		89-90	62	25	60	22	38	13
Garfield	3	88-89	12	47	16	54	25	65
		89-90	32	81	37	83	33	80
	6	88-89	8	50	19	69	25	75
		89-90	8	50	32	85	16	61
Gill, John	3	88-89	66	67	52	43	45	36
		89-90	39	12	32	8	48	34
	6	88-89	73	76	76	83	65	61
		89-90	47	31	57	42	69	65
Hawes	3	88-89	50	66	57	75	36	44
		89-90	15	10	18	10	17	20
Hoover	3	88-89	4	15	4	15	4	8
		89-90	5	29	7	30	7	29
	6	88-89	4	36	14	60	27	77
		89-90	13	61	24	76	22	71
Kennedy	8	89-90	23	32	27	31	23	50
		91-92	33	50	39	65	39	83
McKinley	8	89-90	13	17	53	78	35	73
		91-92	36	42	46	61	36	74
Orion	3	88-89	39	9	18	2	19	3
		89-90	55	41	28	8	45	37

School	Gr.	Yr.	Reading		Writing		Math	
			SR	**RR**	**SR**	**RR**	**SR**	**RR**
	6	88-89	83	71	61	38	76	52
		89-90	50	58	72	82	50	59
Roosevelt	3	88-89	68	75	80	87	60	64
		89-90	52	20	50	16	43	19
	6	88-89	67	30	81	54	88	64
		89-90	72	45	66	34	56	24
Selby Lane	3	88-89	56	35	51	26	74	65
		89-90	67	69	58	56	59	66
	6	88-89	83	87	86	88	84	83
		89-90	61	79	49	64	55	72
Taft	3	88-89	26	22	28	23	22	18
		89-90	24	28	23	23	11	13
	6	88-89	7	11	9	13	16	26
		89-90	22	33	19	22	23	35

SAN BRUNO PARK ELEMENTARY SCHOOL DISTRICT

School	Gr.	Yr.	Reading		Writing		Math	
Allen	3	88-89	43	40	64	72	42	39
		89-90	79	71	64	48	55	47
	6	88-89	43	51	66	81	68	78
		89-90	85	91	66	62	71	70
Belle Air	3	88-89	62	81	73	91	62	79
		89-90	50	74	43	66	36	60
	6	88-89	50	70	31	39	39	48
		89-90	52	76	34	46	40	60
Crestmoor	3	88-89	74	56	91	85	63	44
		89-90	79	47	87	63	71	46
	6	88-89	77	77	50	33	75	67
		89-90	89	81	92	87	96	94
El Crystal	3	88-89	78	69	90	84	76	65
		89-90	90	88	83	78	86	84
	6	88-89	69	89	43	65	77	90
		89-90	50	38	61	53	25	11
John Muir	3	88-89	66	37	73	47	70	49
		89-90	71	46	75	52	69	56
	6	88-89	77	66	88	86	79	64
		89-90	59	52	91	93	46	34
Parkside Int.	8	89-90	69	74	83	84	56	61
		91-92	68	66	79	85	50	60
Rollingwood	3	88-89	66	67	75	78	62	60
		89-90	85	76	72	51	82	77

School	Gr.	Yr.	Reading		Writing		Math	
			SR	RR	SR	RR	SR	RR
	6	88-89	88	83	84	80	75	57
		89-90	92	87	64	36	84	73

SAN CARLOS ELEMENTARY SCHOOL DISTRICT

School	Gr.	Yr.	Reading		Writing		Math	
Arundel	3	88-89	66	25	96	83	95	81
		89-90	86	59	95	80	96	86
Brittan Acres	3	88-89	98	93	97	86	97	87
		89-90	96	82	94	78	95	84
Central Mid.	6	88-89	84	59	90	75	82	51
		89-90	75	40	85	61	91	75
	8	89-90	86	71	96	83	86	69
		91-92	95	83	93	78	84	65
Heather	3	88-89	91	72	96	84	95	81
		89-90	84	54	88	61	86	67
White Oaks	3	88-89	95	83	94	79	97	86
		89-90	92	74	99	97	95	82

SAN MATEO CITY ELEMENTARY SCHOOL DISTRICT

School	Gr.	Yr.	Reading		Writing		Math	
Abbott Mid	6	88-89	65	28	81	53	86	61
		89-90	72	49	61	32	78	59
	8	89-90	61	43	50	18	70	73
		91-92	78	75	84	87	73	86
Audubon	3	88-89	96	84	97	88	93	77
		89-90	86	58	87	60	75	47
Bayside Mid.	6	88-89	49	73	41	62	46	63
		89-90	44	56	37	42	27	26
	8	89-90	44	51	74	88	25	33
		91-92	49	36	53	42	23	14
Baywood	3	88-89	82	54	87	62	69	36
		89-90	81	48	73	33	69	40
Borel Mid.	6	88-89	75	65	83	79	74	58
		89-90	78	77	59	41	63	52
	8	89-90	80	66	94	87	78	65
		91-92	87	75	63	23	63	43
Bowditch	6	88-89	80	48	84	61	82	51
		89-90	84	57	71	34	80	51
	8	89-90	92	80	79	39	92	80
		91-92	95	82	95	83	92	78

School	Gr.	Yr.	Reading		Writing		Math	
			SR	RR	SR	RR	SR	RR
Foster City	3	88-89	87	64	92	74	86	63
		89-90	86	59	84	53	84	62
George Hall	3	88-89	69	65	76	73	64	59
		89-90	66	68	47	38	56	61
Highlands	3	88-89	96	85	93	76	91	75
		89-90	97	95	98	94	96	91
Horrall	3	88-89	75	78	57	52	62	60
		89-90	80	80	68	66	60	62
Laurel	3	88-89	93	91	90	83	93	86
		89-90	82	83	82	84	72	77
Meadow Hts.	3	88-89	77	77	67	63	80	78
		89-90	88	86	75	69	95	94
N. Shorevw.	3	88-89	29	33	43	53	24	24
		89-90	57	73	61	76	58	77
Park	3	88-89	78	81	64	64	68	70
		89-90	83	86	86	89	66	72
Parkside	3	88-89	75	67	89	85	94	90
		89-90	57	29	47	16	40	21
Sunnybrae	3	88-89	79	76	89	86	85	81
		89-90	79	76	67	60	85	85

SAN MATEO UNION HIGH SCHOOL DISTRICT

School	Gr.	Yr.	Reading		Writing		Math	
Aragon	12	88-89	84	52	95	87	88	76
		89-90	84	58	89	69	90	88
Burlingame	12	88-89	83	66	87	78	87	91
		89-90	69	36	86	67	74	63
Capuchino	12	88-89	17	4	43	35	33	33
		89-90	42	36	38	34	41	69
Hillsdale	12	88-89	68	33	70	40	79	74
		89-90	70	50	82	72	79	87
Mills	12	88-89	68	45	90	95	82	90
		89-90	67	40	94	93	90	96
San Mateo	12	88-89	80	30	95	83	89	69
		89-90	81	37	92	68	88	69

School	Gr.	Yr.	Reading		Writing		Math	
			SR	RR	SR	RR	SR	RR

SEQUOIA UNION HIGH SCHOOL DISTRICT

School	Gr.	Yr.	SR	RR	SR	RR	SR	RR
Carlmont	12	88-89	88	89	91	97	90	98
		89-90	80	68	90	87	90	98
Menlo-Ath.	12	88-89	91	61	90	65	94	87
		89-90	93	84	92	69	97	96
Sequoia	12	88-89	50	47	67	80	58	82
		89-90	50	47	63	69	59	83
Woodside	12	88-89	55	33	76	85	57	64
		89-90	73	69	75	64	70	83

SOUTH SAN FRANCISCO UNIFIED SCHOOL DISTRICT

School	Gr.	Yr.	SR	RR	SR	RR	SR	RR
Alta Loma	8	89-90	65	66	50	33	40	33
		91-92	60	39	44	13	54	55
Buri Buri	3	88-89	81	52	77	41	69	36
		89-90	80	68	79	62	82	75
	6	88-89	70	62	46	22	49	28
		89-90	66	69	55	45	78	79
El Camino	12	88-89	68	64	70	75	49	40
		89-90	54	49	60	62	30	21
Foxridge	3	88-89	90	72	89	67	75	45
		89-90	89	83	87	76	77	66
	6	88-89	77	80	49	36	61	55
		89-90	70	50	73	53	56	31
Hillside	3	88-89	43	45	53	60	30	27
		89-90	82	78	88	86	68	65
	6	88-89	68	89	65	89	54	73
		89-90	87	81	95	93	75	60
Junip. Serra	3	88-89	82	71	78	61	71	55
		89-90	88	86	92	89	86	85
	6	88-89	74	68	39	16	68	56
		89-90	76	82	61	57	56	55
Los Cerritos	3	88-89	61	61	72	74	68	69
		89-90	30	10	42	21	36	26
	6	88-89	72	91	81	95	61	81
		89-90	72	85	54	59	38	38
Martin	3	88-89	64	83	68	88	50	67
		89-90	75	86	68	82	89	95

School	Gr.	Yr.	Reading		Writing		Math	
			SR	**RR**	**SR**	**RR**	**SR**	**RR**
	6	88-89	34	46	53	74	44	55
		89-90	39	73	28	53	46	78
Monte Verde	3	88-89	72	66	72	66	76	72
		89-90	72	54	57	29	44	27
	6	88-89	72	59	59	40	57	34
		89-90	45	25	40	16	39	21
Parkway	8	89-90	26	29	20	20	23	40
		91-92	33	29	41	49	44	75
Ponderosa	3	88-89	75	49	77	49	55	23
		89-90	88	81	82	65	57	40
	6	88-89	83	87	56	44	34	16
		89-90	88	86	68	52	67	55
Serra Vista	3	88-89	87	64	88	63	55	18
		89-90	82	62	75	45	52	26
	6	88-89	71	50	64	41	64	36
		89-90	70	53	51	21	70	51
Skyline	3	88-89	89	88	79	72	66	56
		89-90	78	53	76	48	65	46
	6	88-89	70	59	74	68	76	63
		89-90	69	67	62	53	72	69
S. San Fran.	12	88-89	45	66	53	77	36	69
		89-90	55	56	49	48	42	60
Spruce	3	88-89	25	17	20	10	37	31
		89-90	27	17	11	2	26	27
	6	88-89	37	76	29	64	42	76
		89-90	39	59	34	46	35	54
Sunshine Grd.	3	88-89	70	32	60	18	62	27
		89-90	89	88	91	89	45	36
	6	88-89	70	81	44	45	31	22
		89-90	60	83	42	61	61	81
Westborough	8	89-90	93	94	92	90	89	93
		91-92	78	62	86	81	80	81

WOODSIDE ELEMENTARY SCHOOL DISTRICT

School	Gr.	Yr.	Reading		Writing		Math	
Woodside	3	88-89	96	84	82	51	94	79
		89-90	99	99	99	98	99	99
	6	88-89	96	90	99	97	98	96
		89-90	98	94	97	90	94	84
	8	89-90	97	90	98	92	93	80
		91-92	99	97	99	99	98	93

SAT SCORES

Many four year colleges and universities use the SAT to help them assess the abilities of prospective students. High SAT scores are usually an indication of an affluent, well-educated community; therefore these scores should not be used to judge the effectiveness of individual schools. However, high scores and a large percentage of students taking the test probably indicate that these schools have an academic and social environment that values academic success, a wide range of advanced level classes. and many students who plan to go on to college. At the time of this book's publication, the scores for 1993 were not yet available. To obtain more recent scores, contact the California Department of Education at (916) 657-2273.

AVERAGE SAT SCORES FOR SAN MATEO COUNTY HIGH SCHOOLS

HIGH SCHOOL	% Of Takers in '92	'92 Verbal	'91 Verbal	'92 Math	'91 Math
STATE-WIDE	41.0%	416	415	484	482
ARAGON	52.0%	456	450	517	530
BURLINGAME	65.3%	428	445	517	520
CAPUCHINO	46.9%	413	381	492	464
CARLMONT	67.8%	435	429	500	500
EL CAMINO	31.1%	399	414	495	502
HALF MOON BAY	49.4%	454	441	506	509
HILLSDALE	51.7%	422	425	561	522
JEFFERSON	26.0%	342	336	437	411
MENLO-ATHERTON	79.5%	486	479	530	526
MILLS	56.4%	423	421	549	526
OCEANA	34.8%	393	420	440	445
PESCADERO	20.0%	353	345	493	410
SAN MATEO	51.9%	445	484	528	540
SEQUOIA	43.0%	411	394	465	462
S. SAN FRANCISCO	31.7%	395	394	525	501
TERRA NOVA	29.2%	421	445	465	501
WESTMOOR	27.2%	385	389	472	469
WOODSIDE	56.2%	427	418	487	458

AVERAGE SAT SCORES FOR SANTA CLARA COUNTY HIGH SCHOOLS

HIGH SCHOOL	% Of Takers in '92	'92 Verbal	'91 Verbal	'92 Math	'91 Math
STATE-WIDE	41.0%	416	415	484	482
BLACKFORD	14.2%	377	419	446	510
BRANHAM	NA	404	445	472	497
CUPERTINO	69.8%	454	433	550	549
DEL MAR	36.4%	420	423	497	497
FREMONT	46.9%	435	419	537	521
GILROY	26.1%	410	402	470	454
GUNDERSON	35.2%	418	453	502	528
GUNN	83.8%	501	512	610	604
HILL	32.1%	363	348	462	437
HOMESTEAD	66.3%	480	482	582	585
INDEPENDENCE	42.5%	375	370	460	457
LEIGH	34.0%	484	452	529	538
LELAND	66.4%	462	456	556	547
LICK	25.7%	411	397	455	454
LINCOLN	27.7%	453	446	489	492
LIVE OAK	36.8%	436	437	505	503
LOS ALTOS	65.0%	485	482	571	563
LOS GATOS	62.2%	487	480	540	537
LYNBROOK	79.2%	491	483	579	578
MILPITAS	40.7%	394	390	484	483
MONTA VISTA	85.1%	471	486	590	600
MT. PLEASANT	35.4%	374	393	447	457
MTN. VIEW	61.5%	462	456	546	549
OAK GROVE	35.8%	403	399	487	466
OVERFELT	18.0%	378	354	478	440
PALO ALTO	87.9%	534	514	601	593
PIEDMONT HILLS	48.9%	406	397	484	464
PIONEER	46.4%	414	418	483	490
PROSPECT	40.3%	436	430	511	527
SAN JOSE ACADEMY	30.2%	481	519	541	553
SANTA CLARA	45.8%	379	389	487	493
SANTA TERESA	37.1%	435	421	505	483
SARATOGA	82.7%	514	504	588	570
SILVER CREEK	31.6%	364	369	474	466
WESTMONT	40.4%	442	452	519	515
WILCOX	40.7%	408	377	532	508
WILLOW GLEN	34.8%	423	414	476	482
YERBA BUENA	28.7%	353	331	461	459

1991-92 REVENUE PER ADA

SANTA CLARA COUNTY SCHOOL DISTRICTS

Alum Rock	$4021	Milpitas	$4135
Berryessa	$3844	Montebello*	$6939
Cambrian	$3789	Moreland	$3960
Campbell Elem.	$3818	Morgan Hill	$3918
Campbell H.S.	$5173	Mt. Pleasant	$3950
Cupertino	$3845	Mountain View	$4473
East Side H.S.	$4814	Mtn. View-Los Altos H.S.	$5677
Evergreen	$3682	Oak Grove	$3912
Franklin-McKinley	$4048	Orchard	$5707
Fremont H.S.	$5487	Palo Alto	$6317
Gilroy	$3980	San Jose	$5063
Lakeside	$5194	Santa Clara	$4323
Loma Prieta	$4554	Saratoga	$4335
Los Altos	$4445	Sunnyvale	$4317
Los Gatos	$4529	Union	$4142
Ls. Gatos-Saratoga H.S.	$5039	Whisman	$4730
Luther Burbank	$4236		

Source: Santa Clara County Office of Education

SAN MATEO COUNTY SCHOOL DISTRICTS

Bayshore	$3624	Millbrae	$4231
Belmont	$4070	Portola Valley	$4770
Brisbane	$3813	Ravenswood	$4518
Burlingame	$3859	Redwood City	$3925
Cabrillo	$3978	San Bruno Park	$3897
Hillsborough	$5508	San Carlos	$3828
Jefferson Elem.	$3567	San Mateo H.S.	$5352
Jefferson H.S.	$4773	San Mateo-Foster City	$3885
La Honda Pescadero	$5521	Sequoia H.S.	$5856
Laguna Salada	$3634	South San Francisco	$3914
Las Lomitas	$5418	Woodside	$5165
Menlo Park	$4493		

Source: San Mateo County Office of Education

*Necessary, small school.

INDEX

ORDER FORM FOR PARENTS' GUIDE TO SCHOOL SELECTION

Haskala Press
640 Orange Avenue
Los Altos, CA 94022
(415) 948-4648

Group Discount Rates (for books sent to same address)
5 - 9 copies	10%
10 - 19 copies	20%
20 or more copies	30%

Shipping: $1.50 for first book, 50 cents for each additional book.
Please allow 2-3 weeks.

Please send me _____ copies of *Parents' Guide to School Selection*
@ $14.95 each. $ _____

Subtract discount (_____ %) $ _____

Net Order $ _____

Sales Tax (add 8.25%) $ _____

Shipping $ _____

Total $ _____

Name _____

Address _____

City _____ State _____ Zip _____

NOTES

NOTES

NOTES